THE
MONGOL
ART OF WAR

THE

MONGOL
ART OF WAR

Chinggis Khan and the
Mongol Military System

TIMOTHY MAY

WESTHOLME
Yardley

Published in North America under arrangements with Pen & Sword Books, Ltd.

Westholme Publishing, LLC
Eight Harvey Avenue
Yardley, Pennsylvania 19067
Visit our Web site at www.westholmepublishing.com

10 9 8 7 6 5 4 3 2

ISBN: 978-1-59416-046-2
ISBN 10: 1-59416-046-5

Printed in United States of America

Contents

List of Illustrations

A gallery of photographs follows page 114.

Maps

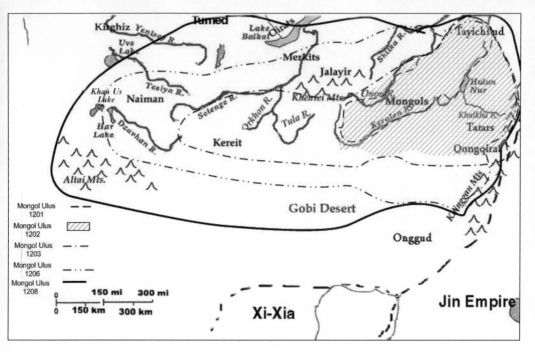

Mongolia 1201–1208

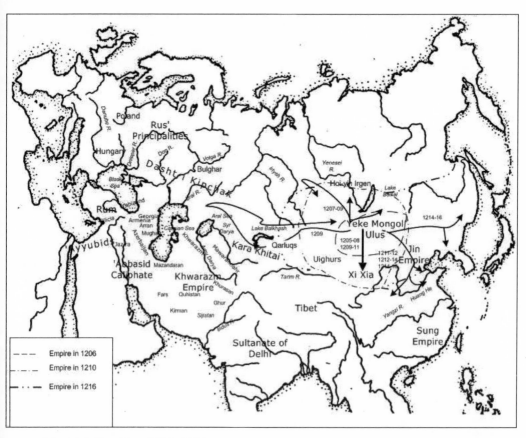

Mongol Empire 1206–1216

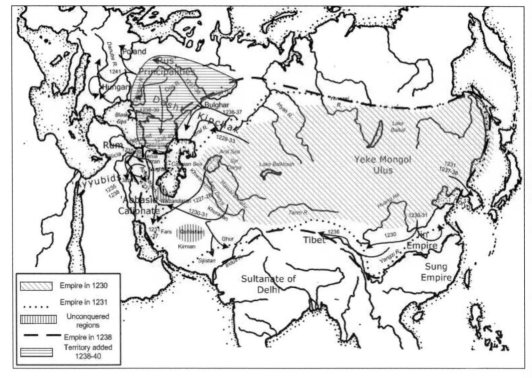

Mongol Empire 1230–1240

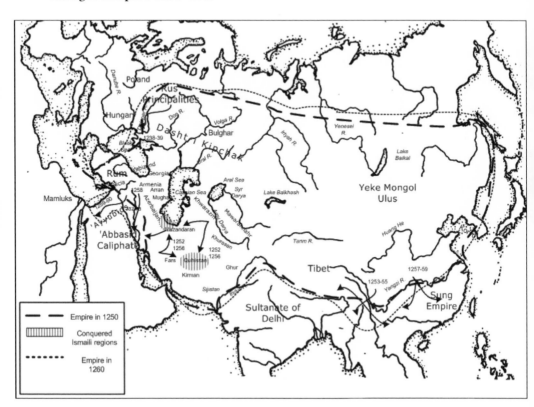

Mongol Empire 1250–1260

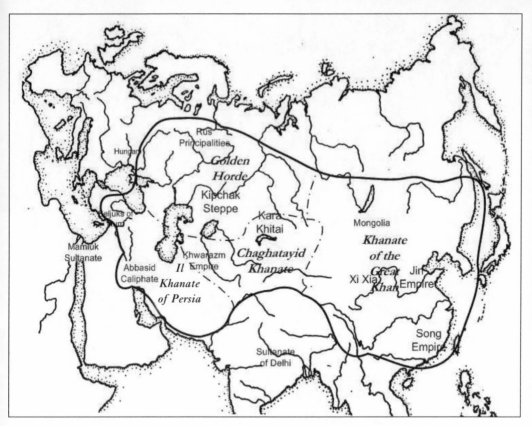

Mongol Empire in the Thirteenth Century

Pronunciation and transliteration guide

The greatest difficulty in studying the Mongols is that mastery of a number of languages is requisite. Since the primary sources were written in Mongolian, Chinese, Arabic, Persian, Russian, Latin, Old French, Armenian, Georgian, Japanese and even other languages, names of people and locations appear in a wide variety of forms. I have attempted to adhere to the forms that have been more or less accepted in the scholarly community while also limiting the use of diacritical marks. Unfortunately, those who primarily use Russian forms have some preferences over those using Chinese or Persian sources, but all of the spellings should be clear enough to identify key persons, terms, and locations for specialists in any area.

As most of the names that appear in this text might be somewhat bewildering to those encountering them for the first time, this rudimentary pronunciation guide will hopefully alleviate some of their difficulties:

'Kh' is pronounced like 'ch' in the Scottish 'loch', or the German 'ach'.
'Ch' is pronounced like 'ch' in 'church'.
'Ö' is pronounced in the back of the throat, similar to 'uh' as in 'ugly'.
'Ü' is pronounced 'oo', as in 'goose'.
'Ts' is the same sound as these letters have in 'cats'.
'ci' at the end of a word is a Mongolian and Turkic suffix pronounced as 'chee'.

Prologue

In Bukhara, one of the great cities of the Khwarazmian Empire, the Friday mosque was filled. It was the year 1220. The throng had gathered not to hear a sermon, but to listen to the words of the man who had just captured their city. The warrior who climbed up into the pulpit after dismounting from a small horse was a foreigner. His clothing and armor indicated he originated in a distant land. The assembled audience of religious leaders, doctors, scholars, and other eminent men waited for the stranger to speak. When he finally did, it was through a translator, who said:

> O people, know that you have committed great sins, and that the great ones among you have committed these sins. If you ask me what proof I have for these words, I say it is because I am the punishment of God. If you had not committed great sins, God would not have sent a punishment like me upon you.[1]

The self-styled scourge of God, however, did not come simply to lecture the citizens of Bukhara. His soldiers plundered the city, and did so in a highly organized fashion. After that the people were herded into groups, and those who were not killed were forced to march with the conquerors. The entire process bewildered the inhabitants, for most had little idea of who the man was or why he and his army had appeared before the walls of Bukhara. But shortly afterwards their conqueror, who was called Chinggis Khan, would go on with his army of Mongols to conquer the rest of the region and much more. The captives marched off with the victorious army must have wondered how this disaster had come about.

The conflict had begun the previous year. The governor of the border city of Otrar had massacred a caravan from the nascent Mongol Empire, probably with the consent of the Khwarazmian ruler, Muhammad Khwarazmshah II. In retaliation, the Mongol ruler Chinggis Khan abandoned his war in Northern China against the Jin Empire, and, leaving only a token force in China to hold Mongol gains, he gathered an army estimated to be 150,000 strong.

In the autumn of 1220, Chinggis Khan led his armies to the city of Otrar and laid siege. The Mongols attacked day and night until the city fell and its governor Inal Khan was captured. While the role of the Khwarazmian ruler in the massacre of the caravan remained uncertain, it was known that Inal Khan had been directly involved. Chinggis Khan ordered him to be executed by having his ears and eyes filled with molten silver.

After the capture of Otrar, Chinggis Khan divided his army. One force marched towards the city of Urgench, south of the Aral Sea; others crossed the Amu Darya River and ravaged the countryside. Chinggis Khan led his own division through the Kizilkum Desert and marched on the important city of Bukhara.

Although his armies were spread out across the Khwarazmian Empire, messengers kept the Mongol ruler informed of their activities. As he approached Bukhara, his army fanned out and began a wide encircling movement which cut communications between the city and Muhammad Khwarazmshah. At the same time separate attacks by the other Mongol armies prevented Muhammad from concentrating his forces.

Bukhara was well defended. Twelve thousand horsemen reinforced its normal garrison to well over 20,000 troops, and an impressive citadel dominated the city's defenses. However, the information the defenders received was disheartening, for as the Mongol forces approached and surrounded the city, the people from outlying districts fled towards Bukhara bringing disturbing news of massacres, alarming surprise attacks, and equally abrupt and unexplained retreats by the Mongols. As the refugees poured in, their increasing numbers put an increasing strain on the city's resources, and its reserves of food and water began to dwindle. The people of Bukhara would soon learn how effective their defenses were.

Having captured other cities along the way, Chinggis Khan and his army arrived and laid siege to Bukhara in February or March of 1220. The Bukharan commander, Kok-Khan, who was rumored to be a Mongol renegade, led an attack on the Mongols at sunrise to prevent them from erecting siege engines. His attack may also have been an effort to break through the Mongol lines in order to make contact with a relief force. The Khwarazmian cavalry surged through a gap in the Mongol lines, which had perhaps been intentionally left open, and when the Mongols realized the Khwarazmians were not coming back they set off in pursuit, attacking them from the rear and flanks. Kok-Khan survived and made his way back to the citadel, but the majority of the Khwarazmian cavalry were cut down before they reached the Amu Darya River.

The next day, the Bukharans sent a committee of imams and officials to Chinggis Khan to discuss terms. Kok-Khan and the garrison in the citadel were excluded from this meeting, which was perhaps conducted without his knowledge. The Bukharans submitted, Chinggis Khan harangued the population from the pulpit in the mosque, and then the Mongols systematically plundered the city.

However, the Mongol victory was not yet complete – the citadel had not surrendered. Chinggis Khan gave the order for the Khwarazmian army to be driven out and the citadel to be taken. However, whereas in the open field the Mongols were without peer, in street fighting they were more vulnerable and could be defeated. Kok-Khan's garrison conducted a determined resistance, often launching night attacks into the city which were aided by the citizens.

Frustrated by this resistance, Chinggis Khan ordered Bukhara to be razed. The resulting inferno lasted for several days, and only buildings constructed of brick – such as some of the palaces and the Friday mosque – survived.

While the fire raged, the Mongols were not idle. They organized the population into a workforce and set up their siege engines, and when the mangonels, ballistae, ladders, and battering rams were ready the Mongols assailed the citadel. The population of Bukhara now served as arrow fodder, manning the rams and carrying debris to fill the moat. The garrison shot at them with their bows, hurled stones from their own mangonels, and dumped pots of burning naphtha on them, but the conscripted Bukharans went on with their work, for to refuse meant certain death at the hands of the Mongols.

The siege lasted for days. Kok-Khan and his men put up a desperate defense. Several times they sallied out in order to break the Mongol lines, only to be beaten back. The moat was filled with stones, faggots, rubble, and the bodies of the Bukharan populace and the Mongols advanced relentlessly, seizing the outer defenses. Then they broke into the citadel itself, hurling naphtha and explosives over the walls and forcing the defenders to retreat. Once inside, the Mongols cut down everyone they found. They were especially severe with the Turks. These nomadic warriors were viewed as renegades by the Mongols because they had refused to submit to Chinggis Khan, who saw himself as lord of all the steppe tribes.

According to the chronicles, 30,000 Khwarazmians perished in the seizure of the citadel alone. Yet Chinggis Khan did not stop there. To ensure that Bukhara could never rebel again the walls were razed and other defenses leveled.

Then the great conqueror planned the next stage of his campaign: an assault on the Khwarazmian capital of Samarqand. For this purpose, he ordered his men to drive the surviving Bukharans out from the burnt remnants of their city and selected young and strong men from among them to serve as laborers and arrow-fodder. Then, leaving a commander named Tausha as the *daruqaci* or governor of the ruins of Bukhara, Chinggis Khan assembled his army and marched on Samarqand.

When Sultan Muhammad II learned of the fall of Bukhara he was horrified. Not only had the great city fallen relatively easily, but other Mongol forces were reported to be rampaging across Mawarannahr (as the land between the Syr Darya and Amu Darya rivers was known). Fear crept into Muhammad's heart as he realized that, in his greed and pride, he had unleashed a wolf into the fold. He therefore decided to abandon Samarqand and the rest of Mawarannahr in the hope that he could thereby preserve the remainder of his empire. However, his actions only served to provoke Chinggis Khan, who dispatched two generals to pursue him to the ends of the earth. Muhammad's decision also undermined his authority and the loyalty of his army, and 7,000 men defected and joined the ranks of the Mongols.

One man who escaped the carnage at Bukhara reached the nearby region of Khurasan. News of the Mongol invasion had spread quickly, and the people pressed him for information. Exhausted from his journey, the man replied simply: 'They came, they sapped, they burnt, they slew, they plundered, and they departed'.[2]

Twenty years later, a European chronicler received news of another Mongol invasion. This was Matthew Paris, a monk in England, who collected the news and gossip of Europe while compiling his great chronicle, the *Chronica Majora*. He included reports of the Mongol invasion of Poland and Hungary as well as information about events in the Middle East. His account is similar to, albeit more detailed than, that of the refugee from Bukhara:

> They razed cities to the ground, burnt woods, pulled down castles, tore up the vine trees, destroyed gardens, and massacred the citizens and husbandmen; if by chance they did spare any who begged their lives, they compelled them, as slaves of the lowest condition, to fight in front of them against their own kindred.[3]

Chapter One

The rise and expansion of the Mongol Empire, 1185–1265

The Mongol Empire founded by Chinggis Khan (also known as Genghis Khan in the West) became the largest contiguous empire in history, stretching from the Sea of Japan to the Mediterranean Sea and the Carpathian Mountains. At its peak, more than a million men were under arms and enrolled in the armies of the Khan, or the emperor of the Mongol Empire. The Mongol Khans became determined to conquer the world, and, indeed, with the resources at their disposal there was little reason why they should fail. Eventually, however, their empire collapsed, partially under its own weight. The following is a brief history of the rise of the Mongol Empire and its subsequent expansion across Asia and into Europe, until it fragmented into four smaller yet still powerful kingdoms.

The rise of Chinggis Khan

The most difficult stage in the evolution of the Mongol empire was the unification of Mongolia itself under Chinggis Khan. There was no clear reason why Temüjin, as Chinggis Khan was known, should become the supreme power in the Mongolian steppe. Indeed, there were many more significant leaders and tribes. The Mongols themselves were a broken power, having suffered defeats by their hereditary enemies – the Tatars in eastern Mongolia, and the Jin Dynasty, which ruled Northern China – in the 1160s. The ramifications of these defeats were immense, and resulted in the Mongols declining to the status of a minor power in the steppe, often requiring the support of more powerful tribes to withstand the continued aggression of the Tatars. Nonetheless, although the Mongols were now without a true khan a few clan leaders still maintained the struggle. One such leader was Yisügei Bahadur (*bahadur* meaning 'hero', 'brave'). Not only did Yisügei prove to be an ardent enemy of the Tatars, but he was also the catalyst for many of the changes that would sweep through Mongolia for the rest of the twelfth century.

Yisügei fathered Temüjin by his wife Hö'elün, who he had acquired through the nefarious, yet traditional, means of kidnapping. Hö'elün, a member of the

Onggirat tribe, had been accompanying her new husband, Chiledu of the Merkit, back to his pasturelands, when Yisügei and his brothers attacked. Chiledu escaped, but Hö'elün was abducted and became Yisügei's first and senior wife. She gave birth to Temüjin around 1165, and then to Jochi-Kasar, Kachun, and Temüge, as well as a daughter, the youngest child, named Temülün. In addition, Yisügei had married a second wife named Ko'agchin, who gave him another two sons.[1] These two boys, Bekhter and Belgütei, appear to have been slightly older than Temüjin, despite being the issue of Yisügei's second wife.

The children knew their father for only a brief time. When Temüjin was 8 or 9 years old Yisügei took him to find a future bride. Along the way they encountered Dai-Sechen, a leader among the Onggirat, who convinced Yisügei that his own daughter, Börte, only slightly older than Temüjin, would be a good wife for the boy. Furthermore, and perhaps the deciding factor, Dai-Sechen prophesized greatness for the young Mongol lad, saying:

> 'This son of yours is a boy,
> Who has fire in his eyes,
> Who has light in his face.'[2]

Dai-Sechen also described to Yisügei a dream he had had the previous night, about a white gerfalcon that clutched the sun and the moon as it flew to him. The Onggirat chieftain's interpretation of the dream was that Temüjin was the gerfalcon, and by clutching the sun and moon it was obvious that he would rule the world.[3]

Yisügei accepted this as a good omen and left his son with the Onggirat before setting out for home. During his return journey he stopped at a camp to rest, since among the steppe nomads there was, and even today still is, a custom of hospitality towards wayfarers. If someone comes to your camp seeking food or shelter, you are obliged to grant it. This was typical behavior and was reciprocal. Unfortunately for Yisügei, the particular camp he had come to was that of some Tatars. Despite their animosity, the Tatars were still obligated to receive their visitor and tend to his needs. Nonetheless, these particular Tatars, having recognized the Mongol chieftain, poisoned his food and drink, and by the time Yisügei reached home he was near death. His last request was that Temüjin should be brought home, although he passed away (in 1175) before Temüjin arrived.

The death of Temüjin's father had grave ramifications for the Mongols. Yisügei had been the leader of the Borjigid, one of the major divisions among the Mongols, but although Temüjin had returned home none of the other clans, understandably, would accept the leadership of a 10-year-old boy. Thus most of the clans that had followed Yisügei now flocked to the Tayichiut, another major Mongol group, while the rest found leadership elsewhere. As a result, Temüjin's family became impoverished.

It was during this period that Temüjin became embroiled in a contest over seniority with his elder half-brother Bekhter. While Temüjin and his brother Jochi-Kasar killed Bekhter in an argument over food, the quarrel was ultimately about power.[4] As the eldest son of Yisügei's senior wife, Hö'elün, Temüjin was the most likely to become leader of the family when he obtained his majority at the age of 15, but Bekhter was a few years older. Thus Bekhter would naturally obtain his majority first, and as such was unlikely to accept inferior rank to his younger half-brother Temüjin. Bekhter might also assume the leadership by Levirate marriage, a common tradition among the nomads being that the sons or brothers of a deceased man could marry his wives (excluding, of course, their own mother). It was consequently feasible that Bekhter might marry Hö'elün, and thus become Temüjin's father and effectively his lord. In all likelihood Temüjin's murder of his brother had more to do with this possibility than the theft of a little food.

While Temüjin staved off a threat to his primacy among his family, Bekhter's death triggered a reaction among the other Mongols. The murder of his half-brother violated nomadic custom, and although Temüjin's family was no longer a major player in steppe politics it still demanded attention. As a result, the Tayichiut raided Temüjin's camp. While Temüjin and his brothers avoided capture for several days, he was ultimately taken prisoner and brought to the Tayichiut camp, where he was held for perhaps several years.[5]

Eventually escaping, Temüjin gradually established himself as leader of a small but loyal following outside of his family. It was during this period that he claimed his bride from Dai-Sechen. This was in 1182/3. In addition to marrying Börte, he used her dowry to develop a client relationship with the powerful leader of the Kereits, Toghril Ong-Qan. As ruler of the Kereit, Toghril dominated central Mongolia in the basin of the Selenge, Orkhon and Tula rivers. Temüjin demonstrated a flair for politics by using his father Yisügei's ties to Toghril to gain his patronage, Yisügei having, on more than one occasion, assisted Toghril in gaining or regaining his throne. Furthermore, the two had been blood-brothers, or *anda*, and it was on the basis of this relationship that Temüjin now called for Toghril's help.

Less than a year after gaining his bride and the protection of the powerful khan of the Kereit, the Merkits belatedly avenged the abduction of Hö'elün by raiding Temüjin's camp. As Temüjin and the others fled, uncertain who was attacking them, Börte was inadvertently left behind and carried off

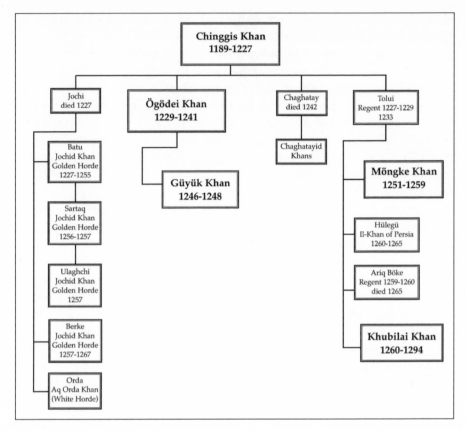

Rulers of the Mongol Empire

by the Merkits. Temüjin therefore turned to Toghril for assistance. Although, in the grand scheme of things, Temüjin was a minor figure in Toghril's hierarchy, the latter agreed to assist him, probably because of the opportunity it provided for plunder. Toghril also called upon another Mongol leader, Jamuqa, to join in the campaign. Jamuqa was not only a client of Toghril, and quite possibly the leader of his armies, but was also an *anda* (blood-brother) of Temüjin, and earlier in his life had been another victim of the depredations of the Merkit.[6] The subsequent attack on the Merkit was tremendously successful, not only regaining Börte but disrupting and weakening Merkit power for several years.

Yet there were some unforeseen consequences. One was that by the time Börte had been rescued several months had passed, and on the return journey she gave birth to a son, named Jochi. The very name means 'guest', and was chosen because Jochi appears not to have been a son of Temüjin, his actual father being a Merkit to whom Börte had been given. Although Temüjin accepted Jochi as his legitimate eldest son throughout his life, it became a source of tension among his offspring.

Another ramification of the Merkit attack was that Temüjin joined Jamuqa for a year. During this time, Temüjin served as a lieutenant to Jamuqa and learned much about the techniques of steppe warfare.[7] Yet rivalry between Jamuqa and Temüjin eventually drove the two apart. It is at this point that the charisma of Temüjin becomes very apparent, since when he and his followers separated from Jamuqa they were joined by several members of Jamuqa's own forces. Although a few members of the Borjigid nobility joined Temüjin, most of those who rallied to him were commoners, many of them barely above the status of slaves. In Temüjin, they saw someone who did not cater only to the interests of the aristocracy.

His separation from Jamuqa accelerated Temüjin's ascension to power, and in 1185 his relatives elected him Khan of the Borjigids. While his patron Toghril, and even Jamuqa, congratulated him on his new title, the election was disingenuous. Typically, a ruler in the steppe was selected from among the leading figures of the nomadic aristocracy based on experience and the ability to provide for and protect the tribe. In 1185 Temüjin was perhaps 20 years old and had relatively little experience compared to his uncles and the other relatives who elected him, but he did possess enormous charisma. In truth, those that selected him did so because he was thought to be malleable and could be manipulated to serve their needs. Much to their chagrin, they would soon find that Temüjin was no puppet.

Yet Temüjin's troubles had only just begun. Tensions increased between Temüjin and his *anda* Jamuqa and eventually war broke out between them. Toghril, as patron of both, did not participate. The two armies met in 1187 at the Battle of Dalan Balzhut, where Jamuqa was victorious. Though Temüjin fled after his defeat, perhaps into China,[8] in some respects the battle strengthened him, as many former followers of Jamuqa joined his ranks when the victor exacted a terrible vengeance on those who had left his following in previous years, thus alienating many of those who had remained with him.

It was not until the early 1190s that Temüjin regained enough power to be a force in the steppe again. Although Jamuqa remained a threat, Temüjin felt the time was right to deal with the Tatars, who had steadily increased in power. Indeed, even the Jin Empire in Northern China was concerned about their strength. Thus the Borjigid Mongols and the Kereit, working in concert with the Jin, launched an attack on the Tatars in 1197, and caught between the pincers of the Kereit and Mongols on one side, and the Jin armies on the other, the Tatars were defeated. Although their power was not completely destroyed, they ceased to be an immediate threat to all parties for the time being. As a result, the Jin recognized Toghril as the principal steppe ruler and Temüjin as one of his important vassals.

For the rest of the 1190s, Temüjin's strength and influence continued to grow. He and Toghril continued to fight the Merkit, as well as the Naiman in Western Mongolia, and Temüjin developed into a capable military leader. On more than one occasion he rescued his overlord, once from the Naiman and a second time by restoring him to his throne after a rebellion. In 1200 Temüjin also established himself as the undisputed ruler of the Onan-Kerulen river basin, the territorial homeland of the Mongols. Conflict between the Borjigids and the Tayichiut was renewed and led to a major battle, from which, in the end, Temüjin emerged victorious. Typically, defeated tribes were added to the strength of the victorious tribe, and many Tayichiut were thereby added to Temüjin's following. However, his victory was not complete, as the majority of the Tayichiut escaped.

A final confrontation between Temüjin and the Tayichiut was not long in coming. Fearing the growing power of Toghril, due partly to Temüjin's own success, a number of smaller tribes banded together in a confederacy against the two allies. As their leader they chose Jamuqa, who in 1201 they elected Gur-Khan or Universal Ruler. They then marched against the Kereit and Mongols, but, on encountering them at Köyiten, Jamuqa was defeated. While Toghril pursued Jamuqa and brought him back to submission, Temüjin followed and overthrew the Tayichiut, although he nearly died from an arrow wound in the throat. The bulk of the Tayichiut were then incorporated into the Borjigid Mongols, but to ensure that the tribe would never threaten him again Temüjin executed its leaders. As an unexpected bonus, the Onggirat also joined Temüjin's following.

Riding a wave of success, he then decided to finish the Tatars once and for all, as they had taken part in the confederation against the Kereit and Mongols. With the addition of the Onggirat and Tayichiut, the Mongols' strength was greatly enhanced. Before attacking, Temüjin issued a remarkable order: that no one was to stop to plunder until he gave the order.[9] Traditionally, once nomadic forces reached the enemy's camp they plundered it and then rode off with their gains, the point of raids and attacks being not to decimate an enemy but rather to enrich themselves. Temüjin, however, saw a new purpose to war: as a means of guaranteeing security against outside threats. He saw the wisdom – or what modern observers would see as common sense – of securing complete victory over an enemy before enjoying the spoils.

In 1202, Temüjin defeated the Tatars at Dalan Nemürges in Eastern Mongolia, near the Khalkha River. Much as he had done with the Tayichiut,

Temüjin ordered the destruction of the Tatar aristocracy, while the commoners were assimilated into the Mongols and distributed among the various clans to ensure that they would not prove troublesome. Having completed this, Temüjin next dealt with his relatives. Since they had elected him as ruler, the Borjigids had considered Temüjin to be their puppet and consequently paid no attention to his prohibition on plundering during the attack on the Tatars. Temüjin therefore confiscated their booty and redistributed it among the rest of the Mongols.

Although still a vassal of Toghril, Temüjin had now become master of Eastern Mongolia. His sudden rise to power began to alter his relationship with Toghril, who naturally became wary of his protégé and was increasingly concerned that Temüjin sought to oust him. Others fed his paranoia, among them Temüjin's senior relatives, who had fled to Toghril after Temüjin had confiscated their booty. Jamuqa had also rejoined Toghril, and spoke ill of his *anda*. Furthermore, Toghril's son, Senggüm, saw Temüjin as a rival for the succession to Toghril's throne. Indeed, Temüjin sought to secure his relationship with Toghril by proposing that his son Jochi should marry Senggüm's daughter; Senggüm was outraged by his audacity. The conspirators considered using the wedding proposal as an opportunity to destroy Temüjin,[10] but the Mongols saw through their designs. Nonetheless, conflict between the Kereit and the Mongols ensued. Although Temüjin suffered a defeat, he managed to rally his forces and made a surprise attack on the Kereit camp as they celebrated their victory.

With this defeat of the Kereit in 1203, Temüjin's power and prestige increased tremendously, since it meant he now dominated both Central and Eastern Mongolia. Furthermore, assimilating the Kereit further increased the strength of his forces. He did not, however, exterminate the Kereit aristocracy. Instead many of Toghril's relatives were treated honorably and given high positions, since, having himself served as a vassal of Toghril for a number of years, many of these men were well-known to Temüjin, and there was no true animosity between the Kereit and the Mongols, unlike the Mongols and the Tatars. Furthermore, Temüjin married many of the daughters and grand-daughters of Toghril to his sons and followers, thus linking the Kereits closely to the Mongol royal family. Toghril and Senggüm escaped the defeat. However, Toghril's flight was short-lived, as a Naiman tribesman came upon the old khan and killed him without realizing who he was. Senggüm, on the other hand, fled south into the kingdom of Xi-Xia (Ningxia and Gansu provinces of modern China).

Final opposition to Temüjin's mastery of the steppe came from the Naiman confederacy. The Naiman initiated the war. Having a low regard for the

Mongols, they believed that if they struck first they would easily defeat Temüjin's armies.[11] However, as the Naiman collected their forces and attempted to find allies among other tribes hostile to the Mongols their plans became known to Temüjin. After considerable debate, Temüjin led his forces westward. Meanwhile the Naiman had collected not only their own considerable strength, but also the Merkits and an army led by Jamuqa, composed of Mongol elements opposed to Temüjin's rule.

Despite their aggressive disposition, the Mongols were outnumbered by the Naiman coalition. Thus upon arriving in Naiman territory, Temüjin ordered every man to light a campfire at night to conceal the relative smallness of their numbers. The ruse worked and delayed the Naiman from attacking. The resultant confusion regarding the Mongols' true strength caused dissension among the Naiman leaders. Their senior khan, Tayang Khan, wanted to lure the Mongols across the Altai Mountains, further into the Naiman's own pasturelands, while his son, Güchülüg, and others urged a direct attack. Tayang Khan finally assented to this, but the decision proved disastrous. The Naiman were crushed by the superior generalship of Temüjin and the disciplined forces that he had developed as he conquered the steppe.

The Battle of the Sa'ari Steppe was the crowning achievement of Temüjin's army. The Mongol victory here, and in a few subsequent skirmishes, crushed the Naiman and the Merkit, although Güchülüg and Toqtoa Beki, the Merkit chieftain, both escaped westward into modern Kazakhstan. The victory also broke Jamuqa's power. He was eventually taken prisoner through treachery, as his own followers took him captive and turned him over to the Mongol ruler. Temüjin rewarded the men who had betrayed their former master by executing them, and offered to pardon Jamuqa, but he, sensing that the rift between them would remain great, requested an honorable death. Respecting the taboo against shedding the blood of the aristocracy, Jamuqa was therefore rolled into a carpet and suffocated.

With the defeat of the Naiman, Temüjin's mastery of the Mongolian steppe was complete, and with relative peace established he was crowned as Chinggis Khan (meaning Firm or Fierce Ruler) in 1206, at a grand *quriltai* or congress. Also at this *quriltai*, Chinggis Khan, as he was henceforth known, began organizing his new empire as well as his army.

Having stabilized the steppes of Mongolia, Chinggis Khan next began to look at his neighbors. There were several immediate threats, most of these being posed by groups that had fled from Mongolia as Chinggis Khan's power grew, such as Senggüm of the Kereit, Toqtoa of the Merkit, and Güchülüg of the Naiman. The Jin Empire continued to meddle in the affairs of the steppe as it attempted to control the various tribes. In addition there was one other group, to the north of Mongolia. This consisted of a number of tribes known collectively as the Hoy-in Irgen or Forest People, which included tribes such as the Oyirad, Buriyad, and Kirghiz. These tended to live a semi-nomadic lifestyle, often establishing permanent villages and living more by hunting, fishing, and limited agriculture rather than pastoral nomadism. In general the Hoy-in Irgen tended to remain neutral in the wars among the nomadic tribes of Mongolia, though there were inevitably exceptions, as a few tribes had joined Jamuqa's coalition.

In 1207 Chinggis Khan sent Jochi with an army to subjugate the Forest People. Quduq-beki of the Oyirad submitted and then acted as a guide for Jochi to the Tümen Oyirad, who submitted to the Mongols at Shiqshit.[12] In addition to the Oyirad, Jochi quickly secured the submission of the rest of the Hoy-in Irgen.[13]

The Kirghiz dominated the upper part of the Yenesei River Valley, while the Kem-Kemjiüts resided along its Kemchik tributary. Economically, it was sensible for Chinggis Khan to incorporate this valley into his realm, as Muslim and Uighur merchants had imported furs and grain from this fertile region for years. The Kirghiz and Kem-Kemjiüts both submitted rather than resist the Mongol army,[14] as did the Tümeds, who controlled the area of the Ija and Angara rivers.[15]

The first sedentary power that the Mongols invaded was the kingdom of Xi-Xia, which lay to the southeast of the nascent Mongolian Empire.[16] The invasion of Xi-Xia is often considered as having been carried out as either a stepping stone towards the invasion of the Jin Empire or for economic reasons, but it was actually invaded for reasons relating to the security of Mongolia.[17]

Although militarily inferior to the Jin dynasty to the east, Xi-Xia was still a powerful state. In addition, it exercised some influence in the steppe, particularly among the Kereit, and had often served as a safe haven for deposed Kereit leaders.[18] Indeed, Senggüm had found refuge in Xi-Xia before being forced to leave after pillaging within the kingdom.[19]

Chinggis Khan invaded Xi-Xia in 1205, using Senggüm's presence there as a pretext.[20] It is also possible that his attack was intended to destabilize Xi-Xia, and thus keep a potential enemy – which also harbored a rival – off balance, and his own army away from Mongolia, while he secured his hold over his newly won kingdom.

The invasion began in the form of raids, in which the Tangut of Xi-Xia made only limited attempts to repel the more mobile Mongol armies. It was not until 1209 that Chinggis Khan began a true invasion of conquest. Several cities had already been taken when the Mongols reached the capital of Zhong-Xiang in May 1209. After the siege of Zhong-Xiang – one of the Mongols' first endeavors at siege warfare – had dragged on into October, Chinggis Khan resorted to building a dyke to divert the Huang He River into the city, and by January the diverted river had almost collapsed the walls. However, the dyke then broke and flooded the Mongol camp, forcing them to withdraw to higher ground. Nonetheless, the Tangut decided to surrender rather than to continue to resist.[21]

Meanwhile, tension had also increased between Chinggis Khan's new state and the Jin dynasty of Northern China. Several tribes that bordered the Jin Empire had switched their allegiance to the Mongols, while others, such as the Juyin, simply revolted against the Jin.[22] The Mongol invasion of the Jin Empire commenced in 1211, partially to avenge past transgressions, but also simply to obtain plunder, as they could no longer raid in Xi-Xia since it had become a Mongol client state. Although the Mongols devastated much of the Jin Empire, they withdrew in 1212 and retained only a small portion of Jin territory, primarily to control the mountain passes back into the steppes. They also compelled the Jin to pay a handsome amount in tribute.[23]

Peace between the two states was short-lived. In the autumn of 1212, Chinggis Khan once again invaded the Jin Empire in a two-pronged attack, the second army being led by Tolui, Chinggis Khan's youngest son. Both forces took siege engineers with them. The Mongols withdrew in 1214, once again having been paid a sizeable tribute and taken a considerable amount of plunder. Perhaps more importantly, the Mongols had demonstrated that the Jin forces could not defeat them in open combat; nor could they rely on their fortifications to protect them, as the Mongols took numerous cities, slowly blockading the capital of Zhongdu (near modern Beijing). As before, the Mongols maintained a presence in strategic passes after their withdrawal, thereby preventing the Jin from launching an attack into Mongolia.

As the Mongol presence crept south and remained a threat, the Jin Emperor, Xuan Zong, moved his capital from Zhongdu to Kaifeng. This, however, breached the terms of his peace treaty with the Mongols, and Chinggis Khan ordered a new invasion later in 1214, not long after his forces had left. While Zhongdu continued to resist all efforts to capture it, Mongol armies continued to be successful in the field. Zhongdu, however, could only hold out for so long without relief, and in June 1215 it surrendered. During the course of invasion several Jin generals switched sides, as it seemed apparent that the Emperor and his advisors had no concept of how to deal with the Mongols. Furthermore, after the fall of Zhongdu other provinces began to rebel.

Following a Mongol invasion of Manchuria, the ancestral lands of the Jin, the Mongols controlled the northern and northeastern portions of the Jin Empire. Although Chinggis Khan himself withdrew in 1216 to deal with a rebellion among the Hoy-in Irgen, by 1218 most of the Empire was in Mongol hands, and more and more Jin generals, including ethnic Jurchen (the founders of the empire) and Khitans and Han Chinese, were changing sides. It seemed that the Empire was on the verge of collapse until events in the west staved off defeat for another fifteen years.

These events occurred in Central Asia. While the Mongols had invaded Xi-Xia and the Jin Empire, Chinggis Khan had not forgotten about the Naiman and Merkit refugees who had fled west. Indeed, when he invaded the Jin Empire he took the step of placing an army on the western borders of his empire to protect it from any possible attack by Güchülüg. In addition he had gained new vassals in the west, the Uighurs of Turfan and some smaller tribes having submitted between 1206 and 1209 as his power grew. Many of these had suffered from attacks by the Merkit and the Naiman.

After Güchülüg fled Mongolia he had eventually made his way into Central Asia and usurped the throne of the Kara Khitai empire, in what is now Kazakhstan. However, he and his Naiman tribesmen were no longer supported by the Merkit, since following the Mongols' defeat of the combined renegade Naiman and Merkit forces on the Irtysh River in 1209 the Merkit had fled westward and found refuge among the Qangli, a Turkic group living north of the Aral Sea. Although the Naiman were able to avoid the Mongols for a few years more, the Merkit were not as fortunate. An army led by two of Chinggis Khan's most gifted generals, Jebe and Sübedei, pursued them into Qangli territory and defeated them. Jebe and Sübedei did not attempt to incorporate the Qangli into the Mongol Empire at this time – they merely completed their task and turned for home.

However, this was not as easy as they had hoped, since on their return journey they encountered a Khwarazmian army led by Sultan Muhammad II. The Mongol generals had strict orders to avoid confrontation with the Khwarazmian Empire, but Sultan Muhammad viewed them as a threat and initiated a battle. The fighting continued until evening, when both sides retired for the night and the Mongols withdrew under cover of the darkness. Although it was the Mongols who had retreated, Muhammad was clearly shaken by the encounter, as his forces had outnumbered the Mongols but were unable to defeat them. According to one chronicler 'the Mongols had filled Muhammad's heart with terror', as he had never before seen an army as ferocious in battle.[24]

This fear faded over time as Muhammad extended his own empire into Afghanistan and Persia, and his sycophantic courtiers called him a second Alexander the Great. Thus when the governor of the city of Otrar on the Syr Darya River massacred a Mongol-sponsored caravan in 1218 for espionage, Muhammad did not worry, even though the Mongols were now his neighbors.

(Earlier in 1218, Jebe had ended Güchülüg's usurpation of Kara Khitai and pursued the prince to his death. The former empire of Kara Khitai was then absorbed into the Mongol Empire.) Undoubtedly the governor of Otrar's suspicions were accurate, as the Mongols used merchants as spies in addition to gathering intelligence from them through conversation. Chinggis Khan initially demanded compensation through diplomatic channels, but Muhammad refused to deal with him as an equal. Furthermore he executed one of the envoys and burned the beards of the remaining two. Perhaps he believed that since the Mongols were involved in a war against the Jin Empire in China, they would not be willing to fight in Central Asia too. Or perhaps he believed his courtiers' flatteries and had faith in his own abilities and the strength of his 400,000-man army. In either case, he chose his course of action poorly.

Once news of the ill-treatment of his envoys reached Chinggis Khan he put his own plans for the Jin on hold and ordered his lieutenant Muqali to take command in Mongol territory and, if possible, to finish off the Jin. Muqali had just 30,000 Mongol troops, but was augmented by thousands of Khitans, Jurchen, Tangut, and Han Chinese who had joined the Mongols. Meanwhile, Chinggis Khan gathered an estimated force of 150,000 horsemen and marched on the Khwarazmian Empire.

The invasion began in the late summer or early autumn of 1219, with the Mongols descending on Otrar, the scene of the massacre. The city fell quickly and the governor was executed, ostensibly by having molten silver poured into his eyes and ears to sate his avarice. From Otrar, the Mongol army split into five forces, each division striking against different targets to prevent the Khwarazmians from using their superior numbers in the field by obliging them to defend the empire's numerous cities. One by one the cities of Mawarannahr fell. When Muhammad eventually fled across the Amu Darya, Chinggis Khan sent his trusted generals Jebe and Sübedei in pursuit while he prosecuted the war. Muhammad eventually escaped to an island in the Caspian Sea, where he died in 1221 in a most un-regal fashion, clothed in rags and suffering from either dysentery or pleurisy. Meanwhile, his son Jalal al-Din attempted to halt the Mongol advance. After some success he attracted the attention of Chinggis Khan himself, who pursued him to the Indus River and defeated him in battle. The prince, however, eluded capture and fled into India.

Although the Mongols thoroughly defeated the Khwarazmians, they gradually began to withdraw their armies from Persia and Afghanistan. Rather than trying to incorporate the entire Khwarazmian Empire, the Mongols annexed only Mawarannahr, and set the Amu Darya River as their frontier. Only retaining a portion of their conquests, so as not to overextend their armies, subsequently became common practice during the expansion of the Mongol Empire.

Meanwhile Jebe and Sübedei continued to ride westward, crossing the Caucasus Mountains and defeating a Georgian army. Indeed, this encounter in 1221–2 had larger ramifications, as the Georgians had planned to participate in the Fifth Crusade, but were prevented from doing so by the Mongol invasion. Although Jebe died crossing the mountains Sübedei continued the campaign, and before eventually rejoining the Mongol armies in the steppes of modern Kazakhstan he defeated the Kipchak Turks and, later, a combined army of Turks and Rus' or Russian princes at the Battle of the Khalkha River in 1223. Not only did he defeat several armies and complete a circuit of approximately 5,000 miles, but he accomplished this without the aid of reinforcements or modern navigational devices. Indeed, many of the nations he encountered were baffled regarding who the Mongols were and from whence they came. One puzzled Russian chronicler wrote of the mysterious opponents of the Rus' at the Khalkha River: 'In the same year, for our sins, there came unknown tribes, and some people called them Tartars. . . . Only God knows who these people are or from whence they came'.[25]

Indeed, the Mongols vanished as quickly as they had appeared. One of the reasons for their withdrawal from the Khwarazmian Empire was the arrival of news that the Tangut of Xi-Xia had rebelled. Although it is often said that Chinggis Khan destroyed Xi-Xia for good because the ruler of the Tangut refused to provide troops for the Khwarazmian campaign, this is not quite accurate. In fact the Tangut served the Mongols against the Jin until 1223, when they rebelled and joined the Jin against the Mongols. Muqali died the same year, forcing Chinggis Khan to return to deal with the situation. Even so, he did not invade Xi-Xia until 1225 but had nevertheless overrun the greater part of the kingdom by late 1226. Only the capital remained unconquered by 1227. The survival of the Tangut was extended by a short span when Chinggis Khan, now in his sixties, fell from his horse while hunting. His injuries slowed the siege as his princes and generals were more concerned with his health, and they urged him to end the siege and return to Mongolia. Chinggis Khan refused, however, and died of his injuries on 18 August 1227 after ordering his commanders to conceal his death until the Xi-Xia capital was taken. When it finally fell no clemency was shown to its inhabitants, just as he had ordered.

Dreams of world conquest: the Empire under Ögödei
With the death of Chinggis Khan and the destruction of the Tangut, the next matter at hand for the Mongols was the selection of a new ruler. Although Tolui was possibly the best candidate in terms of military ability and leadership, Ögödei was ultimately chosen to succeed and was raised to the throne in

1229/30. The prime reason for his selection was his temperament: he was wise, calm, and had a talent for finding compromises between his more quarrelsome brothers, Jochi and Chaghatay.

Ögödei did not rest on his throne long. In 1230 he ordered the Mongol armies back into the Jin Empire. Since Muqali's death many of the Mongols' former allies had wavered, and some had even joined the Jin. In addition Muqali's lieutenants proved to be less capable than he, obliging the Mongols to give up much of the territory they had previously held. Rather than simply attempting to recover these losses, Ögödei was more concerned with the destruction of the Jin once and for all. With this in mind, he and Tolui led armies into the Jin territory and then split up and struck against multiple targets.

Although Tolui died in 1231, the Mongols pressed on. By then the Jin held only Eastern Honan, and the Mongols took the new capital of Kaifeng in 1233. Shortly before its fall the Jin Emperor, Ai-Tsung, fled to Caizhou, ignoring the warning of his commanders that it was poorly protected. The emperor learned just how unprepared the city was once the Mongols arrived. The siege began in October 1233 and continued until February 1234, when, starving and flooded by a diverted river, Caizhou surrendered.

Even while Ögödei invaded the Jin Empire, the Mongols were active on other fronts. In 1230 he ordered the Mongol general Chormaqan to cross the Amu Darya river and resume the war against Jalal al-Din. Jalal al-Din fled before Chormaqan's forces into Transcaucasia (the area south of the Caucasus Mountains). While one army pursued him, Chormaqan quickly gained the submission of the various kingdoms of Persia by 1231, excluding only Isfahan, which finally fell in 1237. Jalal al-Din was killed by Kurdish peasants in 1231, but the Mongols gave Transcaucasia only a brief respite. After consolidating Mongol dominion in Persia, Chormaqan invaded Transcaucasia in 1236. Because of the invasions of Jalal al-Din as well the previous Mongol invasion of 1221–2, the Georgians and Armenians made no attempt to confront the Mongols in the field, and after a series of sieges Georgia, Armenia, and what is now Azerbaijan had all fallen to the Mongols by 1239.

In 1236, an army of 150,000 Mongols, including several grandsons of Chinggis Khan, invaded the lands of the Kipchak Turks and the Bulghars on the Volga River. This invasion was led by Sübedei and Batu, son of Jochi (who had died in 1225). Despite a determined resistance, neither the Kipchaks nor the Bulghars could resist the Mongol onslaught. Many of the Kipchaks fled before the Mongols, some of them reaching Hungary. Others were incorporated into the Mongol military machine.

In the winter of 1238 the Mongols advanced against the Rus' principalities, using the frozen rivers as roads. The fragmented Rus' discovered that they could not defeat the Mongols in open combat, and that they were equally adept at siege warfare, so that one by one the northern Rus' cities fell. In late 1238 and 1239 the southern Rus' cities also succumbed to Mongol attack, as did the tribes of the southern steppes. The great city of Kiev, the center of Rus' civilization, was among the last cities to fall, after days of continual bombardment. Of the major Rus' cities that did not submit when the Mongols approached, only Novgorod was spared from attack, due to a timely thaw that deterred the Mongol cavalry from advancing further. Nonetheless, the Novgorodians saw the wisdom of submitting peacefully to the Mongols rather than incurring their wrath.

In 1241 Sübedei led the bulk of the Mongol army westward. It divided into two forces, of which the smaller, commanded by Baidar and Qadan, invaded Poland while the larger, under Sübedei and Batu, crossed the Carpathian Mountains. At most Baidar and Qadan led just 20,000 men. Thus they sought to avoid direct engagements and conducted numerous raids. Eventually they fought a pitched battle at Liegnitz against a combined army of Poles, Germans, and Teutonic Knights (a military religious order that had been formed during the Crusades), the Mongols destroying this force before it could be reinforced by King Vaclav (Wenceslas) of Bohemia. Baidar and Qadan then moved south to rendezvous with the other Mongol army.

Batu and Sübedei had meanwhile forced their way across the Carpathians along five different routes. Unlike the Khwarazmians, the Hungarian King, Bela IV, did not wait for the Mongols in his castles. Rather, he marched with his army to a point along the Sajo River on the plain of Mohi. The Hungarian army was considered by many to possess the finest cavalry in Europe. However, it proved to be of little use against the Mongols, who decimated it in April 1241. Using a rolling barrage of arrows and catapult shot, the Mongols seized a heavily defended bridge. Then another force made a rear attack by crossing another point of the river, so that before long the Hungarians found themselves trapped in their camp. The Mongols did not launch a final assault yet. Instead, they left a gap in their lines. The Hungarians took this to be an error on the part of the Mongols and began to flee through it, but it was a ruse. With the Hungarians fleeing in a disorderly fashion, the Mongol cavalry descended upon them and destroyed them. Mongol forces then spread throughout Hungary and into Wallachia and Serbia. King Bela IV himself barely escaped to the Adriatic Sea before pursuing Mongol troops arrived.

It appeared to contemporaries that the Mongols were on the verge of invading the rest of Europe, but then, suddenly, they withdrew from Hungary.

The exact reason for this remains a point of debate among scholars, but one factor that certainly played a part was the death of Ögödei in 1240/1.

Ögödei's death drastically altered the Mongol Empire. It was during his reign that the Mongols began to conceive of conquering the world. Although this idea is often attributed to Chinggis Khan, in truth his actions seem to belie it. His goal appears to have been to secure the steppes of Mongolia from external threat rather than to dominate sedentary cultures. Raids and forcing sedentary states to pay tribute helped this and was economically profitable. Ögödei, by contrast, embraced and encouraged the idea of conquest. In addition he endorsed the creation of an effective administrative apparatus to rule the empire.

His death, however, caused a crisis, as he had not chosen a successor. Indeed, his death, due either to alcoholism or poison, revealed the strains between the grandsons of Chinggis Khan.

Signs of strain: Güyük Khan and the regents

Ögödei's widow and sixth wife, Töregene, assumed the role of regent after his death. Among her first obligations was the organization of a *quriltai* in order to select a new Khan. Her private choice was her own son, Güyük. However, Töregene was slow to organize the meeting, in part because of her own ambition for power. As regent, Töregene essentially ran the empire. Those who disagreed with her ambitions, including many high-ranking ministers, ran the risk of death. In 1246, however, Güyük was elected Khan. Although he did correct many of the corrupt practices introduced during Töregene's regency, all was not well within the empire.

Güyük and Batu, the son of Jochi, did not agree on many things. Much of their animosity stemmed from Jochi's questionable ancestry. Furthermore, the two clashed during the Western campaign, when only the presence of Sübedei had prevented physical conflict. Güyük was sent back to Ögödei, who became furious with his son. Previously, it had been thought that Güyük was the undisputed heir to the throne, but by the time Ögödei died Güyük had fallen far from favor. Nor had Güyük had forgotten his feud with Batu, which was intensified by Batu's refusal to come to the *quriltai* for Güyük's ascension to the throne. Güyük actually prepared an army, ostensibly to complete the conquest of Europe, but many suspected that it was to wage war against Batu. In the end, however, it did not matter, as Güyük died in 1248.

His wife Oghul-Qaimish then assumed the regency, which lasted until 1250. During this time very little occurred in the Mongol realm. Indeed, she demonstrated very little interest in arranging a *quriltai*, until a coup led by members of the family of Tolui finally ended the regency and led to the election of Möngke Khan.

Despite the brief reign of Güyük and the, at times, ineffective leadership of the regents, the Mongols actively continued to expand their empire. War against the Song dynasty of Southern China began during Ögödei's reign and continued in a sporadic manner throughout the 1240s. In the Middle East, Baiju, the lieutenant of Chormaqan (who also died in 1240), conquered the Seljuk Sultanate of Rum (modern Turkey) in 1243. Mongol armies in the Middle East raided into Syria and the Crusader states, threatening Antioch, as well as launching numerous raids against Baghdad. But without political stability the Mongols were unable to organize any large-scale campaigns of conquest until the succession of Möngke Khan.

Apogee and dissolution: the Empire of Möngke Khan
The Mongols attained the zenith of their power during the reign of Möngke Khan. Upon ascending the throne with the assistance of his politically wily mother Sorqoqtani and the military power of his cousin Batu, Möngke rectified the corruption that had entered into the empire's administrative practices during the regencies of Töregene and Oghul-Qaimish. In addition he purged many of the descendants of Ögödei and Chaghatay after they attempted a coup. Any threat to the ascendancy of the Toluids was dealt with aggressively.

Having stabilized the empire, Möngke then sought to expand it. By this time the Mongols had approximately a million men under arms, ranging from the nomadic horse-archers who made up the core of their armies, to engineers, siege artillerists, and, of course, infantry for garrisoning cities and fortresses.

Möngke planned to carry out two major campaigns, designed to mop up those powers that had not submitted when called upon. The first campaign, led by Möngke himself, with the assistance of his younger brother Khubilai, was the invasion of the Song Empire of Southern China. The Mongols had been at war with the Song since the reign of Ögödei, but had made little headway. Not only was Southern China unsuitable for cavalry warfare due to its geography, which ranged from mountains to flooded plains used for rice cultivation, but the Song had strongly fortified cities. Although the Mongols had become exceedingly adept at siege warfare, the Song defenders were equally talented at defending their cities and using the latest technological advances against the Mongols, such as gunpowder.

The second campaign was directed against regions in the Middle East that had either not yet submitted, or whose rulers had not come in person to demonstrate their obeisance. Two powers in particular concerned the Mongols. The first was that of the Ismailis of Alamut, in the Elbruz mountains of Iran, south of the Caspian Sea and in Quhistan. The Ismailis, Shi'a Muslims who became known in the West as the Assassins, had been allies of the Mongols during the invasion of the Khwarazmian Empire as well as during the period of Chormaqan's rule in the Middle East. After 1240, however, the Ismailis began to view the Mongols as a threat – an accurate perception, as the Mongols had by now determined that Heaven decreed that they should rule the world. Furthermore, the Ismailis had attempted to assassinate Möngke.[26] The second target of the Mongol army that was led by Hülegü, another brother of Möngke's, was the Abbasid Caliphate of Baghdad. In theory, Caliph Musta'sim ibn Mustansir was the ruler of the Islamic world as the successor to the Prophet Muhammad. In reality, the Abbasid Caliphate had shrunk considerably since its creation in the eighth century as secular rulers sprung up in the frontier provinces to take power, at first with the Caliph's blessing but subsequently with little regard for him. By the 1250s the Caliphate was really a small kingdom centered on the city of Baghdad, with little temporal authority beyond the surrounding area.

Hülegü's campaign began at a leisurely pace as his army marched out of Mongolia in 1255. As he advanced, scouts and officials rode ahead to procure adequate pastures. This also caused a redistribution of the *tammacin*, or troops stationed along the border of the Mongol empire. These would advance to new positions, thus leaving their former pastures to be occupied by the prince's army. In addition, troops already in the Middle East commenced operations against the Ismailis. In 1252 Ket-Buqa, one of Hülegü's generals, began raids into Quhistan that thereafter became fairly constant until the arrival of Hülegü in 1256.

While Khwurshah, the Ismaili leader, did seek to submit to the Mongols, he constantly delayed coming before Hülegü, and while the negotiations continued Ket-Buqa overran Quhistan, often using the orders of the Ismaili leader to secure their formidable fortresses. Despite this obvious display of force, Khwurshah still did not come in person to submit to Hülegü, which only served to anger the Mongol prince. As a result, activities against the Ismailis intensified, and before long their greatest fortresses, including Alamut, had surrendered. Seeing that all was lost, Khwurshah finally came before Hülegü, who then used the Ismaili leader to gain the submission of over a hundred other fortresses. Then, having no further use for him, Hülegü had Khwurshah executed, along with the leaders of all the important Ismaili families. Many Sunni Muslims celebrated on hearing this, as they had come to regard the Ismailis with dread, their assassins being masters of disguise who could strike down notable figures however closely guarded they might be.

The Mongols then moved against the Abbasid Caliphate. Although Baghdad had withstood several years of Mongol attacks it remained independent and defiant. In truth, however, the outcome of the coming attack was never in doubt – at least to the Mongols. Their previous attempts had amounted to little more than raids, and there had been no assault on the city itself until now. Even before Hülegü had arrived, the city's defenses had begun to fragment as internal rivalries robbed the Caliphate of effective leadership. Indeed, Ibn Alqami, the Caliph's *wazir* or chamberlain, is thought to have actually been in league with the Mongols.

After a stand-off lasting almost a month, Hülegü launched his attack in January 1258, defeating the Caliphate's army in the plain before the city walls after flooding the Muslims' camp. As the Muslim forces were driven from the field, the Mongols approached Baghdad from all sides and began their siege in earnest. Negotiations for surrender began at the end of the month, but Hülegü was not in any mood for leniency and continued his attack. The Caliph only finally submitted after the Mongols had breached the walls. Hülegü then had him executed by rolling him in a carpet and having him trampled on, although some sources give a more colorful story in which the Caliph is starved to death surrounded by the treasure he had failed to spend on the defense of the city.[27] Baghdad was then given over to pillaging for more than 30 days.

Having brought the Caliphate under Mongol rule, Hülegü next moved his armies to lush pastures in modern Azerbaijan. Most of the local princes came and offered their submission, but the ruler of Aleppo and Damascus, al-Nasir Yusuf, was not among them. Hülegü's army therefore descended upon Aleppo in January 1260. Despite its stout defenses, the Mongols broke through after six days of concentrated fire from 20 mangonels. The citadel itself held out for another month, but the city was turned over to pillaging for a period of five days.

After the fall of Aleppo, other Syrian cities quickly surrendered, and al-Nasir, upon hearing of the Mongols' approach, fled from Damascus. Although Hülegü himself returned to Azerbaijan after the capture of Aleppo, his general Ket-Buqa continued operations. Damascus wisely surrendered without a fight when the Mongols arrived in March 1260. Another Mongol force caught al-Nasir outside of Nablus after a brief skirmish and used him to gain the submission of other fortresses. Then he was sent to Hülegü in Azerbaijan to show proper obeisance, while Ket-Buqa remained in Syria with a small army.

Though Mongol control of Syria was ephemeral, the Mamluks of Egypt – a dynasty of former slave soldiers who had seized power in 1250 – realized that they stood little chance of defeating a determined invasion, and therefore decided to take the battle to the Mongols while they were unprepared. Having secured the neutrality of the Crusaders, who had provoked Mongol attacks on Sidon and in Galilee, the Mamluks advanced to Ayn Jalut, or the Well of Goliath, where they defeated Ket-Buqa in a hard-fought battle. The desertion of some of the Mongols' Syrian troops may have been the pivotal point in the engagement. While this battle is often viewed as marking a turning point in history, since the Mongols' advance was halted, it owes its claim not so much to the Mamluk victory itself, as tremendous as it was, as to events that occurred in China.

Möngke, having been unable to break through the northern defenses of the Song Empire, had decided to hit them from the southwest, thereby obliging them to redistribute their troops, and Khubilai was sent to open this new front. In 1252–3 Möngke ordered two out of every ten troops in the empire to serve under Khubilai and another two out of every ten to serve under Hülegü, although Khubilai's army was only one of four sent against the Song.[28] The attack began in earnest in 1257, although mobilization had begun in 1255.

The invasion started off well, with all four armies making good progress on their respective fronts. However, it eventually became bogged down due to the terrain. In 1258–9 Möngke led a corps in a three-pronged attack from Shanzi into Sichuan. He captured Chengdu, Tongchuan and several mountain forts after determined attacks in 1258. When Möngke moved against Hezhou the following year, the prefect of the city moved the government to Diaoyucheng, which resisted the Mongols and stalled their offensive. During the course of this siege Möngke died, either from an arrow wound or dysentery, and Diaoyucheng held out until 1279.[29]

During Möngke's invasion, the other Mongol forces operating elsewhere in the Song Empire were not very effective except as raiders.[30] Khubilai laid siege to the city of Yauju and experienced many difficulties.[31] Many of the Mongols' problems during the Song campaign stemmed from the terrain. While they used many infantry units, the primary offensive arm of the Mongol army remained its cavalry, and the hills and rice paddies of Southern China placed many limitations on mounted warfare.

Haojing (1223–75), Khubilai's minister, believed that the movement of the Mongols' armies in Sichuan was restricted by the mountains and valleys as well as by the Song occupation of strategic places. This forced them to take circuitous routes, which were further complicated by guerrilla attacks that slowed their advance further. The difficulty in capturing the mountain forts resulted in Sichuan province only being captured after the rest of the Song Empire had fallen.[32] The Mongols encountered similar problems in the mountains and islands of Korea.

The Song campaign stalled further when Khubilai received news of Möngke's death. Initially he dismissed the report as false and pressed on, crossing the Yangtze River to capture O-Zhou. Only afterwards did Khubilai receive confirmation (from his wife, Chabai) of his brother's death.[33]

Tensions then arose between Khubilai and his brother Ariq Böke, who had been left as regent in Mongolia while Möngke went on campaign, as each sought the throne. Both were chosen to succeed at separate *quriltai*s – Ariq Böke at a council held in Mongolia, and Khubilai at another held in China. Civil war ensued, with Khubilai emerging the victor in 1264, although the unity of the Mongol Empire was destroyed forever.

As Ariq Böke and Khubilai fought the rest of the empire fragmented. Central Asia, the area bequeathed to Ögödei's brother Chaghatay, became a separate khanate and resisted Khubilai's rule: it would be ruled at varying times thereafter by Chaghatayid princes or by Qaidu, a grandson of Ögödei and Khubilai's most formidable opponent. Meanwhile, Batu, son of Jochi, had died in 1255, and his brother Berke had succeeded to the Kipchak khanate after a short reign by Batu's son, Sartaq. Berke instantly came into conflict with Hülegü. The stated reason was that Berke, a Muslim convert, was angered by the destruction of the Abbasid Caliphate, but in truth the reason had more to do with Jochid claims to territory in the Middle East that Hülegü now claimed as part of his own kingdom, known as the Il-Khanate of Persia. Hülegü and his successors therefore found themselves in the unenviable position of fighting not only the Golden Horde, as the Jochids became known, but also the Chaghatayids. In addition the Golden Horde entered into an alliance with the Mamluks, so that the Il-Khanate was surrounded by enemies with no direct route to its sole ally, the Great Khan's Empire ruled by Khubilai's new dynasty, the Yuan.

The civil wars between these Mongol kingdoms undermined the Empire. Their rulers continued to fight until the khanates in turn disintegrated into smaller kingdoms or disappeared altogether amid unabated internecine warfare. The Il-Khanate collapsed in 1335, while the Yuan dynasty lost control of China in 1368. The Yuan would continue to hold Mongolia for a little longer, but here too its authority would eventually evaporate as the Mongols continued to fight amongst themselves. The Chaghatayid kingdom eventually became subordinate to the Central Asian conqueror Timur, or Tamerlane, in the later part of the fourteenth century. The Golden Horde, however, survived in one form or another into the eighteenth century. Over the course of centuries it progressively Balkanized until the Russians slowly but steadily absorbed its remnants. The Kazan Khanate and Astrakhan fell to Ivan the Terrible in 1552 and 1556 respectively, while the Crimean Khanate succumbed to Catherine the Great in 1798.

After the dissolution of their Empire, the Mongol art of war evolved to meet the regional needs of each khanate. Khubilai's armies, while still buttressed by horse archers, included massive units of Chinese infantry. Meanwhile the Il-Khans gradually came to depend more on heavy cavalry like their Mamluk opponents than the light cavalry of Chinggis Khan's day. The only parts of the old Mongol Empire in which light cavalry continued to constitute the principal element of their armies were the Golden Horde and the Chaghatayid kingdom, as both remained in the steppe, where the necessary abundance of pasture remained available. However, it is not apparent whether they were able to maintain the same rigid discipline and training as their predecessors.

Chapter 2

The recruitment and organization of the Mongol Army

An understanding of the organization of the Mongol army provides insights into the underlying command structure and philosophy of command as well as the process of recruitment, and helps to explain the Mongols' approach to tactics and strategy. Military organization was perhaps more crucial to the Mongols than it was in other contemporary armies because of the wide-ranging nature of their campaigns, and because their armies did not rely on central control by a single general or khan. In addition their military organization was important to the evolution of the Mongol state, since under Chinggis Khan's direction it became the basis for a new social structure in which the military unit of a thousand men replaced traditional tribal identities and, in the process, transformed a steppe confederation into an army that conquered an empire.

Recruitment

The process of recruiting or conscripting soldiers for the Mongol army was not quite as simple as is often thought. For instance, not every male in Mongolian society rode off to war. Nor was it a matter of just enlisting every male among conquered nomadic tribes and incorporating them into the army. In order to maintain the troop reservoir of the steppes and yet have sufficient resources available during a campaign, it was necessary to have a highly organized system to provide the Mongol armies with the manpower they required.

The size of the Mongol army varied with the extent of the Mongol empire. For instance, during the Great Khan Möngke's campaign against the Song in the mid-1250s he possessed roughly 90 *tümet* or units of 10,000 men. As *tümet* are usually approximated at 60 per cent strength, Möngke therefore had theoretically 540,000 men for the purpose of conquering Southern China. At the same time in the Middle East, Hülegü led 22 *tümet*, not including Armenian and Georgian auxiliaries who probably filled an additional *tümen*. Hülegü's units provided him with approximately 132,000 men. Furthermore, there were at least 43 *tümet* in the Jochid Ulus.[1] Making the cautious assumption that the Jochid *tümet* were also at 60 per cent strength at any given point, they possessed

258,000 soldiers. There is no available information for the approximate strength in the Chaghatayid Ulus.[2] Finally, these figures do not include the troops that Möngke left in Mongolia under the command of his brother Ariq Böke. Even so, it is clear that at the pinnacle of the Mongolian empire's power the Khan had at his disposal at least 930,000 men, and if one adds the Chaghatayid forces as well as those in Mongolia and elsewhere, this number easily surpasses one million. Considering the size of the Mongol empire, this figure is not surprising, and one must remember that this total was not and could not be assembled in one location – it was scattered across the entire Mongol empire, from the Sea of Japan to the Black Sea.

That being said, it is uncertain how large the army was on the eve of the Mongol expansion beyond Mongolia in 1209, partly because the size of the population of Mongolia at the beginning of the thirteenth century is hard to calculate: most estimates run from 700,000 to approximately 2.5 million.[3] Why is there such a wide discrepancy between the numbers? It is difficult to estimate the population figures of a region that did not carry out a census until decades later, much less maintain demographic records. Most scholars have taken the census figures for Mongolia around the beginning of the twentieth century and based their calculations on this, as the population then was roughly one million. Such a small population could provide a relatively small army at best. Fortunately, we have precise numbers for the Mongol army at the time of Chinggis Khan's coronation in 1206 courtesy of *The Secret History of the Mongols*, which lists the army as 95,000 men.[4]

As this number is based on the assumption that one male in every family in Mongolia between the ages of 15 and 70 served in the Mongol army, it is fairly simple to extrapolate an approximate population of Mongolia. In 1241, the Mongols conducted a census that yielded a total of 97,575 ethnic Mongol troops and a population of 723,910.[5] This provides roughly 7.4 members per household. With this average of one soldier per seven people, in 1206 the population was an estimated 665,000. However, elsewhere in the empire the typical recruitment figure was one out of ten, for instance amongst the sedentary population of Iran, or even one out of 20, as in China, and it seems odd that an army organized along decimal lines should have used anything other than a decimal recruiting method. Thus the population of Mongolia may have been closer to 950,000 people, perhaps topping one million.

Of course, once Mongol territory expanded their army was greatly increased by the addition of large numbers of Turkic nomads as well as auxiliaries from other regions. Thus a decade after the *quriltai* of 1206, the Mongols assembled sufficient forces to simultaneously fight in Northern China, quell rebellions in northern Mongolia, and send an army of 150,000 men into Central Asia.

In the year 1267 each household of two or three men provided one soldier; four or five males in a household provided two soldiers, and six or seven males in a household provided three men. Later even larger proportions were inducted into the military. However, due to their numbers ethnic Han Chinese were registered slightly differently to nomads, only one adult male being inducted into the military out of every 20. This was determined by the census of 1235. Although the census formally inducted men into the army, a general conscription could take place whenever it was deemed necessary. This occurred, for instance, just a year later, between 4 August and 1 September 1236, when one out of every 20 males was conscripted from 372,972 civilian households to form a *cerik* or non-nomad based army.[6]

It is readily assumed that when the Mongols conquered another tribe the defeated were conscripted into the Mongol military, and in most instances this is true. However, incorporating every male into the army could have led to negative consequences. The size of the army would be so swollen that its logistics would not have been able to support it, and the economy and security of the newly-conquered area would be ruined, being devoid of males. Only by gradually incorporating conquered tribesmen, or even Mongols, into the army could a reliable reservoir of manpower be maintained. To immediately incorporate every male, especially those who had been recently defeated, might create an imbalance in which the victors became outnumbered by the vanquished. Although all nomads tended to be warriors, the newly conquered tribesmen would have still required training in order to operate under Mongol command, particularly in terms of discipline and tactics.

How the Mongols assembled their armies is somewhat uncertain. The Song envoy, Zhao Hong, recorded that 'when the Mongols take up arms, hundreds and thousands come. They form units of tens, hundreds, and thousands and carry out the orders that are delivered to them'.[7] This practice was a result of Chinggis Khan's reorganization of the nomadic society of Mongolia from tribal lines to new units based on the decimal system. Zhao Hong's account supports the contemporary belief that the Mongols were perhaps the nation most easily mobilized for war.[8] The Mongols could form an army at little notice and it would perform as such, and not as a rabble. Yet this description does not explain how the Mongols recruited their warriors and then organized them into effective and competent units.

In the Middle East, the Mongols drafted one out of every ten male adults into the military. Often the men from towns and villages were employed for garrison duty or as corvée laborers, but they underwent military reviews periodically and therefore maintained some discipline and training. Nomads were not suitable recruits for garrison duty, yet as even the Mongols' garrison troops underwent occasional reviews this practice applied to conscripted Turkic nomads as well.

Most nomads were inured to a life of riding and archery, so they integrated into the Mongol military system well. As new recruits often joined existing units or were added to newly created units with a veteran core, they were assimilated quickly by means of military drills.

The key instrument in recruitment was the census, which the Mongols adopted not long after invading Northern China. Besides establishing households as units of taxation, all male adults were registered specifically for the purpose of military conscription. Indeed, registering the entire population was an essential step when a territory submitted to the Mongols. The Armenian chronicler, Grigor of Akner, noted that the census registered men between the ages of 15 and 60 as being suitable for military duty. Chinese sources extend the upper age bracket to 70 years.[9] The age of induction into the military usually ranged between 15 and 20, depending on the need and the number of men required. Not all of the men entered the army upon reaching the appropriate age; some were required to stay at home to tend the herds or oversee appanages. Age was also used as a criterion when new units were formed. In 1229 soldiers between the ages of 20 and 30 in each unit of ten were ordered to assemble and were then organized into new units. Those who failed to report or who hid deserters were executed.[10]

Soldiers were not the only ones drafted by the Mongols. Often engineers and artisans found themselves drafted, along with people from other walks of life. In the year 1235, for instance, the artisans of the Chinese cities of Xuan-de, Xi-ching, Ping-yang, Tai yuan, and the region of Shanxi were drafted.[11]

The process of registering families and the conscription of Mongols and non-Mongols was not meant solely to provide troops for the army or establish tax expectations, but was also utilized as a means of reorganizing conquered societies into a system more familiar to the Mongols. The registering process ensured that men from some households were always enlisted into the military and created hereditary military families among the sedentary population.[12] This process allowed the Mongols to efficiently gather recruits to maintain their garrisons. If a soldier died in a garrison, after 100 days the next eligible recruit from his household replaced him. However, if the soldier died in battle, rather than from an accident or disease, a year's exemption was granted to that particular household.[13]

Once recruited into the army, by whatever means, nomadic recruits became Mongol soldiers. Just as modern soldiers undergo a rite of passage that distinguishes them from the civilian population by receiving a crew-cut, the Mongols made their own soldiers distinguishable from the rest of the empire's population. According to William of Rubruck the Mongols cut their hair in the following fashion:

> The men shave a square on the top of their heads and from the front corners of this they continue the shaving in strips along the sides of the head as far as the temples. They also shave their temples and neck to the top of the cervical cavity and their forehead in front to the top of the frontal bone, where they leave a tuft of hair which hangs down as far as the eyebrows. At the sides and the back of the head they leave the hair, which they make into plaits, and these they braid round the head to the ears.[14]

Thus, with his distinctive hairstyle, the recruit became unmistakably part of the Mongol military, and underwent training in unit tactics and, of course, dressed and armed himself accordingly.

Arban, jaghun, minqan, and *tümen*

Chinggis Khan ordered the Mongol army to be established along decimal lines, in units of ten (*arban*, plural *arbat*), 100 (*jaghun*, plural *jaghut*), 1,000 (*minqan*, plural *minqat*), and 10,000 (*tümen*, plural *tümet*).[15] This was not an innovation on his part, as other North Asian empires – such as the Khitan and the Jurched – had previously adopted decimal organization. Indeed, Chinggis Khan was first exposed to it whilst a subordinate of Toghril Ong-Qan of the Kereit. Nevertheless, the adoption of decimal organization was an important step in the development of the Mongol army.

Chinggis Khan did not simply turn tribes into such units, but rather he created new units out of dispersed tribes and distributed men among different units. As the Mongols expanded their domain in Mongolia, the larger conquered tribes were broken into several *minqat* or units of a thousand. Those that numbered fewer than a thousand were placed into existing *minqat* to augment them. In addition, Chinggis Khan allowed his commanders to keep captives or to assemble scattered groups among other tribes to fill out their own *minqat*.[16] In doing so he created a new system that replaced the pre-existing tribal social structure with one better suited to the needs of his new state and army, as it provided a rationalized military organization that, in effect, increased central control over the independent tribes.

While the Mongols created new regiments and units for their army, they were not fluid. As the Persian bureaucrat Juvaini noted, 'No man may depart to another unit than the hundred, thousand, or ten to which he has been assigned, nor may he seek refuge elsewhere'.[17]

Chinggis Khan erased the old kinship ties of Mongol, Tatar, Kereit, and Naiman. Now all of the steppe nomads of Mongolia were part of the *Qamuq Monggol Ulus*, meaning All of or the Whole Mongol Nation, essentially a supra-tribe. In addition, he divided the entire population of Mongolia into units, called *aurug*, which functioned more or less as the supply system for the army, as they provided both men and equipment. In effect, Chinggis Khan created a state suited to the waging of war.

The army was divided into three basic corps of *baraghun ghar* (right flank), *je'ün ghar* (left flank), and *töb* or *qol* (center or pivot). During the era of Chinggis Khan, Bo'orchu commanded the *baraghun ghar*, Muqali commanded the *je'ün ghar*, and Naya commanded the *qol*. The field armies then mirrored the overall organization of the Mongol command structure.

The command structure made it easy to execute orders, creating a flexible and innovative system that outside observers viewed as noteworthy. According to Marco Polo:

> Well, [the Khan] appoints an officer to every ten men, one to every hundred, one to every thousand, and one to every ten thousand, so that his orders have to be given to ten persons only, and each of these ten persons has to pass the orders to only another ten, and so on; no one having to give orders to more than ten. And everyone in turn is responsible only to the officer immediately over him; and the discipline and order that comes of this method is marvelous, for they are a people very obedient to their chiefs.[18]

Although Marco Polo made his observation in the late thirteenth century, his remarks demonstrate the continuity of Chinggis Khan's administrative philosophy, in which army organization involved not just forming military units, but also establishing central control over the disparate elements of the steppe. This was later extended to sedentary groups as the Mongol empire expanded, yet the intent remained the same. The Mongol Khan melded an inchoate collection of tribes and confederations into a single army with a hierarchical, yet responsive, command structure.

Keshik

The *keshik* or bodyguard of Chinggis Khan had rather humble origins but evolved into one of the Mongol Empire's most important institutions. From a unit of a few hundred men it grew to number 10,000, and during the reign of Khubilai Khan reached 12,000. In addition to guarding the Khan, the *keshik* carried out a variety of tasks, including those of *qorci* or archer; *siba'uci* or falconer; *jarlighci*, who wrote sacred decrees; *biceci*, who recorded annals for the

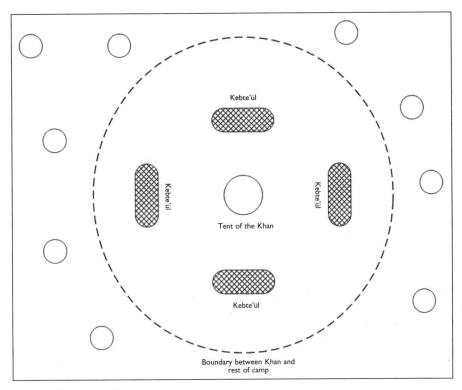

Kebte'ül

Kebte'ül

Kebte'ül

Tent of the Khan

Kebte'ül

Boundary between Khan and
rest of camp

The Keshik *and the Khan*

emperor; *ba'urci*, who cooked and served drinks; *üldüci* or *köldölci*, who assisted
the emperor with his sword and bow; *balaghci*, in charge of the palace gates or
approaches; *daraci*, in charge of the wine; *ula'aci* or *morinci*, in charge of the
wagons and horses; *sügürci*, in charge of garments for imperial use; *temeci* or
camel tender; *qoninci* or shepherd; *qulaghanci*, who captured thieves and seem
to have acted as police; *qurci* (not to be confused with the *qorci*), who played
music; and *ba'adur*, the braves or warriors who all members of the *keshik*
should strive to emulate.[19]

The institution of the *keshik* was founded on Chinggis Khan's four *külü'üd* or
heroes, who served amongst its commanders: Boroghul, Bo'orchu, Muqali, and
Chila'un. It originally consisted of 80 *kebte'ül* or night guards and 70 *turqa'ut*
or day guards, with an additional *minqan* that escorted Chinggis Khan into
battle. At the *quriltai* of 1206 he increased the *keshik* to 10,000 men, which was
achieved by recruiting the sons of the *noyad* (commanders) of the various units,
ranging from those of the *tümen-ü noyad* to the sons of the *arban-u noyad*.
Furthermore, Chinggis Khan always welcomed talented individuals regardless

of rank or social status, including sons of commoners who were 'of able and of good appearance, and who [were] deemed suitable'.[20] The sons of the *noyad* who joined the ranks of the *keshik* were accompanied by a varying number of companions depending on their rank. Sons of the *minqan-u noyad* brought ten companions and a younger brother; sons of the *jaghun-u noyad* brought five companions and a younger brother, sons of the *arban-u noyad* or of ordinary people brought three companions and a younger brother. These recruits were to be fully equipped, along with mounts supplied by their original units, the Khan compensating their units for the material loss. Such a policy would have greatly increased the number of men in the *keshik*, to a level far beyond the point where the illusion could be maintained of the personal contact between ruler and servitor that characterizes a companion-bodyguard.[21] And of course the total number of men involved would have been considerably more than 10,000 if the bodyguards' attendants are counted.

Obviously, not all commanders were able to send the requested number of men. Indeed, some sons were themselves already commanders of units. However, the requirement demonstrates that Chinggis Khan had two overriding aims. The first was to establish a diverse bodyguard, open to all, from the powerful and influential *tümen-ü noyad* to the ordinary shepherd. The second, according to Thomas Allsen, was to create an instrument of political control. By requesting the youngest son in addition to another son, Chinggis Khan gained hostages. This practice was not applied just to his own commanders but was also utilized amongst conquered peoples, a prince or a relative of such vassals often entering the *keshik*. While Chinggis Khan and his successors hoped that such hostages would ensure the loyal behavior of distant governors or clients, they had a longer aim. They saw an opportunity to mold the hostage. Once he had been indoctrinated in the *keshik*, the Mongols possessed a suitable replacement for a vassal or commander who no longer conformed to their demands and expectations.[22]

While service in the *keshik* prepared individuals for duty in the administration of the empire or as commanders of armies, its primary responsibility remained guarding the Khan. For this purpose, the guard was divided into three units: night guards (*kebte'ül*), day guards (*turqa'ut*), and quiver bearers (*qorcin*, singular *qorci*).

The size of the *keshik* having been increased substantially during the *quriltai* of 1206, the *kebte'ül*, commanded by Yeke-Ne'ürin, increased from 80 to 800 men and then to 1,000. The night guards were subdivided under the command of Yisün-te'e, Bügedei, Horqudayi, and Lablaqa. Their duties included taking care of the banners or *tuq*, as well as the drums and tent carts, and they supervised food and drink. Thus members of the *kebte'ül* typically served as *boricin*, *daracin*, and *ula'acin*. Indeed, the night guards were the only ones who prepared the food of the Khan, and typically distributed the food. If other members of the *keshik*, such as the *qorcin*, distributed food, then the *kebte'ül* received it first. Naturally, some of the *kebte'ül* also served as *balaghcin*, or those who guarded the approaches of the Khan's tent. Indeed, the *kebte'ül* guarded far more than just the Khan, guarding in addition the female attendants of the palace as well as the young male slaves, *temecin* and *qonincin*. Essentially they were responsible for the well-being of the entire palace. When the *kebte'ül* came on duty, they not only assumed these responsibilities but also relieved the *qorcin* of their quivers, effectively disarming them.

The *kebte'ül* appear to have been the Khan's most trusted force among the *keshik*. When the Khan hunted, half of them accompanied him at all times. In times of battle, however, the *kebte'ül* did not escort the Khan. Instead, they remained behind to ensure the safety of the royal household and the palace tent. Furthermore, some of the night guards served as *jarlighcin* and were also in charge of the royal armory and the distribution of weapons. This may explain why the *qorcin* handed over their quivers at the end of their shifts.[23]

The *qorcin* or quiver bearers, commanded by Yisün-te'e, the son of Jelme, numbered 400 initially but were increased to 1,000 in 1206. Yisün-te'e's lieutenant was Bügedei, son of Tüge. The *qorcin* primarily fulfilled their duties during the daytime. It is not clear exactly what these duties were, but considering their title of *qorcin* it is likely that they were the only men allowed in the vicinity of the Khan with their bows, as all visitors were disarmed. Thus while other guards protected the body of the Khan, the *qorcin* were expected to keep threats at a distance.

The *turqa'ud* increased from an initial 70 men to a total of 8,000. The chamberlain Ögele-cherbi commanded this element. Its eight *minqat* were commanded by Ögele-cherbi, Buqa (a member of Muqali's family), Alchidai of Ilügei, Dödei-cherbi, Doqolqu-cherbi, Chanai (a member of Jürchedei's family), Aqutai (a member of Alchi's family), and Arqai-Qasar. The 8,000 men of the day guard were further divided into four groups, commanded by Buqa, Alchidai, Dödei-cherbi, and Doqolqu-cherbi.

The guards rotated in shifts every three days. During the time of Chinggis Khan, Boroghul's unit served first,[24] Bo'orchu's division served the second shift, Muqali's division served the third shift, and Chila'un served the final shift, before the whole rotation began again. Positions within the *keshik* were hereditary, but even men of low rank could, over time, achieve a higher position.[25]

In general, the *keshik* had strict orders regarding how it should carry out its primary function of guarding the Khan. The Khan's tent was separated from all others by the length of two arrow flights, or roughly 500m. Furthermore, no one could approach the Khan's tent without the *keshik*'s permission or if armed. Unless they were high-ranking individuals, such as princes or certain generals, the guards required to see evidence that the Khan had summoned them, and the *keshikten* could seize unauthorized persons and hold them until the next shift. The *kebte'ül* were granted further powers of seizing anyone in the vicinity of the Khan's tent at night, or anyone who asked questions regarding the number of night guards or other security matters. They also had the authority to seize animals or even the clothing of apprehended persons.

Finally, the *keshikten* were expected to be present for their shift. If a member did not present himself, he was struck with a rod three times for the first offense. A second offense merited seven blows, and a third offense 37 blows. A third offense also led to the offending guard being sent to a distant post, perhaps meaning that he was banished from the *keshik*. Despite the severe beatings, *keshikten* could be excused from duty if they were ill, or for other reasons if their commander granted permission. Officers received similar punishments to their men if they failed in their duty to muster the guards.

Tamma

While the *keshik* was the most important military institution, producing as it did both commanders for the army and administrators for the governance of the empire, the *tamma* was more important to the expansion of the empire and was the key to maintaining the Mongols' hold on newly conquered territories. One might consider it the cog that allowed the Mongol military machine to function.

Paul Buell described the *tamma* as being 'a special military force comprising selected chiliarchies from the total Mongolian levy and sent into conquered areas to secure and hold them, and if possible, expand Mongolian power and influence'.[26] The Mongols always established the *tamma* in areas bordering nomadic and sedentary spheres. They were expected to remain in specified regions for extended periods, whereas other military units typically withdrew to the steppes after conquering an area. Members of the *tamma* were known as *tammaci* (plural *tammacin*), although the sources are usually referring specifically to the commander of the *tamma* when they use this term.

The *tamma* consisted of a main force, and an advance force known as the *alginci* (plural *algincin*). The *algincin*, consisting of a vanguard and scouts, were stationed closer to the cities, while the *tamma* remained in better pasture-lands. It consisted of troops from various tribes and regions, its commander not necessarily being of Mongolian origin.[27] Although the *tamma* was very important to Mongol expansion, it was not considered part of the regular

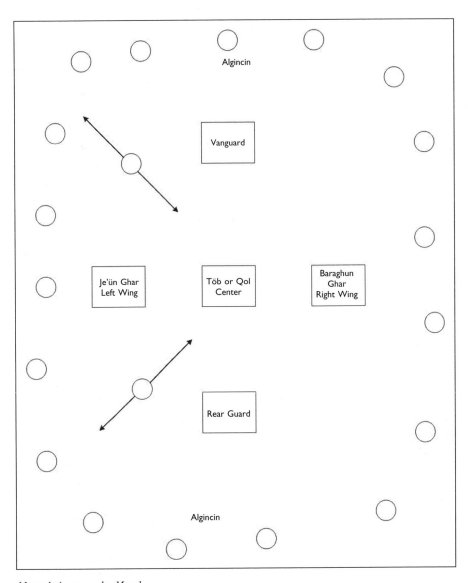

Mongol Army on the March

army. The *Yuan Shi* notes that there were two distinct forces, comprising the *Meng-ku chün* or Mongol army and the *Tan-ma-ch'ih chün* or *tammaci* army. The distinction lay in the composition. The Mongol army solely comprised Mongols, whereas the *tammaci* army consisted of a variety of nomads.[28]

The Mongols used camps of *tammacin* to control occupied regions and repel hostile attacks. Their camps were spread for pasturing purposes and were protected by patrols, while messengers maintained communication between them. In addition, the *tammacin* often devastated neighboring regions to reduce the threat to their camps. The *tamma* essentially served the same purposes as a Western European castle, the various walls of China, or any fortress for that matter. Defensively, the castle might guard a border, as did the *tamma*. Like a castle too, the *tamma* gave the Mongols a base of operations and a means of intimidating neighboring realms.

Although the *tamma* functioned much as fortresses did elsewhere, the Mongols themselves (or most nomads for that matter) did not themselves construct fortresses. The Mongols viewed fixed fortifications with disdain and razed them. *Tamma* units therefore did not serve as permanent garrisons but eventually moved forward to new frontiers as the empire expanded.

Other units

As the empire expanded, conquered peoples swelled the Mongols' ranks. The core component of the Mongol army remained its nomadic Mongol-Turkic cavalry, but their use of infantry raised amongst sedentary populations for garrison and siege duties gave the Mongols greater flexibility and allowed them to expand their empire at a great rate. Among the most important such units was their corps of engineers. Initially, siege engineers consisted of Han, Khitans, and perhaps Jurched engineers, but as the Mongols advanced into Muslim Central Asia and the Middle East they incorporated Arab, Persian, and Armenian engineers too.

The first true corps of engineers in the Mongol army came into existence around 1214. From their encounters with the Jin, as well as in Xi-Xia, the Mongols determined that their own forces were inadequate when it came to dealing with fortifications. Beyond surprising a walled town or fortresses and quickly storming it, they had to rely on blockading a location until it succumbed to famine or to treachery from within. But in 1214 Ambughai of the Barghutai clan became the first commander of an artillery corps consisting of 500 men. In the Chinese sources this unit was known as the *baojun* or catapult corps, but a crossbow or *nujun* unit also existed.[29]

The Mongols did not restrict their engineers' talents to siege warfare. Much like the Romans and countless other armies, the Mongols also assigned them to such tasks as the construction of roads and bridges, such as the bridge that Master Zhang, the chief engineer of Chaghatay, built across the Amu Darya River using approximately one hundred boats.[30] A standard tactic in siege warfare involved the besiegers encircling enemy strongholds with a wall of their own, and the engineers built these too. At Baghdad the engineers even diverted the Euphrates and broke the dykes to flood the camp of the Abbasid army. The Mongols' corps of engineers thereby enabled them to overcome logistical problems that often stymied other nomadic armies.

As well as their corps of engineers the Mongols recruited other non-nomadic troops. The *tamma*, as we have seen, did not function as a permanent garrison, yet the Mongols at times had the need of garrison forces. Such duties were reserved instead for sedentary forces known as *cerik*. The *cerik* comprised armies recruited from the local sedentary population of conquered lands rather than from nomads. Structurally, the *cerik* tended to mirror the *tamma*; however, their primary purpose was to garrison cities and a few fortresses, though in some situations they also served as field armies. The terminology of *cerik* and *tamma* may have simply been used to distinguish between nomadic (*tammaci*) and sedentary (*cerik*) armies. In Mongolian, *cerik* properly translates as 'army', or recruits from a locality or tribe raised for the central government, but in usage it typically meant sedentary forces rather than nomadic *tammaci*.[31]

During the conquest of the Jin Empire, the Mongols created new armies based on Han Chinese conscripts. Even in the initial stages, these *ceriks* played an important role in the conquest. When Chinggis Khan returned north in 1214 one former Jin commander, Po-liu, garrisoned T'ien-ch'eng and held it against Jin attacks before going on to conquer several cities in 1215. He became the first commander of the first official Han *cerik* in 1216. When Muqali received command of the first *tamma* in 1217/18 he also received three *ceriks* commanded by the Khitan generals Uyar, Yeh-Lü-T'u-hua, and Cha-la-erh. Uyar commanded Khitans, mainly of the Pei-ch'ing garrison; Cha-la-erh commanded primarily Juyin toops from the Zhongdu area; and T'u-hua commanded primarily Han troops. The Han *cerik* became increasingly subdivided due to its size, which kept increasing.[32] Initially, these *cerik* were simply the units of individual commanders who had deserted to the Mongols, but as the conquest of the Jin Empire continued and Han Chinese armies surrendered they were organized along Mongol lines by Ögödei, who divided them into three *tümet* and thirty-six *minqat* commanded by the Khitan generals. By 1234 there were three or perhaps more *tümen-ü noyad*.[33] Prior to 1235, these units of Han troops were known as the 'Black Army' or *Hei Chün*. After further drafts in 1236 and 1241 their numbers increased significantly, and over 95,000 were organized as the 'New Army' or *Hsin Chün*.[34]

Many of the posts in the Han Chinese units were inheritable. However, this privilege was greatly reduced in 1262 after a rebellion in Eastern Shandong when the Mongols curbed the power of native officers. They removed kinsmen from the military, and members of the *keshik* served as supervising *tümen-ü noyad* or *daruqaci*.

While the *cerik* forces, like the *tamma*, were positioned along the borders between the steppes and settled lands, or along the borders of the empire, non-*cerik* forces also existed, but were treated in a different way. In part this was because their organization was already modeled on that of the *Meng-ku chün* or Mongol army. Thus armies were created that were based solely on nationalities – the *Ch'i-tan chün* or Khitan army, for instance, and the *Nü-chih chün* or Jurched army.[35]

As the Mongols expanded westward, sedentary Western peoples such as the Rus' and Volga Bulghars were also incorporated into the Mongol army. The Volga Bulghars – like the Jurchens and Khitans – were utilized as heavy cavalry. Having realized that not everyone was suited for service as a horse-archer, the Mongols did not force such peoples to adopt their own mode of fighting, but instead allowed them to fight in their own particular way. This meant that there was less need for the Mongols to fight in close combat. Instead they could use auxiliary troops in that capacity, these being often more heavily armored and better equipped for service as shock troops.

As the Mongols' empire expanded, the application of a census of households in conquered lands enabled them to conscript their sedentary subjects into the military. While those with technical skills became part of the corps of engineers, others became members of the *cerik*, or regular military forces. Though these non-nomadic regular forces typically remained in garrison unless called upon to serve in a campaign, they nonetheless played an important role in the expansion of the Mongol state, for without them the Mongols would have quickly become mired by the need to use nomadic troops to garrison their conquests rather than keeping them active in the field, engaged in new conquests.

Conclusion

Although decimal organization appeared in Inner Asia before the Mongols, its adoption by Chinggis Khan allowed them to restructure Mongolian society, with the *minqan* as the primary unit of tribal and military organization. Through this process Chinggis Khan created a new structure better suited to the needs of his state and army, since it increased central control over the formerly independent tribes. By means of this transformation from tribal army to rationalized military system, nomadic society was remolded through the imposition of such institutions as decimal units. This led to the standardization of Mongol military institutions, from bodyguards to subject peoples. To a certain extent these reforms also transformed the lives of the Mongols' sedentary subjects. In terms of taxation and military conscription, the sedentary population was likewise organized according to a decimal system. Non-nomadic forces could still fight in their accustomed manner, but they were now integrated into the Mongol command structure.

Chapter 3

Training and equipping the Mongol warrior

The military dominance of the steppe nomad horse-archer lasted until the widespread introduction of gunpowder weapons. Although man-to-man comparisons of soldiers are a useful exercise, the Mongol warrior must be examined in his social, cultural, and administrative environments. At the same time he needs to be seen not only as an individual but as a component of a highly organized army. The development of the Mongol warrior also needs to be considered, for his role in the thirteenth century differed from his contemporary nomadic peers as well as his predecessors. Although the Mongols inherited many of the military traditions of previous nomadic empires, they also developed a more refined system of raising their army and developing it.

Training

One of the *biligs* or maxims of Chinggis Khan concerned the training of the army:

> Just as *ortaqs* come with gold spun fabrics and are confident of making profits on those goods and textiles, military commanders should teach their sons archery, horsemanship, and wrestling well. They should test them in these arts and make them audacious and brave to the same degree that *ortaqs* are confident of their own skill.[1]

Although Chinggis Khan placed considerable importance on military training, it was assumed that because nomads learned to ride and shoot arrows from an early age they were already competent warriors. This generalization was applied to all steppe nomads, the most commonly cited example being Ssu-ma Chien's account of the Xiong-nu or Huns. He wrote that little boys learned to ride on the backs of sheep and practised archery by shooting at small game: 'Thus all the young men are able to use a bow and act as armed cavalry in time of war'.[2]

The Mongols learned this at an early age as well, as hunting and riding were essential skills. According to the Franciscan monk John de Plano Carpini:

The men do not make anything at all, with the exception of arrows, and they also sometimes tend the flocks, but they hunt and practise archery, for they are all, big and little, excellent archers, and their children begin as soon as they are two or three years old to ride and manage horses and to gallop them, and they are given bows to suit their stature and are taught to shoot; they are extremely agile and also intrepid.[3]

Chinese sources also note this. The Song envoy and general Zhao Hong wrote that Mongols were born and raised in the saddle and that from spring to winter they spent their days riding and hunting. In addition most of them learned how to fight, thus creating an army trained in cavalry warfare.[4]

The constant exposure to archery from an early age enabled the Mongols to acquire the requisite strength to pull a composite bow and hold it at full-draw. With sustained practice beginning at childhood, an archer could draw a bow with a pull ranging from 100lb up to an extreme and rare level of 160lb.[5]

While this is impressive, other factors in the Mongols' training should be considered, such as how did they practise archery? We know they were superior archers, as the Armenians called them 'The Nation of Archers'. Considering that the Armenians had also endured numerous encounters with other nomadic horse-archers it is noteworthy that they considered the Mongols' ability greater than that of the other tribes.[6]

The thirteenth-century sources concerning the Mongols do not reveal much about their training, so one must examine the training of groups who used similar tactics to gain an insight into their methods – the Mamluks of Egypt and Syria and the Khitans of the Liao Dynasty (945–1125) of Northern China. Both groups originally came from the steppes: the Khitans, linked to the Mongols by ethnic and linguistic ties, ruled part of Mongolia, while most thirteenth-century Mamluks were imported into the Muslim world from the steppes of Russia when they were boys. More is known about their military system than that of the Mongols, and this can be used as a paradigm for the study of the Mongols.

The Mamluks of Egypt instituted a strict regimen of training for their new recruits. Only when they reached their majority did they actually begin military training, in four areas – equestrian arts, lancing, archery, and fencing – and only after successfully completing all four courses could the recruit be considered a *faris* or cavalryman. To understand the training of the Mongol army, only the Mamluks' archery practices need to be reviewed.

One exercise was the *qabaq* drill, in which a gourd was affixed to a pole and a Mamluk shot at while riding past. The height of the pole could be altered, which forced the rider to shoot upwards and from different angles, including the Parthian or backwards shot.[7] An extension of this practice was the Mamluk drill of shooting the *qipaj* or *qighaj*. This drill was similar to the *qabaq*, but involved the rider shooting downward at a target as he rode by, often rising in his stirrups to gain a better vantage point.[8]

These simple training drills originated in the steppe, similar games still being played in Mongolia today. One could easily substitute a bag or other item for the gourd or *qabaq*. One such contest in modern Mongolia is the *bombog kharvaa* or ball shooting, in which three leather balls are mounted on poles. The mounted archer attempts to hit the first one while advancing upon it, then the second as he rides by it. The final ball is targeted using the 'Parthian shot' after the archer has ridden past. The most difficult part of the exercise is controlling the horse solely with the knees, as both hands are occupied with the bow, while the reins are tied to the saddle.[9]

Controlling the horse was vital for medieval horse-archers. The Mamluks practised holding the reins of their horse while shooting. They tied a knot to shorten the reins and unify them into one strand. Then they were slipped over the pommel of the saddle or held by the third finger of the drawing hand, attached by a thong. They could do this because they used a thumb ring and the index finger to draw the string, while the other fingers held the thong. The thumb ring, often made of polished stone, allowed the string to slide off the archer's thumb with less friction. It also allowed the archer to use a higher pull weight, as the string did not cut into his fingers.

The *Liao Shi*, the history of the Liao Dynasty, reveals other steppe training practices. Much like the Mongols, the Khitans attacked in caracole fashion, one wave advancing and firing before retiring as another wave came up.[10] This tactic required regular practice to be performed successfully, a high degree of coordination and discipline being called for if order was to be maintained as wave after wave of horsemen performed their attacks. Without appropriate training mass chaos resulted, with retreating riders impeding the advance of the next wave.

Although the Khitans originated from the steppes and forests, their empire's administration and military developed to high level of sophistication and probably utilized other means of military training besides hunting. Indeed, the Khitans held periodic military reviews.[11] In addition, they practised archery by shooting at willow rods while mounted, perhaps like in the *bombog kharvaa*. It is thought that the Mongols and the Jurchen practised this as well.[12]

There is evidence that the *qabaq* and caracole drills existed in the Western Eurasian steppes prior to the Mongol era. Maurikos, the Byzantine emperor and author of the *Strategikon*, a Byzantine manual of warfare, wrote that the

Alans performed similar tactics and advised that the Byzantines should also practise them:

> In the Alan system the troops, some as assault and some as defenders, are drawn up in a single battle line. This is divided into *moiras*, lined up about two or four hundred feet from each other. The assault troops advance at a gallop as in pursuit, and then turn back filtering into the intervals or clear spaces in the main line. Then, together with the defenders they turn and charge against the enemy. In another maneuver the assault troops turn around in those intervals and charge out against both flanks of the unit, the men keeping their original relative positions.[13]

Further evidence that the caracole method of attack required a high degree of training comes from sixteenth-century Western Europe, where it required training and practice if it was to be performed effectively. When the *Reiter* or German pistol-armed heavy cavalry who used the caracole were deployed alongside non-*Reiter* troops, it was found that the caracole could disrupt the actions of cavalry troops unaccustomed to it. King Henri IV of France

> ordered the 250 Reiters in his pay to dispense with the caracole tactic and charge home with the rest of his cavalry. This was significant, for when performing their customary maneuver the Reiters always wheeled to the left after discharging their pistols. But the danger here was that they often collided with other oncoming friendly cavalry, throwing the latter's attack into disorder and blunting its effect. Indeed, the duc de Mayenne, the League leader, later attributed his defeat at Ivry precisely to this cause in an effort to shift the blame for the debacle onto others. Even so, his claim was not without some foundation: after performing the caracole, his Reiters did collide with the long lines of charging League lancers, destroying their momentum and rendering their weapons useless.[14]

Not everyone believes that the Mongols were well trained. John Masson Smith Jr has contended that in comparison with the Mamluks of Egypt they were poorly trained.[15] In many ways this is a comparison that cannot be made, as the Mamluks were an elite force specifically recruited and trained for no other purpose than to serve as soldiers. Although the Mongols performed admirably in battle, they not could be considered an elite unit. Unlike the Mamluks, they were not individually selected, since all able-bodied men fought in the army.

Certainly, in many respects, Smith is correct: the Mamluks ranked among the most highly trained warriors of the Middle Ages. However, one cannot compare a Mamluk with a random Mongol trooper who, when not on military duty, might very well spend his time minding his flocks. It is especially unrealistic to compare Mongol swordsmanship with that of the Mamluks. The Mongols avoided hand-to-hand combat unless necessary, as they preferred to shoot their enemies, often using an arrow shower tactic which originated in the steppes. Considering that their opponents would be able to fire from a fairly stable platform, it is unlikely that, except in a charge or under favorable circumstances, the Mongols would have had any interest in closing with the enemy. The closer they got, the better the opposing side could use their bows to deadly effect.[16]

Another common observation about the Mongols is that their military maneuvers were based on the practice of the *nerge*, which was a mass hunt often referred to as the *battue*.[17] This involved the Mongols in fanning out over several miles and forming a circle. Gradually this circle would contract until all the animals within it were trapped in a ring of men and horses. After the Khan had killed a few animals others would join in the hunt. Some animals were allowed to escape. A hunt of this size naturally required excellent communication and discipline in order to maintain the circle and prevent animals from escaping until the Khan allowed it.

Nor were the Mongols the only Inner Asian group that considered hunting a valuable technique in military training. The Khitans, even during the period of the Liao Dynasty, used hunting not only for the practical purpose of feeding their troops, but also as a means of training for military maneuvers. Indeed, one Liao emperor once said: 'Our hunting is not simply a pursuit of pleasure. It is a means of practicing warfare'.[18]

The experience of the *nerge* gave Mongol warriors the ability to function as a single unit on the battlefield. One source noted that:

> The Mongols from among the Turkish people accustomed their people [to fight as] a single squadron of cavalry, so that they struggled together against the enemy. Retiring [from the battle] and returning [to it] was denied to each of them. They gained from this great experience which was not [duplicated] by others.[19]

Certainly the *nerge* contributed to a well-disciplined force capable of complex maneuvers over a broad front. That the Mongols were competent horsemen and archers due to daily exposure to both almost from birth is undeniable. Their discipline in maneuvers and coordinated moves across great distances was enhanced by the seasonal migrations of nomadic life.

Another, and perhaps the most important, key element to the success of the Mongols was their instilling of discipline into the otherwise individualistic nomad warrior. Anecdotes of the discipline of the Mongols are numerous. For the Mongols, discipline meant not only adhering to the orders of their commanders but also not straying from the parameters of an operation. While the Mongols plundered and raided, they also completely bypassed areas that had not been designated as targets. Furthermore, discipline instilled order among their armies so that generals, princes, and the common soldiery all understood their roles. Discipline allowed the Mongols to operate at great distances without their armies disintegrating into marauding bands bent more on their own interests than those of the Khan.

Indeed, discipline was essential to the successful execution of both the caracole and the *nerge*. Warfare in the Mongolian steppes prior to Chinggis Khan's empire frequently degenerated into individual combats, in which victory was often thrown away as the victors stopped fighting in order to plunder their enemy's camp, thereby allowing the defeated force to counterattack. Consequently instilling discipline into the tribes of Mongolia may have been Chinggis Khan's single greatest achievement. Even before his rise to absolute master of the Mongolian steppe, Chinggis Khan expected his orders to be obeyed, even by his relatives. While still a vassal of Toghril Ong-Qan, he introduced a radical departure from traditional steppe warfare when, attacking the Tatars at Dalan Nemürges in 1202, he ordered his men not to start plundering the enemy until they were defeated. Furthermore, he commanded his men to regroup at a predesignated location if they suffered defeat, rather than dispersing across the steppe. Those who disobeyed would suffer the consequences:

> If we conquer the enemy, we shall not stop to plunder. If the victory
> is complete, that booty will be ours in any case and we will share it
> among ourselves. If we are forced by the enemy to retreat, let us turn
> back to the point where we began the attack. The men who do not
> turn back to the point where we began the attack will be cut down.[20]

This absolute discipline also assured the Khan that his commanders could carry out their operations without subordinates questioning their authority, and without the Khan needing to be present on all campaigns.

Chinggis Khan expected absolute obedience to his commands. Much like other steppe leaders before him, he desired his followers to place him above all other ties, whether familial, clan, or tribal. Upon his enthronement in 1206, Juzjani wrote that Chinggis Khan declared: 'If you are obedient to my mandates, it behooveth (*sic*) that, if I should command the sons to slay the

father, you should all obey'.[21] In addition, the discipline instilled in the Mongol
army permeated Mongolian society, which further benefited from a tendency
to be more egalitarian than its sedentary counterparts.

Certainly with the great Khan present, few dared to risk offense, but as the
Mongol armies ranged across a continent troops might have been tempted to
plunder rather than to maintain their discipline and destroy the paltry forces of
a city-state in Rus' or a distant town in China. One of the most commonly held
hypotheses is that draconian measures held the warriors in check while on
campaign. An example involves an expedition against the Merkit and Naiman
on which Sübedei was sent by Chinggis Khan. Sübedei was instructed to spare
his remounts so that they would not be overworked and become too lean. In
addition he prohibited Sübedei from allowing his troops to hunt except in
moderation in order to maintain their provisions. Even orders on daily routines
were to be carried out in strict obedience. He further instructed Sübedei:

> Do not allow the soldiers to fix the crupper to the saddle and put on
> the bridle, but let the horses go with their mouths free. If this order
> is issued the soldiers will not be able to gallop on the way. Once you
> have so ordered, then whoever transgress this command shall be
> seized and beaten. Send to Us those who transgress Our command if
> it looks that they are personally known to Us; as for the many who
> are not known to Us, just cut them down on the spot.[22]

This example illustrates several points. The first is that Chinggis Khan gave his
general authority to deal with misconduct and that disobedience was a serious
crime. Secondly, he realized that princes, other relatives, and those in Chinggis
Khan's favor could undermine the authority of a campaign commander by
flaunting their special rank. Thus if they did disobey the general they were to
either return to Chinggis Khan on their own accord, or else one can be sure
that news of the violation would come to his attention. Even after Chinggis
Khan died princes were unable to usurp the authority of the army generals.

Outsiders confirmed that the Mongols maintained discipline in the ranks
and among their officers by draconian measures. Carpini wrote:

> If anyone is found in the act of plundering or stealing in the territory
> under their power, he is put to death without any mercy. Again, if
> anyone reveals their plans, especially when they intend going to war,
> he is given a hundred stripes on his back, as heavy as a peasant can
> give with a big stick.[23]

Carpini also noted that in battle, if a few men from an *arban* fled but the entire
unit did not, the entire *arban* was still put to death. Likewise, if an *arban* fled

but the *jaghun* to which it belonged did not, all 100 men were nevertheless executed. Also, if members of a unit were captured the rest of the unit must rescue them.[24] It is not known if these measures were carried out, but the moral was that the Mongols were expected to function as a unit.

Valery Aleexev, however, questions the idea that only draconian punishment maintained discipline in the Mongol army:

> Without doubt, harshness played a role. But in the conditions of nomadic life, harsh measures, if none others were used, could well lead to the disintegration of military units ... It would be far more realistic to presume that the discipline in the army rested on some deeply held collective psychology.[25]

Other factors were involved in maintaining discipline. One was simple loyalty. As Chinggis Khan elevated men from all levels of nomadic society to positions of importance, his followers became devoted to him out of gratitude and loyalty. This is how Chinggis Khan rose to power, through the development of personal ties to his commanders. In return they ensured that their own units remained disciplined. Another factor was the growing sense of collective destiny during Ögödei's reign, when the Mongols came to believe that Heaven had decreed that they should rule the world.[26]

In the end, their training produced skilled and disciplined soldiers whose capacity to withstand difficult conditions was unmatched. Marco Polo observed, decades after Carpini and Zhao Hong had made their own observations, that 'of all troops in the world those are they which endure the greatest hardship and fatigue, and which cost the least; and they are the best of all for making wide conquests of country'.[27]

Equipment

Opinion regarding the quality of a Mongol warrior's equipment is divided. One school of thought takes the view that Mongol warriors were well armed, albeit primarily with a composite bow, in a manner similar to the soldiers of the Liao dynasty in tenth and eleventh century Northern China and, probably, the warriors of the Kara Khitai Empire in Turkistan. According to the *Liao Shi*, Khitan soldiers were required to possess nine pieces of iron armor, saddle clothes, leather and iron barding and other accoutrements for their horses, four bows and 400 arrows, as well as a long and short spear, club, axe, and halberd. In addition they were to be equipped with a small banner, hammer, awl, flint and knife, a bucket for their horse, rations of dried food, a grappling hook with 200 ft of rope, and an umbrella.[28] It is uncertain if the soldiers were furnished with these items or if they were expected to acquire them. John de Plano

Carpini, who traveled through the Mongol Empire in the mid-1240s, recorded that he saw similar equipment as standard among the Mongol soldiers:

> They all have to possess the following arms at least: two or three bows or at least one good one, three large quivers full of arrows, an axe and ropes for hauling engines of war. As for the wealthy, they have swords pointed at the end but sharp only on one side and somewhat curved and they have a horse with armor, their legs also are covered and they have helmets and cuirasses.[29]

The second school of thought is that the Mongols were poorly and haphazardly armed. Adherents of this school believe that beyond a composite bow, most of their equipment was acquired by looting the battlefield, and only in their later period did the Mongols establish a professional system of equipping their armies.[30] The actual procurement of weapons, armor, and other equipment will be discussed in chapter four, which is concerned with logistics and the supplying of the army.

Weapons

The main weapon of the Mongols was a composite bow. Made from layers of horn, wood, sinew, and glue this weapon possessed a maximum range of 300m, with an extreme range of 500m.[31] Of course, accuracy and penetrating power increased at closer ranges. Still, this was significantly better than the cross-bow used in Western European armies and among the Franks in Palestine. The crossbow had an accurate range of approximately 75m, although it had considerable penetrating power. In order to shoot further, one had to elevate the crossbow in order to achieve a better arc. This in turned forced the archer to look upward and not at the target. The bow, however, was accurate at longer ranges as, though the archer still had to elevate the bow, he looked under his hand to aim. To get a better idea of the effectiveness of the Mongol composite bow, its range should be compared to Welsh and English longbows of the fourteenth century and later, which possessed an accurate range of 220m.

Unlike the longbow, or any other Western bow for that matter, the Mongols and other nomads and Middle Eastern archers used a thumb ring to pull the bow-string back. The use of a thumb ring prevented strain on the thumb. Ralph Payne-Gallwey noted that he could bend even a strong bow 'much easier and draw it a great deal farther with the Turkish thumb-ring' than with the standard European finger grip. Furthermore, he noted that with the thumb ring there was less drag on the release, which was therefore quicker.[32] Like Europeans, the Mongols held the bow in the left hand, but they set the arrow on the right-hand side as the thumb ring affected how the arrow flew. If placed on the left-hand side of the bow the shot tended to be less accurate.[33]

Although the Mongols' bows were powerful, the archer's accuracy diminished at 300m. In most forms of combat shooting from such a range tended to consist of disrupting the enemy's ranks. Actual combat, in which the archer intended to wound or kill his opponents rather than disrupting their formations, took place at a closer range, certainly under 150m. Of course, the closer the target was, the more accurate and more lethal the shot.

Latham and Paterson also noted that the composite bow possessed exceptional power:

> Since such composites can withstand an enormous amount of bend, shortness of length could be achieved in design, and this feature made them very suitable weapons for the mounted archer.
>
> In a well-designed bow the weight should increase quickly during the first few inches of the draw, after which the rate of increase should diminish as the draw progresses. This quality was achieved in the East by the fitting of a rigid end-piece (in Arabic, *siyah*, pl. *siyat*) to each end of the bow. When the bow was about half-drawn, the *siyat* began to act as levers so that the draw could be continued with less increase in the weight than would have been the case without them ... For a given weight at full draw – this quantity depending on the archer's strength – the composite bow stores a great amount of energy which is then available for transfer to the arrow when the string is loosed.
>
> When the *siyat* project away from the archer before the braced bow is drawn, as in the case with the Manchu and Mongolian bows ... a string-bridge is fitted to prevent the string from slipping past the knee of the bow; for should this happen the latter would violently assume its unbraced shape and virtually turn itself inside out.[34]

While the bow provided the power to kill at a distance and even the power to penetrate armor, much of its lethality depended on the type of arrowhead used. The Mongols utilized numerous styles of arrowheads made from iron, steel, horn, or bone. Their soldiers carried files to sharpen the edges. Each arrowhead had a different function, ranging from armor piercing and signal arrows that produced a whistling sound to knobbed stun arrows and more.[35] The arrows themselves tended to be a little over 2 ft in length. The arrowhead possessed a tang that was stuck into the shaft. In general, for armor penetration, a tapered spiked arrowhead or a tempered chiseled arrowhead performed better than others, as the force of the bow focused at one point. A broad-headed arrow dispersed the force along the edge of the arrowhead, so that it performed admirably against unarmored targets. The shafts tended to be made from river reeds or willow wood and tended to be larger than those used in Europe. Mongol troopers usually carried 60 of them. It is also possible that the fletching on Mongol arrows was set slightly asymmetrically, as was observed among Mongols in the early twentieth century.[36] Thus when shot, the arrow rotated as it flew, much like a bullet from a rifle, allowing it to penetrate deeper into the target.

In addition to the warrior's own personal quiver, extra quivers were attached to their remounts' saddles to ensure a supply of arrows. The quivers them-selves were constructed from birch bark and willow wood and fastened to the archer's belt by a hook or loops.[37] Although there has been some speculation concerning whether the Mongols poisoned their arrows, this seems unlikely, as their weapons were sufficient in power and accuracy to kill without the aid of poison.[38]

Although the composite bow was an excellent weapon, it did have some drawbacks – the primary one being that damp weather was detrimental to it. Using a bow in the rain could ruin it.[39] Thus when the nomads encountered a rainy battlefield they had to either close for mêlée combat or flee. Usually they retreated, as their hand-to-hand combat skills were often inferior to those of their sedentary opponents. The Mongols nevertheless possessed weaponry for close combat, including a lance or spear with a hook on one part of the shaft that was used to pull riders from their horses. They also carried sabers and other swords, but the accounts are contradictory regarding whether these were universally used. Their sabers were curved and very light. Higher quality weapons tended to be lighter in weight, but weight was not always an exact gauge of quality. The Mongols may have helped spread the use of the saber in the Middle East, although the arguments are not completely convincing.[40]

One weapon that may have been used, but is not directly mentioned, is the *ughurgh-a* or lasso. The lasso used by the Mongols in their herding activities is not the same as that used on ranches and in rodeos in the American West. Rather it consists of a long pole with rope running along its shaft and forming a loop at the end furthest from the herdsman. This loop could be slipped around the head of a wayward animal and tightened, the rigid staff providing greater control over the animal than a rope. As a weapon, the *ughurgh-a* may have been used to capture opponents, or to drag them from their saddles. The pole would have allowed the rider to maintain his distance from an opponent and could also have served as a means of defense. Carpini mentions that the Mongols carried rope, but he speculated that its purpose was for the pulling of siege weapons. Denis Sinor, however, posits that it may have been used for a lasso, as other nomads are known to have used the lasso in combat.[41] However, it is unclear if he is referring to the lasso in its American sense or to the *ughurgh-a* that the Mongols traditionally used. If it is to the *ughurgh-a*, then it should be noted that Carpini did not record anything that resembled it.

Armor

Although the Mongols were primarily light cavalry they often wore armor, as Carpini indicated:

> Some have cuirasses and protection for their horses, fashioned out of leather in the following manner: they take strips of ox-hide or the skin of another animal, a hand's breadth wide, and cover three or four together with pitch, and they fasten them with leather thongs or cord; in the upper strip they put the lace at one end, in the next they put it in the middle and so on to the end; consequently, when they bend, the lower strips come up over the upper ones and thus there is a double or triple thickness over the body.[42]

When the Mongols wore armor they preferred lamellar, as it provided better protection against arrows than mail. According to David Nicolle 'tests have shown that mail can absorb arrows shot from a reasonable distance, but it could not prevent them causing minor wounds. Lamellar armor, however, was much more effective against arrows'.[43] Carpini also noted that the night guards in the *keshik* carried large cane or wicker shields. At the same time the Mongols' backs were generally unarmored and the left armpit was exposed when the arm was raised to fire the bow. In addition to its protection from arrows, the Mongols also preferred lamellar armor because of its simplicity of manufacture.[44]

Many Mongols did not wear armor at all, but simply wore the traditional *deel*, or *degel*, a knee-length coat that fastened on one side.[45] In addition to the *degel*, the Mongols carried treated coats to protect them from the rain as well as felt coats to combat the cold. They carried these even during the summer.

They wore helmets of simple construction, similar in shape to an upside-down acorn. On the sides were slots where flaps could be attached to better protect the ears and neck. These helmets were generally constructed of bronze or iron, often comprising an iron framework with a bronze skin.

It is notable that while John Plano de Carpini opined that the armies of Western Christendom should adopt Mongol military attributes, Eastern European states, particularly those that primarily faced opponents from the steppe, actually transformed their armies along Mongol lines. As well as the more widespread use of the composite bow, Mongol-style lamellar armor became common in Eastern Europe after the Mongol conquests. In addition 'it has also been suggested that the Mongols' *khatanghu degel* large scale-lined fabric or felt coat lay behind the development of the 14th century Western European brigandine jacket'.[46]

Horses

The Mongols owed much of their success to their horses, which were sturdy, strong, and raised in a harsh environment. Though small in stature compared to the warhorses of Western Europe or even the horses used in the Middle East, the Mongol horse was strong and surpassed all others in endurance.

During the thirteenth century, each Mongol took several remounts on campaign in order to avoid exhausting their horses. Beyond the purposes of maintaining the speed of troop movement, there existed the necessity of keeping their mounts fresh simply due to the nature of steppe warfare. Their caracole attacks and the *nerge* maneuver required constant movement to be successful and could wear out a horse over time. Thus in order to maintain their actions, the Mongols changed horses at regular intervals. Being nomads, they had the resources to provide large numbers of remounts for their armies. Indeed, the Song envoy Zhao Hong noted that Mongolia had an abundance of the grass and water essential to support livestock. Furthermore, he observed that the herds of the Mongols consisted of hundreds of thousands of animals.[47]

The maintenance of their herds was critical to the Mongols' success, and as such it was carefully organized, further demonstrating the extent of Mongol military efficiency. The Mongol court and individual princes owned a number of herds as well as pasturelands. In addition, the government allotted horses to each *yam* or post station. However, it is unclear to what extent they mobilized their herds or if they created a system of acquisition for military needs.

The sources vary regarding the number of horses that each Mongol soldier was required to take with him on campaign, but an estimate of five is reasonable. Yet supplying even five horses was not a simple task. According to one scholar, in order to provide five battle-ready mounts to maintain an archer, a man required a herd of 30 horses.[48]

For military use, the Mongols preferred geldings, which had been castrated at around the age of four years. This produced a full-grown but gentler horse, mature enough for warfare. For much the same reasons as they used geldings, the Mongols often rode mares, which had the additional benefit of providing milk for the warriors' rations. This use of geldings and mares in warfare was contrary to European practice, in which stallions dominated the battlefield.[49]

Grazing comprised the entire diet of their horses. However, the horses were not allowed to graze while being ridden. Only after the horse had been unsaddled, tied and cooled off, and its breathing had returned to normal, was it permitted to roam free and graze. In addition the Mongols allowed their horses to fatten in the spring, during which time they were not ridden. Once autumn arrived, they were allowed to graze for shorter durations so that they became leaner, hardier, and sweated less. The Mongols considered autumn as the best season for war, for both man and horse: from an invader's perspective it had the further advantage of being harvest time among the sedentary states. The destruction of crops during raids could induce famine, and peasants were reluctant to leave their fields during harvest time, thus reducing the number of troops available for defense against the invaders.

If each soldier possessed a string of several horses, which grazed for their feeding requirements rather than eating fodder, a constant source of pasture had to be found. Despite the need to graze, this does not appear to have reduced the Mongols' own readiness for combat or marching the following day. According to Marco Polo, the Mongols' policy about their horses not being allowed to graze while being ridden changed on campaign:

> Their horses also will subsist entirely on the grass of the plains, so that there is no need to carry store of barley or straw or oats; and they are very docile to their riders. These, in case of need, will abide on horseback the livelong night, armed at all points, while the horse will be continually grazing.[50]

The Song envoy Zhao Hong likewise remarked that the Mongols never fed their horses fodder, beans, or grain.[51]

J.M. Smith argued that reliance on pasture impacted on the Mongols' rate of movement. In his estimation, Mongol armies moved slowly – often less than 15 miles per day – because their horses grazed.[52] However, his argument is countered by Zhao and Polo, who state that their horses were only released to pasture at night. They grazed where the grass was green and dry, and then at daybreak the Mongols saddled up and rode on again until nightfall.[53] This is not to say that Smith is mistaken. Ideally the Mongol armies would move at a leisurely enough pace to ensure that their horses arrived in peak condition. This is borne out by Hülegü's deliberate pace en route to the Middle East.[54] Hülegü, however, was also accompanied by large numbers of non-combatants, his march being not only a military campaign but a migration to his new appanage. Smith does not take into account that the Mongol cavalry could and did conduct rapid marches when necessary, as indicated by the sources, such as during a pursuit or in an attempt to gain a tactical or strategic advantage as, for example, during Jebe and Sübedei's pursuit of Sultan Muhammad Khwarazmshah.

Nevertheless, the Mongols secured appropriate pasturelands for their base camps. In the Middle East two such locations were the Mughan plain in modern Azerbaijan and the Biqa' Valley in modern Lebanon. In some situations, however, such as when additional forces arrived, more pasturage became necessary. This often upset the local political and military balance, in some cases causing conflict between Mongol troops and local client rulers.[55] The availability of pasturelands also had strategic implications, particularly regarding whether or not the Mongol mode of warfare (or even their way of life) could be successful in certain regions. Without sufficient pasturelands the Mongols could not station enough troops in regions like Syria for long before the available resources were exhausted.

For all of their resistance to harsh environmental conditions, the resilient horses of the Mongols also underwent intensive training. Marco Polo remarked that 'their horses are trained so perfectly that they will double hither and thither, just like a dog, in a way that is quite astonishing'.[56] Indeed, the Chinese believed that the training the Mongols gave their horses provided them with incredible endurance, and that a Mongol horse ridden into battle would not become exhausted for eight to ten days, even in conditions where food and water were insufficient. Although this is an exaggeration, it does illustrate the perception that the Mongol horses' stamina exceeded that found in the sedentary world. Overall, the care and treatment the Mongols provided for their horses made outside observers comment on its significance.[57]

Every day the Mongols rode their horses 30 *li*, or 15km, and then when they dismounted they fettered the horses so tightly that they could not move. As stated above, they were not allowed to eat or drink until they were suitably calm. This practice made the fat tighter on the horse's back, the belly small but strong, and the croup large but firm.[58] The Song emissary Zhao Hong noted:

> When their horses are only one or two years old they ride them harshly in the steppe and train them. They then maintain them for three years and after that mount and ride them again. Thus they train them early and for that reason they do not kick or bite. Thousands and hundreds form herds but they are silent and are without neighing or calling. When they dismount they do not rein them in and tether them, but they do not stray. Their temperament is very good.[59]

In general, the saddle as well as other equipment remained light. According to the *Meng Da Bei Lu* of Zhao Hong, the Mongol saddle weighed 9.5lb to 11lb. It was constructed from wood, into which the Mongols rubbed sheep fat in order to protect it from swelling and other water damage. It possessed a high back and front, thus providing the rider with stability while his hands were occupied with his bow or other weaponry. The stirrups were short and designed so that the weight of the rider was placed on the center of the stirrup and not the sides, thus allowing him to turn and shoot.[60] The hooves of their horses were protected by shoes of iron or wood.

Although the trading and selling of horses in exchange for goods that the nomads could not manufacture had been a vital component of steppe economy for centuries (there being many records of steppe nomads trading horses to China, the Rus' and even India), the Mongols restricted this. Both Ögödei and Möngke issued decrees to prevent horses from being smuggled to Song China, for instance, and at one point it was a capital offense for anyone but a Mongol or a messenger to ride a horse along the border. Such restrictions were possible because, with Northern China, Central Asia, Dasht-i Kipchak and much of the Middle East at their disposal, the Mongol Khans were no longer dependent on their sedentary neighbors for manufactured goods and could indulge in the luxury of banning the export of horses.

Conclusions

While the thirteenth-century Mongol soldier had much in common with warriors of previous steppe empires such as the Khitan, or even with contemporary nomads, he was also substantially different. This difference was in the militarization of Mongolian society. In order to carry out their conquests and maintain their military advantages, the Mongols created a system of regular training rather than simply assembling a mass army. This process fostered a strong sense of discipline that gave them a considerable edge against their opponents, particularly at moments of defeat. They could maintain their composure and regain the advantage whereas their opponents often dispersed in rout or in order to loot rather than pursuing victory. Through their methods of training both men and horses, and the proper procurement of weaponry, food, and other necessities, the Mongols created an army that could carry out long campaigns and, as a consequence, extended conquests.

Chapter 4

The care of the army: logistics, supply, and medical care

Central to the success of every army is the science of logistics, or that part of a military organization that plans the movement and supply of the army. This includes not only supplying the army with equipment, but also feeding it. Without proper nutrition, soldiers weaken through illness and discipline disintegrates as they attempt to find food. It is easy to fall into the trap of thinking that the Mongols were simply a rampaging horde that lived off the land, not only gathering food in this way but also acquiring their equipment by stripping the dead. While elements of this view are accurate, an examination of the Mongols' attempts to provide food and equipment, as well as to tend to their wounded, reveals a more complex picture.

Nutrition and rations

According to one study, 3,600 calories of food per day are necessary for active males, 70g of it consisting of protein, in order to avoid starvation and malnutrition.[1] For the Mongols, this was provided through a simplistic system of rations supplemented by hunting and the seizure of supplies from the cities that submitted to them.

During the campaign against the Khwarazmian Empire (1219–22), every *arban* carried between three and three-and-a-half dried sheep with them, along with a cauldron.[2] The Mongols also brought flocks of sheep and goats; however, as sheep travel slowly the soldiers carried dried rations while the livestock followed after them. Every man also had a skin of water. Although the Mongols carried their own rations, they did not rely solely on their provisions, particularly during long campaigns in distant regions. Instead they normally looked to the countryside they invaded to provide them with sustenance, and typically saved their own rations for periods when no other nourishment was available. When they camped during a siege or simply to rest, the outlying areas were thoroughly combed for supplies.[3]

In a study of pre-modern logistics, Donald Engels illustrated how Alexander the Great maintained the logistics of the Macedonian army while it campaigned far from its native territory. In the process of procuring adequate supplies for his army, Alexander secured alliances in order to set up supply depots beforehand. He ensured their security by taking hostages and paying gifts to local rulers, and issued requisition orders for, as well as purchasing, foodstuffs. 'Not to have surrendered to Alexander before he entered a district was considered a hostile action, and special operations were required to assure the army's food supply in such cases.'[4] The Mongols undertook similar, yet slightly different measures.

While obtaining the submission of regions adjoining their theatre of operations, the Mongols requested food and pastureland in addition to tribute. If a region resisted their demands the Mongol army devastated it, reducing competition for pasturage, and possibly creating new pastureland by the destruction of agricultural lands. This practice might be compared to the medieval European *chevauchée*, a method of not only living off the land but also of laying waste to the surrounding region. In addition to obtaining food, the raiders acquired plunder and lured enemies out of their fortresses, thus avoiding lengthy sieges.

European travelers recorded many observations about the Mongols and their culinary habits, not all of them favorable. The Franciscan monk John de Plano Carpini wrote:

> Their food consists of everything that can be eaten, for they eat dogs, wolves, foxes and horses and, when driven by necessity, they feed on human flesh ... They eat the filth which comes away from mares when they bring forth foals. Nay, I have even seen them eating lice. They would say, 'Why should I not eat them since they eat the flesh of my son and drink his blood?' I have also seen them eat mice.[5]

While it is possible that Carpini may have witnessed Mongol troops eating rodents or even lice, it is fair to say that this did not constitute their regular diet.

Their rations differed according to the season. Their preferred drink was fermented mare's milk or *airagh*, more commonly known as *kumiss*. Mare's milk was ideal for making this because, according to Rubruck, it does not curdle unlike other animals' milk. Rubruck, having sampled and enjoyed it, took an interest in producing the beverage and left detailed instructions. He described how milk was poured into a large leather sack and then churned with a specially crafted stick or club, the head of which was hollowed out. Part of the mixture turned to butter, and the milk fermented and soured. The butter was then removed. More churning increased the fermentation and produced a clear and more potent liquor.[6] Of course, the unprocessed milk was also drunk or processed into other dairy products.

Indeed, dairy products comprised most of the Mongols' diet. A mare produces 2.25–2.5 quarts of milk per day above the requirement necessary for a foal. This is roughly 20kcal/oz, approximately 1,440–1,600kcal/day or roughly half of the typical 3,000kcal diet required for proper nutrition. Thus two ponies could support one soldier for their normal five-month lactation period. The Mongols typically had five to eight horses per soldier on campaign. However, ensuring that the ponies were lactating required planning.[7] Zhao Hong, on the other hand, noted that usually the milk from one horse was sufficient for three men. Often a Mongol's rations would consist exclusively of mare's or sheep's milk.[8] During winter, when their horse herds could eat less, mare's milk became scarce and other foods became more important. One such ration was a paste made from powdered milk called *qurut* that was reconstituted in water and served as a staple in the Mongol soldier's diet. This was observed by both William of Rubruck and Marco Polo. According to Polo,

> They also have milk dried into a kind of paste to carry with them; and when they need food they put this in water, and beat it up till it dissolves, and then drink it. It is prepared in this way; they boil the milk, and when the rich part floats on the top they skim it into another vessel, and of that they make butter; for the milk will not become solid till this is removed. They put the milk in the sun to dry. And when they go on an expedition, every man takes some ten pounds of this dried milk with him. And of a morning he will take a half pound of it and put it in his leather bottle, with as much water as he pleases. So, as he rides along, the milk-paste and the water in the bottle get well churned together into a kind of pap, and that makes his dinner.[9]

John Masson Smith Jr noted that this particular form of rations provided 800kcal and 80g of protein, providing a quarter of the necessary ration of 3,000kcal per day.[10] In the fourteenth century in the territory of the Golden Horde, each soldier possessed ten sheep or goats to provide for his needs. Ten ewes provide approximately five quarts of milk or 3,000kcal a day during their five-month lactating period.[11] Thus it was possible to survive on a dairy-based diet.

Of course, the Mongols consumed other food products. Rather than the stereotypical image of a medieval 'barbarian' devouring a haunch of meat, the Mongols appear to have consumed most of their non-dairy meals in the form of soups. According to Carpini, in winter

> They boil millet in water and make it so thin that they cannot eat it but have to drink it. Each one of them drinks one or two cups in the morning and they eat nothing more during the day; in the evening, however, they are all given a little meat, and they drink the meat broth. But in the summer, seeing they have plenty of mare's milk, they seldom eat meat, unless it happens to be given to them or they catch some animal or bird when hunting.[12]

William of Rubruck observed how the Mongols made the most of their rations. Indeed, if a horse or oxen died they promptly dried the meat or made sausages; some they ate there and then, and the rest were smoked for later use. He noted that 50 to 100 men fed off a single sheep cut into pieces and cooked in water and salt. Although each man received but a few mouthfuls of meat, all received similar portions regardless of rank.[13] This soup or stew, known as *shülen*, was the standard meal of the Mongols. Marco Polo verified that, almost 50 years later, the Mongols still maintained a Spartan diet on the march:

> When they are going on a distant expedition they take no gear with them except two leather bottles for milk; a little earthenware pot to cook their meat in, a little tent to shelter them from rain. And in case of great urgency they will ride ten days on end without lighting a fire or taking a meal. On such occasion they will sustain themselves on the blood of their horses, opening a vein and letting the blood jet into their mouths, drinking till they have had enough, and then staunching it.[14]

It has been calculated that a horse can donate one third of its blood without serious risk to its health. Thus a horse could provide roughly 14 pints of blood with approximately 156kcal/pint, or approximately 2,184kcal, two-thirds of the projected 3,000kcal ration. So the five to eight mounts that a Mongol soldier took with him on campaign could provide him with several days of rations. Eight mounts could provide six days of a full 3,000kcal ration. Polo wrote that the Mongols could survive ten days on this. Eventually, however, it would take a toll on the horses, and was used only as a last resort.[15]

As the Franciscan friar Carpini observed, the Mongols also consumed grains. While the Mongols' diet is typically depicted as meat and dairy based, often with liberal doses of alcohol, the addition of cereals should not be surprising. Although cereals have rarely if ever been a dominant source of food in Mongolia, they can be cultivated there. In the eleventh and twelfth centuries millet, barley, and wheat were grown along the Selenge, Khalkha, Orkhon, Kerülen, and Zavkhan rivers, as well as in the region of Lake Buir. *The Secret History of the Mongols* describes how Ögödei Khan assigned guards for the granaries into which grain flowed in the form of tax payments. It is possible that this grain came from Northern China; however, all other references in section 279 of *The Secret History of the Mongols* refer to the nomads and to programs and reforms instituted in Mongolia, and newly conquered territories such as China are not discussed.[16] Cereals were used in fashions similar to that described by Carpini – as a thickener for soup or as porridge. Indeed, Zhao Hong hints that the Mongols may have commandeered considerable supplies of rice, wheat, and millet, leaving the populace with only bread and water for nourishment.[17]

Of course, the Mongols, particularly while on the march, did not rely solely on their rations. While hunting served as a training exercise, it also fed the army. Various animals were hunted, especially marmots, which are found in large numbers on the steppe. This prairie-dog-like animal, which Carpini found unsavory, served as a key source of nutrition. Marmots weigh about 10lb and carry about 3.3lb of fat, at 250kcal/oz or 13,200kcal total, while the meat provided approximately 3,400kcal, a total of 16,600kcal or 5.5 rations per marmot. Marmots, however, were only used to supplement the diet. Also there was a certain risk in eating marmots, as they were often infested with fleas carrying bubonic plague.[18]

Naturally, the Mongols hunted other animals too. The use of the *nerge*, as discussed in the chapter on training, virtually guaranteed the Mongols a variety of animals ranging from marmots and deer to antelope and even bears or tigers. However, this was a time-consuming process and not ideal for rapid marches.

Organization of logistics
Although the Mongols often foraged for food through raiding or hunting, or brought it along en masse in the form of herds and flocks, they still required supply lines, if not for foodstuffs then for other goods. These could include materials for siege equipment, additional weapons, horses, and more mundane materials. Although many of these goods might be procured by raiding, not all of the troops in a Mongol army were involved in predatory raids, particularly as the empire became larger and better organized. For instance, the armies assigned to garrison duties required supplies, and regardless of how goods were obtained a coherent plan for ensuring their supply to the armies had to be maintained. The Mongols had the capability of doing this, as it required 900 wagonloads of provisions a day to support their capital at Karakorum.

Supplies were normally carried to the army by camel or on horseback. A Bactrian camel can carry 200–240kg as a pack animal and pull 400–600kg as a draught animal, traveling 30 to 40km per day.[19] Thus a sizeable amount of food and equipment could be delivered to Mongol armies on the march. It was not always delivered at the rapid pace that one associates with the Mongols, but their forces did not always travel quickly either (see Chapter 5). Their main armies could and often did travel at a more leisurely pace while flying columns and vanguards pushed swiftly ahead. Thus baggage trains could keep up with the rest of the army. This practice confused their enemies. The Mongol vanguard and flying columns often devastated a region before the baggage train arrived, and their opponents were perplexed by the damage the Mongols could do, seemingly without carrying any heavy supplies.

It is unclear if the Mongols organized special units devoted to supplying the army with food or equipment and also to what extent they provided equipment to individual soldiers. For instance, Juvaini noted that a unit would be punished if any man failed to provide his share of implements, including banners, needles, ropes, mounts and pack animals.[20] Yet, as will be seen in the section on weaponry, the court purchased large amounts of weapons.

Providing pasture for the immense number of livestock on which the Mongol armies depended was paramount. Advanced planning was essential to ensure that grasslands were available along the route, and the problem of supplying the army was solved by making similar arrangements. Also, as the vanguard or flying columns forced cities to submit they captured supplies that could be given to the following army or to other columns.

The key element, however, was ensuring that the troops were properly equipped before the march began. While many items necessary on campaign were ubiquitous and could easily be obtained in any nomad's household, weapons beyond the basic composite bow and a supply of arrows were another matter.

The supply and manufacture of weapons, armor, and siege engines

Mongol soldiers were not solely responsible for the acquisition of their arms and armor. While it is possible that the khan may have contributed other equipment, each man brought much of his own equipment with him, thus providing his *arban* with the basic necessities of campaign life. Nonetheless, an army that is bent on world domination could not expect individual soldiers to procure all their weaponry or bear all of the cost.

There is too much data in the sources that negates the argument that the Mongols failed to equip and arm their soldiers properly. Thus the Mongol rulers did not leave them to equip themselves in the same way as bandits and roving plunderers. Indeed, the Mongols moved hundreds of craftsmen and artisans from Central Asia, Persia, and China to other locations such as Chinqai Balasghun purely so that they could benefit from their skills. There are at least three other known colonies of artisans, at Besh Baliq in Uighurstan on the northern slopes of Tien Shan; at Xinmalin or Simali, north of Beijing; and in Hongzhou, 180km west of Beijing. All were staffed mainly by artisans from Central Asia who were captured in the Khwarazmian War and mixed with Chinese counterparts. While Thomas Allsen notes that all three colonies made gold brocade known as *nasij*, they also made other goods, as many of the artisans sent to these cities were specialists in other arts. The thirteenth-century Daoist traveler Li Chih-Chang noted that the town of Chinqai Balasghun was a military colony that also possessed a granary.[21]

These cities, while not thriving metropolises such as Zhongdu or Samarqand, were industrial and agricultural centers whose raison d'être was to supply the Mongol armies and the court. Archaeological studies of these centers reveal that a fledgling industry existed in Mongolia prior to the rise of Chinggis Khan. The Khitans, during their own rule of part of Mongolia, established at least ten garrison towns that included facilities – smithies, for instance – for the maintenance of their garrisons. The archaeological evidence demonstrates that this practice continued after the Khitan, although on a more limited scale, until, with the rise of Chinggis Khan, other military-industrial colonies were established such as Chinqai Balasghun.[22] The Mongols focused their manufacturing on military needs as well as luxury and quotidian goods in specially constructed centers away from their capital.

The Mongols were quick to adapt to siege warfare once they understood it, and after seeing the benefits of regular taxation they adopted this too. In a similar manner, they recognized the value of possessing a regular supply of arms and armor. In addition to creating industrial centers for the manufacture of weaponry and armor, as well as luxury goods and other items for trade, the Mongol Khans also dealt with weapons merchants. The Persian chroniclers Juvaini and Rashid al-Din are replete with examples. On numerous occasions, Ögödei purchased bone arrowheads, bows, and even more mundane items such as leather thongs and bags for the military.[23] Thus, while the exact workings of this system of procurement remain vague, it is quite clear that the Mongols saw the merit of acquiring arms and armor in a regular fashion. Of course, gaining them as plunder was never ruled out, but in order to gain plunder one must first be properly outfitted.

This is not to say that the Mongols under Chinggis Khan were so well organized as to have the office of a quartermaster. It is evident that during the reign of Ögödei in the 1230s, when the Mongols were purchasing weapons for their military needs, the typical Mongol soldier still possessed the skills to make much of his own equipment. Arrows could be constructed fairly easily to replace lost ones, and most nomads learned to make their own bows from horn, wood, and sinew. The same could be said about their leather armor. While a smith would have to rivet thousands of links of metal rings together to make a mail shirt, the lamellar and leather armor of the Mongols was much simpler to manufacture. Of course, the quality of their bows would not equal those made by master artisans. Indeed, while the Mongols saw the talents of sedentary artisans as useful for their empire, they valued nomadic artisans in a similar way.

Maintaining communications

Maintaining effective lines of communication is essential in all aspects of war. For the horse-based army of the Mongols there were certain advantages and challenges. As horsemen, the Mongols could send messengers to maintain contact between units with relative ease. However, as their armies were extremely mobile there always remained the possibility that communications between armies or units could be broken.

To avoid this, the Mongol armies operated according to predetermined time schedules. This helped to coordinate efforts to resupply troops with horses, and to make sure pastureland was available. In addition, communications between columns on the march were maintained through the continual dispatch of riders. Yet the most important tool for maintaining logistics for the army, and indeed for communications throughout the empire, was the *yam*.

Essentially a post system, the *yam* had stations set up at intervals where official messengers could exchange their horses for fresh ones or, at times, the riders themselves could be changed. The *yam* system extended as the Mongols expanded their empire, and it was possible to relay information to the Mongol capital at Karakorum in a matter of days as the riders traveled non-stop. In many respects it was a forerunner of the nineteenth-century American Pony Express.

Medical care

Medical care in the medieval world was not an advanced art. Nor was it a pretty sight. Native Mongolian medical care involved shamans and healers who sought to cure illnesses through the spirit world or by the use of plants. However, as their empire expanded the Mongols encountered new and more sophisticated medical techniques which they incorporated into their medical arrangements.

There is no record of a true medical corps, but it is probable that doctors, surgeons, healers, and shamans traveled with the Mongols to tend to the needs of the sick and wounded. In addition to their native techniques, the Mongols adopted elements from Islamic medicine, traditional Chinese dietary medicine, and even Tibetan Ayurvedic medical techniques. Specialists from all over the empire were brought in to practice each type of medicine and over time many of their methods intermingled.

Islamic methods, largely developed from Galenic practices, were applied to injuries such as broken bones, burns, and combat wounds.[24] Of course, doctors had to deal with maladies as well, such as dysentery, bubonic plague, and milder illnesses. In addition to herbal treatments, which were a standard practice throughout the pre-modern world, Muslim doctors used cauterization and surgery. Cauterization rather than sutures appears to have been the usual technique for closing wounds. Unfortunately there is no conclusive evidence regarding Mongol attitudes to medical care, and we do not know which tradition they preferred.

In combat, the wounded were removed from the forefront of battle and apparently received care. Recorded incidents in the wars that waged across Mongolia before Chinggis Khan came to power indicate this. While most of the individuals mentioned were leaders, it is reasonable to assume that any wounded warrior would attempt to extricate himself from danger. In the early years of the Mongol empire, women appear to have been the primary care-givers, while later specialists were recruited. However, non-specialists were probably sufficient for the most common injuries such as broken bones and arrow wounds.

A lifetime of riding animals, dealing with livestock and breaking horses frequently resulted in broken bones, so that the Mongols, like other societies involved in such activities, were adept at setting fractures. Similarly, since arrow wounds were common in their battles attending to them appears to have been a widespread skill.

Several incidents in Chinggis Khan's rise to power include references to sucking blood from wounds. The primary danger from such puncture wounds was not the bleeding, but rather internal hemorrhaging. According to the research of Sophia Kaszuba, the main benefit of sucking the blood from such a wound is the prevention of an air embolism, or the formation of air bubbles in the blood stream that can lead to pulmonary embolism. As Kaszuba points out, it is doubtful that the Mongols were aware of this, but probably they learned that a wounded man had a higher chance of recovery when the wound was sucked. Sucking also aided in cleaning the wound by removing debris and possible poisons.[25]

Of course, with arrow wounds there is also the matter of removing the arrow. As the Mongols and other nomadic tribes used a wide variety of arrowheads, extraction was not easy. In most instances, pushing the arrowhead right through was preferable, so as not to enlarge the wound with the barbs on the back of the arrowhead. Yet some arrowheads were wider at the tip and would create a more grievous wound if pushed through rather than pulled out.

The Mongols may have attempted to alleviate some of the trauma associated with arrow wounds. Not long after invading Northern China they adopted the practice of wearing tightly woven silk undershirts. James Chambers, in his *Devils' Horsemen*, speculated that this shirt prevented the arrowhead from completely penetrating the body. The silk, in Chambers' estimation, wrapped around the arrowhead, thus allowing surgeons to simply unwrap it and pull the arrow out rather than having to push the arrow through the patient. Since Chambers' work first appeared in 1979 numerous other authors have accepted this interpretation as fact. Unfortunately, none of the medieval sources indicate that the shirt had a function beyond that of being a simple (though luxurious) garment. Indeed, if it were, the armies of the Jin and Song may have fared better against the Mongols.

Individuals who had been severely wounded, such as with multiple wounds or injuries caused by a bolt fired by a ballistae siege engine, received a special treatment. An ox, buffalo, or other suitably large animal (but rarely a horse) was disemboweled, and the patient, who had had arrows and other fragments removed from him, was placed inside the carcass. The undigested vegetable matter found in the animal's stomach then served as a poultice for the wounds.[26] Many of those who underwent this treatment seemed to have recovered well. It is doubtful that the blood of the animal had any inherent healing properties, but it is possible that by providing warmth its body helped to stave off shock.

When dealing with illnesses, shamans were of great importance, especially if herbal remedies failed. In the belief system of the Mongols, and many other Eurasian nomads at the time, the causes of illness originated in the spirit world. They thought that a sick individual's soul had been somehow lost or abducted, and a shaman was brought in to retrieve it. After entering an ecstatic state, the shaman's astral spirit would enter the spirit world and attempt to bring it back. If the sick person recovered, then the shaman was successful. If not, then it was beyond the power of the shaman to work a cure.

As the Mongols became more cosmopolitan it was not unusual for them to attempt various more practical measures to cure the sick. It is also notable that the Mongols had a system of quarantine. Friar John de Plano Carpini observed that if someone was seriously ill, a spear wrapped with black felt would be planted outside their *yurt* or tent. This was a clear signal that the end was nigh and no one would enter the tent except a select few, such as family members. These individuals were then prevented from coming into contact with any high-ranking persons.[27]

In addition to their attempts to treat the sick the Mongols took steps to prevent the spread of disease, often through a crude form of hygiene. They were not noted for their cleanliness, at least when it came to personal hygiene, yet when one considers the lifestyle of a medieval nomad the typical Mongol warrior was in excellent physical condition. Indeed, those born with severe illnesses were not likely to survive their childhood simply because of the rigors of the environment.

They were careful not to foul running water with urine or by washing their hands, clothing, or dishes in it. Water had to be drawn off in a vessel before it was used. Their apparent lack of cleanliness even by medieval European standards repulsed the thirteenth-century monk, John de Plano Carpini.[28] However, he failed to realize that the Mongols were concerned with maintaining the purity of water. If the water became foul through bathing, urination, or cleaning, then it would have a detrimental effect not only on their own health, but also the health of their flocks and herds. It was particularly important to prevent the water from being fouled upstream of their camp. Also, perhaps inadvertently, they reduced the chance of disease spreading in their large camps by pitching their *yurts* a considerable distance away from each other.

Conclusion

The greatest difficulty in assessing the logistics and supply of the Mongol army is in determining how much of it was organized by the government and how much by individuals. The answer is not clear cut. It is evident that while individuals were responsible for much of their own equipment and rations, the Great Khan of the Mongol empire did take measures to feed and equip his armies. It is also apparent that as the Mongol empire expanded, the Mongols were willing to incorporate new techniques and practices into their existing logistical and medical arrangements.

Chapter 5

Espionage, tactics, and strategy

As the Mongol army evolved, it developed tactics that were no longer wholly derived from pastoralist steppe warfare. While many of their tactics were common on the steppe, the Mongols' use and integration of them into their more complex military system demonstrates their success in transforming traditional steppe warfare into the more sophisticated operational concepts characteristic of a permanent army. More importantly, their tactics provided the foundation for an operational strategy that enabled them to fight on several fronts and allowed the Mongol empire to expand at a steady and planned rate rather than by means of haphazard conquests scattered over vast territories.

As part of their military system, the Mongols planned their strategy before commencing a campaign. Juvaini noted this:

> Whenever a khan ascends the throne, or a great army is mobilized, or the princes assemble and begin [to consult together] concerning affairs of state and the administration thereof, they produce these rolls and model their actions thereon; and proceed with the disposition of armies or the destruction of provinces and cities in the manner therein prescribed.[1]

The 'rolls' that Juvaini refers to were the Great Book of *Yasa*, on which all the ordinances of Chinggis Khan were written. Although the document has not survived, there is sufficient evidence to show that the Mongols chose a particular strategy and maintained it throughout the empire's existence. As their methods of conquest and warfare became increasingly well-organized, the Mongols were transformed from a tribal force into a true army.

Espionage and intelligence

The Mongols did not begin a campaign without accumulating intelligence. This they gathered in a variety of ways, from merchants, from their own spies, from the *algincin* or scouts who rode ahead of their armies, and from the reports of expeditionary forces sent to deal with specific threats. Institutions within the empire facilitated the information gathering process. The famous *yam* or postal system relayed news and other information back to the Khan and his generals at a rapid pace. In his classic study on pre-modern intelligence systems, Francis Dvornik saw this as an integral key to the Mongols' success.[2] It expedited the accumulation of intelligence by enabling messengers to travel quickly from station to station. Furthermore, imperial messengers could also requisition horses from virtually anyone should the need arise. In this way the Mongol court received the latest intelligence from the frontiers of the empire in a matter of days rather than months.

Merchants played an important role. Dvornik noted:

> They controlled all trade between China and Central Asia. They knew all the routes and, being highly cultivated, were good observers and were well acquainted with the economic and political situation of every district with which they traded. By reason of their trade they had numerous contacts in many quarters, and all the lands from Persia to China through which their caravans passed were well known to them.[3]

Throughout the history of the Mongol Empire, the khans patronized merchants and protected the trade routes. In return, the merchants supported the khans and provided them with a wealth of information. Some did so willingly in order to cultivate a relationship with the Khan, while others may have simply been unaware that the Mongols sought to gain intelligence from them. Indeed, the Mongols sought up-to-date news from all travelers who came to their courts. The Mongols also utilized merchants as actual spies, and not merely as passive collectors of information. Indeed, it was on suspicion of spying that the governor of Otrar had infamously massacred a Mongol-sponsored caravan in Khwarazmia in 1219.

The Mongols also collected information by more aggressive means. While campaigning, for instance, it was not uncommon for raiding parties to enter areas beyond the main arena of conflict. When the Mongols reached enemy territory they sent out a screen of scouts, who covered the invading force and constantly relayed information back to their main column. This had been common practice even before Chinggis Khan unified the steppe – *The Secret History of the Mongols* records that during the war of Chinggis Khan and Toghril Ong-Qan against Jamuqa, the Mongols marched down the Kelüren River with a vanguard that had scouts riding ahead of it. They set up observation posts along the way so that the scouts could relay information back to the main body.[4] The scouts or *alginci* often operated more than 50km ahead of each column and on the flanks, making it very difficult for an enemy to launch a surprise attack.[5] They relayed information back through the *yam* system, or a modified version of it, or even by means of signal flags. This practice appears to have evolved over time into a standard operational procedure.

Finally, the Mongols gathered intelligence through the use of expeditionary forces. This was a secondary duty of such forces, since most had a specific task, such as hunting down a fleeing leader. Jebe and Sübedei's historic *reconnaissance en force* began as the pursuit of Sultan Muhammad II of the Khwarazmian Empire. However, after this they continued on through much of Eurasia and collected valuable information about regions beyond the Mongol frontier. Similar opportunities arose during the unification of Mongolia when Chinggis Khan sent armies to pursue leaders who would not submit to him. While these were punitive missions, the generals also accumulated intelligence concerning the politics, military strength, and geography of neighboring regions, thus providing the Mongols with more data for the planning of future invasions.

Tactics

As was the case with most steppe armies, the Mongols were primarily light horse-archers. Their tactics sought to exploit their abilities with the bow and their mobility, usually by staying out of reach of their opponents' weapons and using hit and run tactics in waves while showering the enemy with arrows. Often they retreated before the enemy, utilizing the famous 'Parthian shot' as they went. At the right moment, normally when the enemy's forces were drawn out in pursuit, the nomads would wheel around and annihilate them. These methods of war were augmented with surprise attacks, ambushes, and encirclements. Like the Turkic troops the Crusaders encountered in Anatolia and elsewhere in the Middle East, the Mongols initiated combat at bowshot range and only closed in for the decisive encounter, after the enemy's formation had broken or was weakened.[6] Their tactics ensured that they did not require superior numbers. They relied instead on mobility, firepower, and subterfuge to gain victory.

The Mongols were not necessarily innovative but simply perfected the timeless tactics of the steppe. Training exercises further perfected their execution. They practiced the tactics of encirclement through the *nerge* and hit-and-run tactics through *qabaq* exercises. However, while these tactics were not new, the Mongols' natural inclination towards traditional steppe warfare did not prevent them from adopting other tactics.

Arrow storm and rolling barrage

The arrow storm or shower was the most common tactic practised by the Mongols. They enveloped their enemy, then shot a hail of arrows. The number of arrows that hit was described as a phenomenon of nature.[7] The range from which they mounted such an attack varied. At a long range of 200 or 300m their shooting was less accurate, but it could still disrupt the enemy's formation.[8] Once this broke, the Mongols charged.

In the course of the arrow storm archers did not aim at specific targets. Rather, they loosed their arrows at a high trajectory into a predetermined 'killing zone' or area target. While this practice probably caused few mortal wounds it undoubtedly weakened morale, as soldiers had to watch arrows wound their comrades while being unable to retaliate.[9] On occasion the Mongols found it beneficial to dismount in order to shoot, often using their horses as a protective barrier, as they did in 1230 while battling Jalal al-Din and then again in 1300 under Ghazan against the Mamluks.

Concentrated firepower

While the practice of concentrating firepower certainly existed prior to the Mongols, they were perhaps the first to use it to its maximum effect in all aspects of war, from the arrow storm to batteries of siege weapons. At the siege of Nishapur, the Mongols amassed enough weaponry to overawe its defenders, who were allegedly defended by 300 ballistae and catapults along with 3,000 crossbows. While these figures are probably exaggerated, they indicate that the Mongols' own corps of engineers must have deployed a large number of siege weapons.[10]

Not until the 1300s did Western Europeans begin to fully appreciate the potential of missile fire. Despite the success of their crossbows at battles such as Arsuf (1191), it was not until much later that the military elite of Europe developed the technique of massed firepower. The Mongols, on the other hand, routinely focused on the destruction of military formations by directing their fire by means of banners, fire signals, and whistling arrows.

Caracole tactics

The Mongols combined the arrow storm with hit-and-run tactics, changing horses regularly to keep them fresh. Approximately 80 men in each *jaghun* participated, the remaining 20 acting as heavy cavalry. Each *jaghun* sent 20 men per wave. The waves fired several arrows as they charged, and then circled back to the Mongol lines after completing their charge, having loosed their final shot roughly 40–50m from the enemy line before wheeling around. This distance was close enough to pierce armor, but far enough from the enemy to evade a counter-charge. While circling back, the Mongols often used the 'Parthian shot'. Since each man was equipped with 60 arrows the Mongols could maintain this barrage for almost an hour, perhaps longer if the number of men in each wave varied.[11]

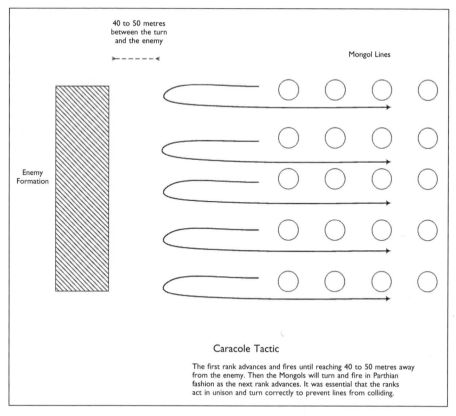

40 to 50 metres
between the turn
and the enemy

Mongol Lines

Enemy
Formation

Caracole Tactic

The first rank advances and fires until reaching 40 to 50 metres away
from the enemy. Then the Mongols will turn and fire in Parthian
fashion as the next rank advances. It was essential that the ranks
act in unison and turn correctly to prevent lines from colliding.

Caracole Tactics

This technique remained in use among the Mongols throughout their era of
dominance, as Marco Polo observed in the late thirteenth century:

> When they come to an engagement with the enemy, they will gain
> the victory in this fashion. [They never let themselves get into a
> regular mêlée, but keep perpetually riding round and shooting into
> the enemy. And] as they do not count it any shame to run away in
> battle, they will [sometimes pretend to] do so, and in running away
> they turn in the saddle and shoot hard and strong at the foe, and in
> this way make great havoc.[12]

This tactic is remarkably similar to the caracole used by European pistol-armed
cavalry in the late sixteenth and seventeenth centuries:

> To perform the caracole, a body of cavalry several ranks deep
> approached the enemy. The first rank fired its pistols, wheeled about,

and rode to the rear of the formation to reload; the succeeding ranks fired and wheeled in turn. By the time the last rank had fired, the first would be ready to discharge its weapons once again. The intention was to blow a hole in the enemy square ...[13]

In *The Secret History of the Mongols*, on one occasion, Chinggis Khan ordered his men to attack in 'chisel' formation, but it is not clear what this was.[14] The name implies that the purpose of the formation was to drive through the enemy's ranks. Dalantai, however, offers an alternative suggestion:

A group of cavalrymen would make a direct charge into the enemy line. If the first charge failed, a second and even third group would attack. No matter how great the opposition, even if they numbered a hundred thousand, they were unable to withstand the charges. Finally, in response to a signal, the Mongol cavalrymen would charge from all directions into the enemy lines in order to destroy their formation.[15]

While Dalantai's description resembles the traditional cavalry charge, that is to say a movement to direct contact, it is more likely that the Mongols advanced, fired their bows, and then wheeled around to make another attack, for they were always reluctant to engage in close combat except to finish off an opponent. Thus, like a laborer with a chisel, constant strikes broke the enemy rather than a single hammer blow. So the 'chisel' attack was probably similar to the caracole and was used in conjunction with other maneuvers such as the feigned retreat.

Feigned retreat

The feigned retreat was a classic tactic of steppe warfare practised since ancient times. A token force charged the enemy and then retreated, drawing the enemy in pursuit. The retreat might extend a great distance in order to stretch the enemy's ranks and formations. Then at a pre-arranged location, other Mongol forces would attack from the flanks while the token force wheeled around and attacked from the front.

Perhaps the most renowned use of the feigned retreat took place in 1223, when Jebe and Sübedei encountered a combined army of Kipchak Turks and Rus' along the Dnepr River. The Mongols promptly retreated, luring the Kipchaks and Rus' deep into the steppe for several days until they reached the Khalkha River. Here the main the Mongol force awaited them, and the pursuing allies were promptly destroyed.[16]

Marco Polo also remarked on the effectiveness of the feigned retreat:

> Thus they fight to as good purpose in running away as if they stood and faced the enemy, because of the vast volleys of arrows that they shoot in this way, turning round upon their pursuers, who are fancying that they have won the battle. But when the Tartars see that they have killed and wounded a good many horses and men, they wheel round bodily, and return to the charge in perfect order and with loud cries; and in a very short time the enemy are routed.[17]

The Mongols used this tactic in the same way as did other pastoral nomadic groups. As with most of their tactics, the feigned retreat allowed them to avoid close combat until they had gained the advantage.

Fabian tactics

At times the Mongols avoided combat with the enemy until they found an ideal location for a battle or had regrouped far-flung forces to confront their opponent. This tactic differed from the feigned retreat in which they attacked and then withdrew with the deliberate intent of luring the enemy into an ambush. Fabian tactics involved the avoidance of all direct contact with the enemy. The Mongol army would often divide into small groups to prevent it from being surrounded when necessary, and then regroup and launch a surprise attack on the enemy at a more opportune time.[18] Fabian tactics also had the effect of exhausting the enemy by avoiding combat. This was particularly effective when the enemy's forces maintained a strong defensive posture, whether in the open or in a fortress. As the Mongols remained in the vicinity, the constant stress of the anticipation of an attack wore down some units.

When the Mongols were confronted by opponents who had planted spears in the ground to prevent cavalry charges, they responded by withdrawing the bulk of their forces while a few detachments remained behind to harass the enemy. Eventually, their enemies would emerge from their defenses, either because of hunger or thirst or because they believed that the Mongols had withdrawn. The main Mongol force would then return and destroy them. Again, in this way the Mongols were able to choose a more opportune time to fight if the initial encounter did not go well.

Flanking tactics and double envelopment

Whenever possible, the Mongols preferred to surround their enemies by using their *nerge* training. According to the Chinese general Zhao Hong, the author of the *Meng-Da Bei-Lu*:

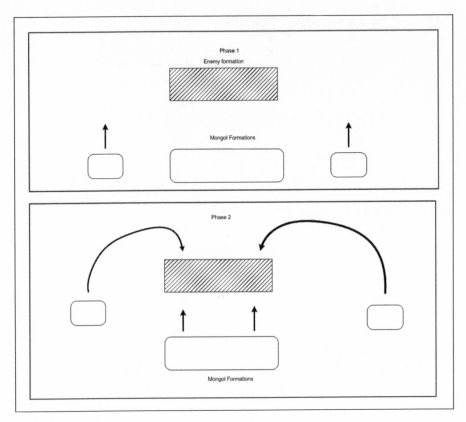

Envelopment Tactics

as soon as the scouting screen of a Mongol army made contact with the enemy, the main body extended in front over as great a distance as possible so as to overlap the flanks of the hostile force. On closer contact and the approach of action, skirmishers went forward, and scouts were called upon to bring in reports about local topography, lines of communication, and the strength and disposition of the opposing troops.[19]

Zhao Hong's description shows a highly organized army with a clear set of operational procedures for engaging the enemy, not a tribal army intending to overcome its foe by force of numbers.

Chinggis Khan used encircling tactics against his enemies on several occasions, especially if their flanks and rear were exposed, and during sieges if the defenders were weak. When he was confronted by an army using such features of the terrain as a river to its advantage, he attempted to encircle it along both sides of the river.

The Mongols sometimes confused an enemy by feinting towards his front and then unleashing their main attack against his rear. By attacking from several directions, the Mongols gave their enemies the impression that they were surrounded. By leaving a gap in their encirclement the Mongols allowed the enemy an apparent means of escape, whereas in reality it served as a trap. In their panic and desire to escape through this gap, the enemy often discarded their weapons to flee faster and rarely maintained their discipline. The Mongols then attacked them from the rear, as in their defeat of the Hungarians at Mohi in 1241. Dalantai called this the 'Open-the-End tactic' and noted that the Mongols used it if the enemy seemed to be very strong and might fight to the death if trapped.[20]

The practice of double envelopment or even encirclement, while a traditional steppe tactic, also stems from the Mongols' training in the *nerge* or *battue* style of hunting. Just as in the *nerge*, the warriors gradually tightened the circle around their prey, forming a dense mass from which it was difficult to escape. The Mongols did not always require large numbers of troops to achieve this, their archery skills and mobility allowing them to encircle an enemy force even when they were outnumbered.

The *nerge* used in military operations essentially served as a double envelopment tactic, in which the wings of the Mongol army would wrap around the flanks of the enemy's battle formation. This, like the feigned retreat, was a standard tactic of steppe warfare, and its use was not limited to set-piece battles. The Mongols sometimes used it as a strategy on a broader front during an invasion, as they did when they attacked the Rus'. After the capture of the city of Vladimir in 1237, 'they turned back from there and held a council, deciding that they would proceed tümän by tümän in järge formation and take and destroy every town, province and fortress they came to'.[21] In this fashion the Mongols encircled an area, then gradually closed in so that avenues of escape narrowed just as they would in a battle.

In some instances the Mongols sent a force of prisoners and conscripted levies to attack the enemy front – backed, of course, by a suitable number of Mongol troops to ensure that they performed their duty. Meanwhile, Mongol columns marched out of sight until they reappeared on the flanks or in the rear of the enemy.[22]

Siege warfare

The army's inability to conduct sieges effectively during the early days of the Mongol conquests was a weakness that Chinggis Khan and his generals knew would have to be overcome if they were to hold territory. So as their successes against sedentary opponents increased, the Mongols incorporated engineers into their armies. These were either conscripted or came over to the Mongols voluntarily. Nonetheless, the Mongols remained dependent on Muslim and Chinese engineers – who both manned and manufactured their artillery and other siege equipment – throughout the entire existence of their empire.

The Mongols delayed beginning major sieges until the later part of a campaign, starting instead with the reduction of smaller outlying places.[23] This ensured that they had sufficient manpower to lay siege to the larger towns when the time came.

When they came up against an inaccessible city or fortress, the Mongols set up a blockade in order to starve the enemy into surrendering. They also dealt with strongholds by bypassing them; once they were isolated they lost their strategic importance. If the Mongols found that they could not reduce a city or fortress, they often built a counter fortress to blockade it and waited until the enemy succumbed to hunger or agreed to a diplomatic settlement.

Nasawi observed that the Mongols laid siege in the following manner:

> According to the custom which they use when laying siege to a citadel that is very fortified, the Mongols constructed around Ilal a wall pierced with openings that they close at night and open during the day.[24]

While the building of a wall surrounding a besieged city became standard practice for the Mongols after the Khwarazmian War, it is unclear if they used the same technique against the Jin or if there were any precedents for this practice among previous steppe powers in Mongolia or North China.

Prior to a siege, the Mongols collected numerous captives and conscripts from conquered cities and villages to serve as corvée labor and arrow fodder. After seizing a city, town, or village, the Mongols divided the population into units of ten, and each Mongol soldier received a unit. These gathered grass, wood, earth and stone. If any of the captives fell behind during the march, the Mongols executed them. When the levies arrived at the city that was to be attacked, they quickly filled the moat or defensive trench with stones and other materials – bundles of straw, wood, and debris – so that the Mongols could reach the walls and pierce them. Prisoners were compelled to build siege engines, presumably under the direction of the Mongols' Chinese and Persian engineers. With these engines and their own bows, the Mongols maintained a constant barrage on the city in order to prevent the enemy from resting. The Mongols also used naphtha and possibly Greek Fire, and the Franciscan friar John de Plano Carpini noted a more gruesome fuel. According to him 'they even take the fat of the people they kill and, melting it, throw it on to the house, and wherever the fire falls on this fat it is almost inextinguishable'.[25]

Prisoners were forced to take an active part in the sieges. They were forced to dig trenches and erect defenses and to undertake whatever other tasks were deemed necessary. They even worked the battering rams, which were operated from the shelter of a canopy or perhaps some more substantial protection resembling the sows and cats used in medieval Europe. If the captives tried to run away they were put to death. Thus they had a choice of certain death at the hands of the Mongols or probable death at the hands of the defenders, some of whom they may have known.

In addition to using catapults and rams to weaken the walls of a city, the Mongols dug tunnels to undermine them. If a river ran nearby – as at Xi-Xia, for instance – they would dam it and flood the streets.[26]

During a siege the Mongols tended to stay out of the range of fire from the city, but once the wall was breached they donned their armor and attacked, often at night to minimize casualties.[27] The conscripted levies did most of the dangerous work and the Mongols only exposed themselves when they were required to engage in combat. Thus they conserved their own troops while letting auxiliaries and local levies perform the most perilous jobs.[28]

These tactics were standard operating procedure for the Mongols throughout their conquests. Russian sources, for instance, note that they surrounded cities with walls and then built catapults, ladders, and other siege weapons.[29] Indeed, the campaign in Russia demonstrated the sophistication and efficiency of Mongol siege techniques by that date. The siege of Vladimir in 1238 is a particularly good example. There the Mongols isolated the city by surrounding it with a wall before bombarding it with catapults, arrows, and fire arrows, and attacking it with battering rams operated by levies. Once they had breached a city wall, the Mongols would mount a swift assault before moving on to attack the next stronghold.

Psychological tactics and means of deception

The Mongols realized it was more efficient to convince a city or fortress to surrender without resistance rather than to be drawn into a siege. As a result the Mongols gained a notorious reputation for massacres. According to some sources, most notably Juzjani and the Rus' chroniclers, the Mongols rarely left a living soul wherever they conquered. However, in general their massacres were not carried out in wanton blood lust – rather they served several useful purposes. The first was to discourage revolts by hostile populations to the Mongols' rear. The second was to discourage resistance. As news of the massacres spread, particularly those that had taken place after the defenders had put up a determined fight, other cities and peoples were sufficiently intimidated to surrender. Finally, since massacre was the punishment for rebellion it served as a powerful deterrent.

Yet such actions were often incomprehensible to contemporary observers. According to Thomas Barfield, the Mongols

> were extremely conscious of their small numbers and employed terror as a tool to discourage resistance against them. Cities, like Herat, that surrendered and then revolted were put to the sword. The Mongols could not maintain strong garrisons and so preferred to wipe out whole areas that appeared troublesome. Such behavior was inexplicable to sedentary historians for whom conquest of productive populations was the goal of warfare.[30]

In addition, the Mongols used propaganda and often spread rumors that exaggerated the size of their army. In 1258, for example, Möngke invaded Szechuan with 40,000 men but spread rumors that he led 100,000. The Mongols also took advantage of dissension within the ranks of their enemies, as they did in their campaign in Khwarazm.[31] This policy, like their calculated use of massacres, helped to weaken resistance through the use of fear, and further lent credence to the idea that the Mongols were an unstoppable force.

They resorted to subterfuge to confuse and intimidate their foes. When he fought the Naiman in 1204, Chinggis Khan ordered his soldiers to set up camp on the Sa'ari Steppe in western Mongolia. In order to conceal the true size of his army he commanded that each soldier should light five campfires, thus giving the impression that the Mongols possessed a numerous army.[32] Similarly, when the Mongols encountered numerically superior forces they often sent troops out to stir up dust behind their own lines by means of branches tied to the tails of their horses, thereby creating the illusion of approaching reinforcements. They also mounted dummies on their spare horses, and rode in single file to mask their numbers at a distance. Shiqi Qutuqtu unsuccessfully attempted this tactic against Jalal al-Din in 1221 at the Battle of the Parvan Valley in Afghanistan.[33]

On other occasions they herded oxen and horses into the enemy's lines to disrupt them. This tactic was especially useful if the enemy appeared to be well organized or strong. The Mongols would then attack amidst the resulting confusion.[34]

The Inner Mongolian historian Dalantai believes that the Mongols sometimes attempted to surprise the enemy by approaching in what were known as 'bush formations'. He wrote: 'These tactics involved dividing the soldiers into many small groups which, although keeping in contact with each other, maintained a low profile as they advanced. Such tactics were also used at night-time, and on dark or cloudy days.'[35]

The Mongols sought to weaken their opponents by promoting rebellion or discord, and by courting the support of oppressed minorities (or majorities). While the Mongols made good use of their reputation for extreme brutality they took pains to portray themselves as liberators when circumstances warranted. They also played rivals off against one another. As the French knight Jean de Joinville wrote: 'Whenever the Mongols wish to make war on the Saracens they send Christians to fight against them, and on the other hand employ Saracens in any war against Christians'.[36]

'Supernatural tactics'

The Mongols even resorted to supernatural means to assure their success. They asked Tenggri, or Heaven, for his favor on the battlefield, in the same way that Muslim and Christian armies appealed to their god. But the Mongols also employed other supernatural tactics, of which the most important was weather magic, conducted by a shaman known as the *jadaci*.

Several accounts mention the use of weather magic. The *jadaci* used special rocks known as rain stones, thought to be imbued with the power to control weather, in order to summon rainstorms, or even snowstorms in the summer, which caught the enemy ill-prepared. The Mongols, who had lured their opponents away from their base, took shelter during the storm and then attacked while their foes were disoriented. A prime example of this tactic was recorded during the war against the Jin after Chinggis Khan's death. Bar Hebraeus relates that Ögödei resorted to using rain stones after he saw the size of a Jin field army. After he had lured the Jin away from any support, he called upon his *jadaci* to summon a storm. The ensuing downpour, in the normally dry month of July, lasted for three day and three nights. The Jin army was caught in the open and drenched while the Mongols donned rain gear and waited the storm out. They then turned around and ambushed the Jin army, annihilating it.[37]

Other sources indicate that Tolui, rather than Ögödei, was the general involved in this episode. Tolui had retreated after encountering a much larger Jin force, and after the Jin had attacked his rearguard he summoned a Turkic rainmaker to perform his magic. Rashid al-Din recorded that 'this is a kind of sorcery carried out with various stones, the property of which is that when they are taken out, placed in water, and washed, cold, snow, rain and blizzards at once appear even though it's the middle of summer'.[38] The rain continued for three days, changing on the final day to snow accompanied by an icy wind.

The Jin troops were exposed to this severe weather while the Mongols found shelter. After four days of snow, the Mongols attacked and destroyed the bewildered and weakened Jin troops.[39]

Strategy

The most effective strategies in war exploit the strengths of the army involved. For the Mongols, this meant a strategy of high mobility. The Mongols' horses were surpassed in strength and speed by those of sedentary armies, but they were superior in endurance, and the Mongols had more of them. Since the average trooper in the Mongol army possessed three to five mounts he could remain mobile even if one or two of his mounts were lost or exhausted. In consequence the Mongols engaged in a style of warfare that was not employed again until the twentieth century, when armies became mechanized.

Timing

When preparing for war, the Mongols took several steps. First, they conducted a census in order to organize the mobilization of their troops. They also accumulated intelligence on their opponents. Only after sufficient intelligence had been obtained did they make a declaration of war. Such declarations varied, but by the peak of the empire they outlined why the Mongols were invading and gave the enemy a few options, such as surrendering and providing tribute and troops when requested or else face destruction. The strategy for the upcoming war and the selection of commanders were agreed at a *quriltai*, points of rendezvous were established, and mobilization began in earnest.

According to Denis Sinor:

> Mongol strategy at its best was based on a very careful planning of the military operations to be performed, and the essence of it lay in a very rigid timetable to which all Mongol commanders were expected to adhere strictly.[40]

While timetables were important to Mongol armies, they were not afraid to alter their plans in order to take advantage of favorable weather and other environmental factors. They sought to attack when least expected. They were not afraid to do so when their horses were lean or weak, or over frozen rivers in the middle of winter.

Although campaigns were meticulously planned, the Mongol generals maintained a high degree of independence. Thus they could fulfill their objectives in their own way so long as they abided by the overall timetable. This form of strategic organization allowed the Mongols to coordinate their armies and concentrate them at prearranged sites.

Travel by columns

Invading Mongol armies followed several routes of advance. Against the Khwarazmian Empire Chinggis Khan used at least four and perhaps five routes, one of which ran through the Kyzyl Kum desert. During the invasion of Russia, Sübedei, Batu, and Möngke approached from three directions. Later, in the invasion of Eastern Europe, another three-pronged advance was made. Ultimately, as in modern warfare, these columns converged upon a single target, usually the enemy's center of power. Against the Khwarazmian Empire it was Samarqand; in Europe, Budapest.

Because of their pre-planned schedule and their skillful use of scouts, the Mongols were able to march divided but fight united. As their forces marched in small detachments their advance was not impeded by columns that stretched for miles. They exploited their mobility and used an indirect approach to such effect that their opponents were rarely able to concentrate their forces before the Mongols appeared on many fronts at the same time. While the Mongols were quite capable of concentrating their forces before a critical point in an enemy's defenses, such as a strategic fortress or a field army, they often overwhelmed their opponents by applying pressure to several points simultaneously.

Annihilation of a field army

A multi-pronged invasion plan suited the Mongols' favored method of engaging the enemy, that is, by destroying the opposing field army before moving deep into enemy territory. Provoking such an engagement was rarely difficult, as their enemies sought to meet the Mongols before their outlying provinces were devastated. Screens of scouts ensured that the Mongols could rapidly locate enemy armies. In addition, the Mongols were normally in a position to unite their forces before anyone realized how many invading armies existed, the troop strengths of the Mongols being concealed. This system of advance also meant that an embattled Mongol force could be reinforced or, in the event of defeat, it could be avenged.

After defeating an army, the Mongols pursued it until it was destroyed. Assaults on enemy strongholds were often delayed by this effort to put the field army out of action, though small fortresses and larger ones that could be surprised easily were taken in the course of the advance. The Khwarazmian campaign is perhaps the best example of this, smaller cities and fortresses being taken before the capital, Samarqand, was captured. This strategy had two obvious advantages. First, it prevented the principal city from communicating with others that might have come to its aid. Second, refugees from the smaller cities fled to the main stronghold, where not only did their reports reduce the morale of both the inhabitants and the garrison, but the refugees themselves became a burden on its resources, food and water reserves being taxed by the sudden influx of people.

With the destruction of the field army, the Mongols were free to commence sieges wherever they wished without fear of interference. Forces from smaller forts and cities could not seriously disrupt the Mongol besiegers, who either foraged or were out on other missions during the siege and were thus beyond their reach. More importantly, the roving Mongol forces prevented the larger enemy cities from assisting their smaller neighbors, as to do so in any strength left them open to attack. Finally, the capture of the outer strongholds and towns gave the Mongols more siege experience, and in the process of seizing them they took prisoners who could then be used to man the siege machines or to act as human shields.

The pursuit of leaders

Once an enemy field army had been defeated, the Mongols concentrated on destroying their opponent's capacity to rally. They targeted all the enemy leaders and harried them until they were killed. Chinggis Khan first pursued this policy during the wars of unification in Mongolia. In his first few campaigns his failure to eliminate the opposing leaders allowed them to regroup their forces and start the conflict anew. He learned from this experience and in his later campaigns the merciless pursuit of enemy commanders evolved into a standard operational procedure.[41] In Khwarazm, for example, Muhammad Khwarazmshah fled to the Caspian Sea with the generals Jebe and Sübedei in pursuit. Meanwhile, Chinggis Khan chased Jalal al-Din to the Indus River. Koten, one of the khans of the Kipchaks, fled from the Dasht-i Kipchak to Hungary and his flight was later used as the political rationale for the Mongol invasion of Hungary. And in Europe, King Bela IV of Hungary received no breathing room after the disaster at Mohi.

Since they were compelled to be constantly on the move, defeated rulers found it difficult to rally their forces. In several accounts, perhaps exaggerated, they were said to be only a few steps ahead of the Mongols. In their pursuit the Mongols took the opportunity to acquire intelligence about new lands and they caused disruption in the regions they moved through. In addition, news of their advance made it advisable for local rulers to keep their forces at home rather than going to help their suzerain. To pursue fleeing rulers, the Mongols dispatched a strike force, while other forces were sent to outlying regions. In some cases these regions were independent of the kingdom invaded by the Mongols, yet that did not protect them from Mongol interference.

Conclusions

The Mongols possessed a highly developed and complex military structure. While this certainly gave them an edge in warfare over their opponents, previous nomadic confederations had possessed equally complex military structures in terms of training, organization, tactics, and strategy. The key to Mongol success in war was their pragmatic melding of traditional and still effective steppe tactics with the new tactics, weapons, and forms of warfare that they encountered during their conquests. They also ensured that their soldiers were properly trained to execute the appropriate tactics when ordered. Finally, due to their extensive planning the Mongols were better organized and informed about their opponents than most medieval armies. Their generals carried out orders without tight supervision from a central command, yet remained obedient to the instructions they were given.

Chapter 6

Leadership

As with all armies, leadership played a pivotal role in the success of the Mongols on the battlefield. Even with a highly organized and disciplined army, it was still necessary for someone to provide direction and to execute the tactics and strategies that were devised in training or during discussions between commanders. What sets the Mongols apart from other armies of their era was not that they produced exceptional brilliance such as that of Chinggis Khan or even his best-known general Sübedei, but rather that they possessed numerous commanders of outstanding ability. Whereas in the rest of the medieval world military genius, or even competence, was rare, among the Mongols it was expected from every commander.

Much of this resulted from how the Mongols selected their commanders and trained them in the performance of their duties. Unlike many of their contemporaries, the Mongols did not base the ability to command on lineage, although this might support one's claim to authority. Instead, throughout his ascent to power, Chinggis Khan demonstrated an extraordinary gift for spotting talent in men, whether they were of noble birth or commoners. Merit was the key to acquiring a position of leadership in the Mongol military hierarchy, and battlefield promotions were not uncommon. Yet at the same time, should a commander fail in his duties battlefield demotions occurred even to generals. Nonetheless, the Mongols saw the benefit of grooming successful commanders rather than relying entirely on either choosing great warriors or spotting the potential in talented shepherds. Instead they used two systems to train their leaders. The first was through the *keshik* or bodyguard of the Khan, while the second – often used in conjunction with the first – was through an apprenticeship of sorts.

The *keshik*
As we have already seen, the *keshik* served as more than the Khan's bodyguard. While the *jaghud* and *minqat* of the regular army were often led by officers of non-*keshikten* origin, the generals who led the armies of conquest typically rose from its ranks. Thus the *keshik* served not only as a training school for officers, but also as a proving ground.[1] Because of the ties forged within the *keshik* and

its focus on serving the Khan, the Mongol ruler allowed his commanders to operate independently in the field without fear of rebellion.

The command abilities and prestige of the *keshikten* were so highly regarded by the Khans that the rank of *arban-u noyan* in the *keshik* was deemed equal to that of a *jaghun-u noyan* in the regular military, and in general held that the rank of a member of the *keshik* was equivalent to the next rank up in the rest of the army. As such, the *keshik* continued to be a reservoir for commanders after Chinggis Khan's death.

The members of the *keshik* remained in the bodyguard until they were specially selected by the Khan to take command of a mission. Unfortunately it is not always clear whether those chosen were also *noyad* within the *keshik*. Nonetheless, those that emerged from the *keshik* demonstrated unparalleled administrative and leadership abilities as they took command of units ranging from a *minqan* to several *tümet*, as in the case of Chormaqan, a *qorci* or quiver bearer, during the Khwarazmian campaign. His first command was an army of 30,000 men.

One of the main benefits of the *keshik* was that the generals promoted from its ranks gained consistent and systematic training in the tactics and strategies used by the Mongols. Thus they were better able to coordinate actions on the battlefield rather than acting as individual commanders directing personal armies, as was the case in European and Middle Eastern armies. This consistency of command was a key distinction between the Mongols and their foes.

Apprentices

An apprenticeship was a commonly utilized technique in the training of Mongol commanders, in which younger officers, including princes, were paired up with senior commanders. This enabled the junior officers to learn, receive advice, and be corrected when necessary without endangering the entire army.

The use of apprentices appears to have originated from Chinggis Khan's own experience. It will be remembered that in his youth, Temüjin, as he was then known, was a vassal of Toghril Ong-Qan, the ruler of the powerful Kereit confederation in central Mongolia, and was paired with another Mongol, Jamuqa, who happened to be his *anda* or blood brother. Jamuqa also served as Toghril's war chief on many occasions. While the sources are not explicit regarding their activities, the two spent well over a year together. Prior to this Temüjin had had a very small following, but when the two eventually parted company not only did Temüjin's own supporters increase in number, but many of Jamuqa's supporters switched their allegiance to him.[2]

By serving as Jamuqa's lieutenant while the latter was the war-chief of Toghril, Temüjin may have learned much of what later became the corner-stones of the Mongol military system. There is certainly ample evidence demonstrating that Jamuqa tutored the future Mongol ruler in warfare, as he was the only opponent that Chinggis Khan did not defeat when their armies met. Indeed, the decimal system was used not only by Jamuqa but also by Toghril himself before Chinggis Khan became an independent ruler. Also, Jamuqa insisted on a tightly organized timetable for gathering troops and launching attacks.[3]

The apprentice system was maintained throughout Chinggis Khan's reign. It was not unusual to see an experienced commander paired with one less experienced and then see the latter receive his own independent command. On numerous occasions Sübedei, possibly the most well-known Mongol general, was subordinate to Jebe, one of Chinggis Khan's most brilliant commanders. Sübedei did carry out independent operations on his own, such as during the Khwarazmian War, but prior to that campaign he usually accompanied Jebe, whereas Jebe is listed as leading operations independently throughout his career.

Such apprenticeships were also used to prepare the sons and grandsons of Chinggis Khan for war. In 1211 Chinggis Khan's middle sons, Ögödei and Chaghatay, were subordinate to his eldest son Jochi during the invasion on the Jin Empire, although Chinggis Khan had also selected *minqan-u noyad* as advisors for the princes. Typically the princes were paired with capable generals who, while technically lower in rank, had the final say throughout the course of a campaign. As was discussed in the section on discipline, generals had the authority to send princes back to the Khan to be reprimanded.

Command structure

Initially, the Mongol army was established with 95 *minqat* commanded by 88 *noyad* (singular *noyan*) or commanders. Each unit possessed a *noyan*. These were called *arban-u noyan*, *jaghun-u noyan*, *minqan-u noyan*, and *tümen-ü noyan* depending on the size of their respective commands (10, 100, 1,000, or 10,000 men).

As discussed in Chapter 2, a Mongol army was typically divided into three corps, consisting of the *baraghun ghar* (right flank), *je'ün ghar* (left flank), and *töb* or *qol* (center or pivot). Each of these corps possessed a separate commander but only one held supreme command. He was known as an *örlüg*, essentially the equivalent of a field-marshal. Originally this term had been applied to just a handful of people, the *yisün örlüg* or Nine Paladins, consisting of nine of Chinggis Khan's earliest companions, all of whom rose to the position of generals.[4]

The Khan assigned the *örlüg* to an army, but the *örlüg* would then select the *tümen-ü noyad*, who in turn selected the *minqan-u noyad*, and so forth, with each commander selecting his own junior officers right down to the *arban-u noyad*.[5] Medieval travelers were somewhat amazed by this process, as well as by the authority that the Khan and, indirectly, his generals wielded. The Franciscan friar John de Plano Carpini, who traveled to the Mongol court a few years after the 1240 invasion of Hungary and Poland, noted:

> The Emperor of the Tartars has a remarkable power over everyone. No one dare stay anywhere except in the place he has assigned to him. It is he who appoints where the chiefs are to be, but the chiefs fix the positions of the captains of a thousand, the captains of a thousand those of the captains of a hundred, and the captains of a hundred those of the captains of ten. Moreover, whatever command he gives them, be it battle, to life or to death, they obey without word of objection.[6]

As already mentioned, in contrast to other contemporary societies commanders did not necessarily come from the nobility. Instead the Mongol Khans encouraged and selected men of talent from among commoners and nobility alike. While the nobility did have the upper hand in this process, commoners also became commanders of *minqat*. Regardless of rank or social origins, each commander was expected to maintain strict order in his respective unit. Indeed, one of the *biligs* or maxims of Chinggis Khan was that 'Commanders of units of ten thousand, one hundred, and one thousand should keep their soldiers in such order and in such readiness that whenever a command is given, they should mount without regard to day or night'.[7] Another *bilig* declared:

> Let any officer who cannot keep order in his own squad be branded a criminal along with his wife and children, and let another be chosen as officer from his squad and companies of a hundred, a thousand, and ten thousand likewise.[8]

It is clear from this that the Mongols expected their commanders, regardless of rank, to keep their units in order, and if they could not, then someone else – even a regular soldier – replaced him. But what qualities were sought? Obviously someone who could maintain discipline and order was essential. Their abilities on the battlefield might also be taken into consideration. However, to assume that the best warrior in a squad of ten would automatically be selected is misleading. Certainly great warriors enjoyed honor and considerable prestige, but the Mongols also believed that the best warriors did not always make the best leaders. Concerning one warrior and his suitability for leadership, Chinggis Khan said:

> There is no warrior like [Yesügei] Bahadur, and no one else possesses the skills he had, but he did not suffer from hardship and was not affected by hunger or thirst. He thought his liege men could tolerate hardship as well as he could, but they couldn't. A man is worthy of leadership who knows what hunger and thirst are and who can judge the condition of others thereby, who can go at a measured pace and not allow the soldiers to get hungry and thirsty or the horses to get worn out.

The proverb 'Travel the pace of the weakest among you' is an allusion to this.[9] In short, commanders were expected to do more than simply execute tactics and strategies. While the typical image of Chinggis Khan and other Mongol commanders is as merciless, draconian warlords intent on destroying all who opposed or disobeyed them, including their own troops, the reality is quite different. From the *bilig* concerning Yesügei Bahadur (not to be confused with Chinggis Khan's father), it is evident that good commanders took care of their men and their horses. While this should not change Chinggis Khan's image from great and terrifying warrior to a teddy bear, it should be noted that he understood how to get the most from his men without exhausting them. Part of the 'draconian' discipline often ascribed to the Mongols stems from the fact that their commanders looked after their troops' interests. In return, the soldiers were more willing to trust and obey the decisions of their officers. Conversely, if the commander marched them and their mounts to exhaustion and then attempted to fight a battle, their performance would be substandard and could possibly result in devastating consequences for the unit, including defeat or annihilation.

Of course, leadership manifests itself in a variety of forms, and different forms are needed to achieve different goals. The decisions that issued from the Mongol capital of Karakorum generally involved strategies aimed at achieving long-range goals, so that more than one front or military operation had to be taken into account. Out on campaign, meanwhile, field commanders had more limited goals and thus needed to be accomplished in other skills.

Imperial leadership and long-term goals

The first and foremost role of the imperial leadership, which included not only the Khan but also the senior princes and generals, was the planning of war. The Khan rarely made his decisions alone. Usually a *quriltai*, or assembly of Mongol princes and generals, gathered to discuss these issues. The *quriltai* was also used to select a new Khan when necessary. These meetings were considered to be of the utmost importance and attendance was mandatory for all major figures throughout the empire.

Of course, the Khan's own decisions and pronouncements carried the most weight. If he truly wanted to carry out a particular invasion, it was done. However, his advisors ensured that the decision was not rash or excessive. The generals obviously did not want to overextend their forces, as Mongol armies typically fought on several fronts throughout the duration of the empire.

Decisions made at the *quriltai* involved not only where to invade, but also the manner in which an invasion should be carried out. Not all of the Mongol invasions were aimed at the conquest and destruction of a rival state. Indeed, the Khwarazmian War did succeed in the latter regard, but the Mongols did not attempt to hold any territory beyond the Amu Darya at that time. In addition, commanders often received a list of objectives. Chormaqan, who would conquer Iran and the modern Transcaucasia region in the 1230s, had as his primary objective the destruction of Jalal al-Din, the last of the Khwarazmshahs. It was also expected that he would bring other domains under Mongol control, but eliminating Jalal al-Din was paramount, primarily because Mongol control south of the Amu Darya would remain elusive until he was permanently removed.

Finally, the *quriltai* assisted in deciding who would participate in a campaign. As most of the major figures within the empire were present, generals were assigned to the campaign on the spot. This process included assigning princes to the command of units. By virtue of their status they held command posts, but as stated previously, they were accompanied by experienced advisors and were under the overall supervision of an *örlüg*. Nor did all campaigns contain a Chinggisid contingent. Generally the princes went on major ventures such as those mounted against the empires in China, and the thrust west into modern Russia. This may have been because the personal troops of the nobility were required for such undertakings, as well as additional commanders. Chormaqan's invasion of the Middle East lacked princely representation from the four major branches of the Mongol royalty.

Decisions made at the level of the imperial leadership focused on overall campaign strategy: where to go, who would go, and when they would go. The commander in charge of the operation, however, had considerable leeway in his interpretation of the execution of his orders. This leads us to the operational decisions of the man on the spot.

Battlefield commanders and limited goals

As the Mongol armies typically split into smaller forces, each commander was expected to achieve certain objectives. Naturally, these goals were more limited than those expected of the entire campaign. One such goal could be to lay siege to a stronghold. Again, how this was carried out was left to the commander's own initiative. The Mongols followed what seems to have been a set of standard operational procedures in carrying out sieges and so forth, but the final decision regarding how they should be carried out was up to the commander on the spot.

Crucial to the battlefield commander, no matter what his rank, was an ability to think quickly and make decisions. As a commander rarely earned the title of *mingan-u noyan* without serving first as an *arban-u noyan* and *jaghun-u noyan*, he knew how these smaller units functioned and what their capabilities were. Rarely did Mongol commanders actively take part in combat. Instead, they remained behind the front line and issued orders through a system of banners, fire signals, messengers, and whistling arrows. Thus they coordinated attacks, retreats, and counterattacks more effectively. Of course, they were not immune to danger and often participated in the fighting at critical moments. Indeed, considering the lack of modern communications equipment they probably placed themselves just slightly out of bow range in order to stay in contact with their units. In doing so, they behaved more like their modern counterparts than their contemporaries.

Biographies

Jebe

One of Chinggis Khan's most brilliant yet overlooked generals, Jebe first encountered Chinggis Khan on the battlefield during the wars of unification in Mongolia, when he was a warrior among the Tayichiut Mongols and thus an enemy. After Chinggis Khan defeated the Tayichiut in 1201 a few of them joined his forces. During the battle a sharpshooter had killed Chinggis Khan's horse with a well-placed arrow to the neck, and one of the warriors who sought to join the Mongols, a man named Jirqo'adai, publicly declared that he was the culprit and was prepared to accept any consequences of his action. This so impressed Chinggis Khan that, because of his archery skills, he gave him the nickname of Jebe (meaning a weapon or, more specifically, a type of arrow) and made him one of his closest companions.

In 1206, when Chinggis Khan formally became the unquestioned master of Mongolia, Jebe was one of 88 commanders named as a *mingan-u noyan*. Throughout the wars in Mongolia he was also known as one of the *dörben noqas* or 'four hounds' of Chinggis Khan along with three other *mingan-u noyad* – Sübedei, Jelme, and Qubilai (not to be confused with Chinggis Khan's grand-son Qubilai Khan). The *dörben noqas* and their units constituted an elite brigade that served with distinction at Chakirmaut, where the opponents of Chinggis Khan's mastery of Mongolia made their last stand.

The *dörben noqas* were particularly noted for their tenacious pursuit of fleeing opponents, which may be one reason why Jebe led so many pursuit missions. In 1209 he and Sübedei pursued the Naiman and Merkit who fled Mongolia to the Irtysh River, and then again to the Chu River. Jebe was also responsible for hunting down Güchülüg, a Naiman prince who became ruler of Kara-Khitai in modern Kazakhstan. From there, Güchülüg would have been a threat to Chinggis Khan's nascent kingdom in Mongolia. But Jebe is perhaps best known for his part in the pursuit of Muhammad Khwarazmshah during the Khwarazmian War. Although Muhammad successfully yet narrowly eluded the two generals, he died alone from illness and exhaustion on an island in the Caspian Sea shortly afterwards. Although Jebe and Sübedei were often paired together on missions, it appears that Jebe was the senior commander of the two, probably due to his experience and innovative strategies.

Yet Jebe did more than hunt down enemy leaders. Against the Jin Empire, he served as commander of Chinggis Khan's vanguard in 1211, capturing the strongly guarded Chabchiyal Pass through a perfectly executed feigned retreat. Jebe also became well known for his deep incursions into enemy territory, feigned retreats that were carried out over days, and of course for the tenacity that allowed him to cover several days' travel in one. Jebe died in 1223 during the famous *reconnaissance en force* that he and Sübedei conducted following the death of Muhammad Khwarazmshah in 1220.

Sübedei[10]

Arguably the most well-known Mongol general, a great deal of his fame must be attributed not only to his undeniable military talents but also to the simple fact of his longevity. He was born in 1176 among the Uriangkhai – one of the so-called Hoy-in Irgen or Forest People who lived in the forests surrounding Lake Baikal and Siberia north of Mongolia – and entered Chinggis Khan's service as a young man, not long after the split between the latter and Jamuqa. Sübedei's brother, Jelme, had been a companion and servant of Chinggis Khan since his youth, and it appears that Sübedei and his brother earned the trust and profited from the wisdom of Chinggis Khan as members of his household, while performing menial tasks such as tending his horses. Sübedei having proved to be talented, he served as a *jaghun-u noyan* and, like his brother, became known as one of the *dörben noqas*. Then in 1206 he became a *mingan-u noyan*, although it is very likely that he already held this position before the official announcement was made at the *quriltai* of 1206.

His first foray outside of Mongolia was conducted under the tutelage of Jebe, pursuing renegade Naiman and Merkit tribes into western Siberia in 1209. It was this campaign that eventually led to a collision with a Khwarazmian army under Sultan Muhammad Khwarazmshah II, who was left severely shaken by the encounter even though the outcome was a draw. With the invasion of the Jin Empire, Sübedei carried out various missions on behalf of Chinggis Khan, including attacks into Manchuria, the homeland of the Jin Dynasty.

Sübedei's talents became obvious during the Khwarazmian War, where he served as one of the vanguard commanders and then, with Jebe, relentlessly pursued Sultan Khwarazmshah. Sübedei and Jebe next set out on the *reconnaissance en force* that took them through Transcaucasia and across the Caucasus Mountains. There, they defeated a combined army of Russian princes and Kipchak Turks at the battle of the Khalkha River in 1223. Jebe apparently died not long afterwards, but Sübedei, now in full command, continued the mission and successfully rendezvoused with Jochi, son of Chinggis Khan, in what is now Kazakhstan. This feat remains an unparalleled accomplishment, as his forces rode approximately 5,000 miles without the assistance of modern communications or reinforcements and always in hostile territory.

After a brief respite – during which he began forming a *tamma* to protect the empire's western flank in Kazakhstan – Sübedei led a Mongol army against the recalcitrant Tangut of Xi-Xia in 1226–7. Although he had a brief falling out with the new Mongol ruler Ögödei, he also served as a commander in the final assault on the Jin Empire and was instrumental in its destruction.

At the age of 60, in 1236 he was chosen to lead the Mongols west towards the Volga River and into the Russian heartland and beyond. Although Jochi's son, Batu, was in nominal command, Sübedei prepared the strategy for the campaign and assumed overall command. One of his most amazing achievements as commander was not only leading an army of 150,000 men against a variety of foes on a wide front, but also managing to keep the egos of dozens of high-ranking Chinggisid princes in check. The fact that they accomplished anything despite constant princely rivalry is a true testament of his abilities. The Volga region fell quickly and by the end of 1237 the Mongols had begun their attack on the Russian cities. Kiev, the grandest of them, fell on 6 December 1240. In three years of campaigning the Mongols extended their empire by 1,000km, from the Volga River to the Carpathian Mountains, conquering not only the Rus' but also the Kipchak Turks.

Sübedei then planned his invasion of Central Europe. Mongol armies struck simultaneously at Hungary and Poland. The invasion of Poland appears to have been little more than a diversion to keep armies there from potentially joining forces with the Hungarians. Sübedei himself led the assault on Hungary. After overpowering the fortresses that guarded the mountain passes, the Mongols encountered the Hungarian army – considered one of the best in Europe – on the Sajo River, at a spot called Mohi. Here, Sübedei demonstrated strategic and tactical genius. The Mongols seized the bridge across the river by means of a rolling barrage of catapult fire, while Sübedei simultaneously outflanked the Hungarians by building a pontoon bridge at another point along the river. The Hungarians were crushed.

Sübedei, however, ordered a general withdraw from Hungary in 1240 upon receiving news that Ögödei Khan had died, since he, as well as the other princes, were needed to select another Khan, which did not occur until 1246. Sübedei's services remained in demand and the new Khan, Güyük, dispatched the now 70-year-old general to lead a force against the Song Empire. When age finally caught up with him he retired to the Tula River basin in Mongolia, where he died in 1248.

Toquchar

A *tümen-ü noyan* since the time of Chinggis Khan's unification of Mongolia, Toquchar is a lesser known commander, yet one of some significance in the development of the Mongol Empire. A member of the Onggirat tribe that had submitted to Chinggis Khan in 1201, Toquchar became a valued commander early in his career. By 1211 he had been placed in command of the western frontier of the Mongol Empire (at that time roughly the current western border of Mongolia). Here, serving as a *tammaci*, Toquchar provided protection to non-Mongol clients who submitted to Chinggis Khan, such as the Qarluqs in modern Kazakhstan, and the Uighurs. He also served as a deterrent to the Naiman and Merkit tribes who had fled Mongolia yet still posed a threat to Chinggis Khan. When the Mongols moved against the Khwarazmian Empire in 1219, Toquchar became one of the three commanders of the vanguard, along with Jebe and Sübedei. While not noted for any particular military greatness, he also became the poster boy for disobedience.

During the Khwarazmian campaign, Chinggis Khan sent Toquchar, Jebe, and Sübedei in pursuit of the fleeing Sultan Muhammad II. As some of the Khwarazmian local rulers around the city of Herat had submitted Chinggis Khan gave implicit orders that their territory should not be disturbed. But Toquchar disobeyed and plundered its environs. As a result, Chinggis Khan stripped him of his command and planned to execute him. In the end, however, the Khan relented and instead reduced Toquchar to the rank of a common soldier. He died in the vicinity of Ghur in Afghanistan in 1221/2.

Muqali

Muqali of the Jalayir tribe was one of the most important military figures of Chinggis Khan's reign. He was known as one of the Khan's *yisün örlüg* or Nine Paladins and was often referred to as one of his *dörben külü'üd* or four steeds, along with fellow *örlüg* Bo'orchu, Boroghul, and Chila'un.

Muqali had entered Chinggis Khan's service in 1196, when he and his brother Buqa were given to the Mongol lord as slaves by their father. Thus they, like Sübedei, were raised in Chinggis Khan's household. As the Mongol Khan had an unrivaled eye for ability, Muqali and his brother soon became members of the Mongol military and rose through the ranks to become *dörben külü'üt* – who, like the *dörben noqas* that was formed not long afterwards, served as an elite brigade that carried out critical missions for the Mongol Khan.

At the great *quriltai* of 1206, Muqali was named a *minqan-u noyan*. Indeed, he was the third to be named, after Münglig, a retainer of Chinggis Khan's family since his father's time, and Bo'orchu, a companion of the Khan since his youth. In addition Muqali was awarded the title of *tümen-ü noyan* in 1206, and made the commander of the *je'ün ghar* or left wing. Unlike his personal *minqan*, which consisted of his fellow Jalayir, the new *tümen* consisted of tribes in eastern Mongolia from the Qara'un Jidun Mountains to the Khingan range, thus bringing his domain to the borders of the Jin Empire. The honors continued for Muqali, who after years of success against the Jin received the title of Gui Ong, or Prince of State. In many regards he stood second in rank only to Chinggis Khan himself.

Chinggis Khan considered Muqali his most trusted and valuable general throughout his short career. During the invasions of the Jin Empire, Muqali almost invariably operated on the left wing of the army, including supervision of operations in Manchuria and eastern China that resulted in splitting the empire so that a number of Khitan, Jurchen, and Han commanders deserted to the Mongols.

Chinggis Khan's trust in Muqali is implicit, as when he took the bulk of the Mongol army to fight the Khwarazmian Empire in 1219 he placed the war against the Jin in Muqali's hands, along with 30,000 men and various *cerik* forces. Somewhat limited by the smallness of his forces, Muqali nevertheless pressed on against the Jin so that by 1221 only a few of their cities remained unconquered. However, while Muqali had hoped to finish the war in 1223, the Jin's scorched earth policy led to his progress being stalled at the siege of Feng-xing. The war thus became a stalemate, which Muqali might have overcome but for the fact that the Tangut chose this moment to revolt. This was compounded by Muqali's sudden death in 1223, since without his leadership the Mongols lost much of the territory they had gained since 1221. Of course, this only extended the Jin Empire's existence by a decade, as it ultimately fell to the Mongols in 1234.

Chormaqan[11]

A member of the Sunit tribe, Chormaqan began his career as a *qorci* in the *keshik* of Chinggis Khan. During the Khwarazmian War in 1221, Chinggis Khan gave him a command position and instructed him to conquer Baghdad and force the Abbasid Caliphate into submission. It is not clear when Chinggis Khan expected this to occur, as Chormaqan did not receive his army at this time. Chormaqan's campaign was placed on hold because of the revolt of the Tangut.

Chinggis Khan's death in 1227 further delayed Chormaqan's rise to the rank of a commanding general. Not until Ögödei became ruler in 1230 were Chormaqan's promotion and instructions confirmed, but now he was also to hunt down Jalal al-Din, the last Khwarazmshah, who had become essentially a bandit king and a menace to his neighbors despite his success against the Mongols.

In 1230 Chormaqan crossed the Amu Darya River with approximately 30,000 men. His army, specifically designated as a *tamma*, carried out its role quite well, and Chormaqan brought the area that is now modern Iran under Mongol control, meeting only token resistance. In addition he sent his lieutenant, Dayir, to pacify much of modern Afghanistan and Pakistan, and ordered another lieutenant, Taimaz, to hunt down Jalal al-Din. Both lieutenants completed their tasks successfully and Jalal al-Din died in 1231, killed by Kurdish peasants as he fled from a Mongol surprise attack.

Chormaqan's own efforts in Iran are overlooked but they are impressive in their own right. It should be noted that the Mongols' reputation preceded them, as much of southern Iran submitted to Chormaqan rather than risk confrontation. Only three regions did not submit: two were held by the Ismailis, Shi'a Muslims popularly known as Assassins, who resided in the mountains south of the Caspian Sea and in Quhistan in central Iran, while the third was the district round the city of Isfahan, which was a strong supporter of Jalal al-Din. Isfahan fell in 1237, but the two Ismailis' areas remained independent until 1256 by making an alliance with the Mongols.[12]

Chormaqan did not move against Baghdad, but in 1233 the bulk of his army moved into the Mughan plain in modern Azerbaijan, a rich pastureland essential to the Mongols' horses. Here the Mongols rested before commencing the invasion of Transcaucasia (modern Georgia, Armenia; Azerbaijan, and eastern Turkey) in 1234. The city of Ganjak was destroyed, and then after a brief *quriltai* with his *minqan-u noyad* Chormaqan divided his army into several columns and conquered the rest of the region between 1235 and 1240.

The most notable thing about this five-year campaign is that the majority of its engagements consisted of sieges carried out in very mountainous terrain. Despite being out of their element in terms of preferred warfare, Chormaqan and his lieutenants successfully brought the region into submission without suffering any major setbacks, thus demonstrating their ever-increasing talent for siege warfare. In many cases the Mongols simply blockaded the fortresses and starved their occupants. Chormaqan also showed a proclivity for diplomacy and psychological warfare that had few rivals among his peers.

While major cities like Ganjak, Ani and Tiflis were destroyed, Chormaqan utilized the sieges against the mountain fortresses as a means of securing the rest of the region with less destruction. During the sieges, he opened negotiations with the various Georgian and Armenian princes who had taken refuge in these strongholds, and through diplomacy managed to coerce several into submitting and paying tribute. In exchange Chormaqan increased the extent of their own territory, and then took the princes and their followers along with him against his next target. Thus the princes' prestige and territory grew, and Chormaqan was able to demonstrate how well the Mongols treated those who were loyal to them. Nonetheless, pragmatism still dominated Mongol military thinking and Chormaqan ordered the walls of several fortresses to be razed to ensure that rebellion did not become an option.

Yet what of Chormaqan's original mission, to conquer Baghdad? He had not neglected this. Throughout his conquest of Transcaucasia, Mongol troops invaded the territory north of Baghdad. In 1235 they sacked the city of Irbil and devastated much of what is now northern Iraq. A Mongol army also suffered a defeat at Jabal Hamrin. However, Chormaqan did not make a concerted effort against Baghdad before his death, probably due to complications from a stroke, in 1240.

On the surface it is a bit perplexing why Chormaqan seemingly ignored his primary orders. However, there was a method to his madness, so to speak. A major objective for any Mongol army was to find grazing land, since without enough of it they simply could not stay in one place for very long. Chormaqan stationed his *tammacin* in the Mughan plain, thus ensuring pasture for the army's numerous horses, and then he subdued the neighboring territories. Even while they did this, the Mongols also raided into the territory north of Baghdad, testing the Abbasids' strength. In this way Chormaqan provided his army with a favorable base of operations while simultaneously eliminating any immediate threat. His armies also threatened the borders of Baghdad, as well as other areas, and if such raids could persuade the region's princes to submit, as had happened in southern Iran, so much the better. Had Chormaqan lived, it is very likely that the Abbasid Caliphate would have fallen a decade earlier than it did. Fortunately for the Caliph, the death of Chormaqan, along with the death of Ögödei Khan, put Mongol operations in the Middle East on hold and left the Abbasid Caliphate on life support for almost 20 more years.

Chapter 7

Opponents of the Mongols

The Mongols fought a wide variety of opponents. While many used similar strategies and tactics, the Mongols also came up against enemies whose approach to warfare differed markedly from their own. They nevertheless defeated all of them bar one, the Mamluks alone successfully resisting them. In order to maintain this extraordinary record, the Mongols skillfully adapted to the challenges that each opponent presented and incorporated the tactics and even the weapons of their opponents into their own military system.

Nomads

Other steppe nomads proved to be among the most difficult of foes for the Mongols, whether they were from the Mongolian Plateau or were made up of the numerous Kipchak and Qangli Turks of the Eurasian Steppe. Most of them resisted Mongol rule fiercely, yet in the end they became a vital component of the Mongol army.

Organization

The nomads were organized along tribal lines in a confederation. Although chieftains within the confederation led their own clans and tribes as individual units, some confederations did create more organized units. Indeed, Chinggis Khan's own decimal system appears to have originated from his contact with the Kereit of central Mongolia.

Nomads existed across the steppes of Eurasia, from the forests of Manchuria to the Carpathian Mountains. Several million nomads lived within this geographic zone, and if they had been united into a state prior to the rise of the Mongols they could have proved a serious challenge. However, distance and tribal rivalries prevented any formal unions amongst them, particularly amongst the various Kipchak tribes. Nonetheless, some areas – such as in the Volga River region – put up a stubborn resistance in the mid–1220s which only ended with the Mongol drive west that began in 1236.

Methods of warfare

The nomads fought in a similar way to the Mongols – primarily as horse-archers. Mobility and encirclement also remained a constant throughout the steppe. Indeed, many Mongol tactics were widespread among the nomads and had been in use since the ancient period. As steppe nomads customarily mastered riding and archery at an early age, they all possessed basic military skills. In addition to composite bows, the Kipchaks and other nomads used a variety of weapons including spears, javelins, and sabers. It is precisely because they and the Mongols were so alike in tactics, mobility, and archery that they were so dangerous. Yet the Mongols held a key advantage over other nomadic armies: the discipline that Chinggis Khan and his commanders instilled into their army. Whereas their opponents would stop to plunder, the Mongols primary goal was to destroy the enemy. Only afterwards was it permissible to plunder.

Mongol adaptation

The Mongols adopted and adapted many steppe traditions. They possessed the archery and riding skills that all nomads developed. In addition, they used and refined the battlefield tactics common across the steppe. The latter is what made the Mongols the example *par excellence* of nomadic armies. Most of their battlefield strategies and tactics were not new, but were simply refined and executed with routine perfection.

The Jin Empire

The Jin Empire of North China staved off complete Mongol domination for almost 25 years, despite numerous defeats and desertions. While the Mongols routinely defeated its armies, the Jin Empire – with a population of approximately 50 million – possessed the resources and strength to create new forces and slow Mongol progress by means of its heavily fortified cities.

Organization

The Jin imperial army consisted of a variety of ethnicities and branches, though the majority of the military came from four major ethnic groups – the Jurchen, Khitan, Han, and Jüyin. The Jurchen, a semi-nomadic people from the forests of Manchuria, had defeated the Liao dynasty in 1125 and established the Jin Empire as the dominant force in northern China. The Khitans had dominated during the Liao dynasty. Although many had fled west rather than be ruled by the Jurchen, a sizeable number of Khitans remained in the Jin Empire, principally in the vicinity of the Liao River. Although they served in the military, the Jurchen scorned them and placed little trust in their loyalty or their abilities. Han Chinese comprised the bulk of the population and the army, their numbers constituting their key military significance in the eyes of the Jurchen. The fourth group, the Jüyin, were Turkic-Mongolian nomads who occupied much of the frontier region between the Empire and Mongolia. 'Jüyin' itself was a term that referred to an assortment of tribes rather than a single people. They primarily served as military auxiliaries, and as a buffer against the nomads north of the Gobi desert.[1]

Cavalry comprised the main force of the Jin army, particularly among the Jurchen. Although a semi-nomadic people, the Jurchen possessed many horses and all males participated in hunting and served as soldiers. However, over time their martial qualities had slowly degenerated as sedentary traditions replaced nomadic ones. Cavalry constituted more than a fifth of the estimated 500,000-strong Jin army. They used a decimal system of organization, with units divided into *meng-an* (thousands) and *mou-k'e* (hundreds), and most men were armed uniformly. Jin soldiers, however, provided their own weapons, thus leading to some units being equipped rather haphazardly.[2]

Methods of warfare
By the 13th century, the Jurchen military had declined. A contributing factor was that they had abandoned hunting as a form of military training.[3] Nonetheless, the Jin cavalry remained a high-quality force, experienced in fighting both nomads from the steppe and infantry forces such as those of the Song Dynasty to the south. Against the Mongols, the Jin primarily fought a defensive war, relying on their cavalry and overwhelming numbers to defeat the Mongols as they tried to penetrate the Jin defensive system, which was based on a string of fortifications, including the 'Onggut' Walls located north of the present day Great Wall. These walls and fortresses served to control the Jüyin and project Jin power into the steppe. The Jin also relied on their fortresses guarding the mountain passes between Mongolia and China.

While their cavalry was made up of Jüyin, Jurchen, and Khitans, the larger part of the Jin army consisted of Han infantry armed with crossbows, pikes, and other weapons. Their primary duty became defending the fortresses once the Jurchen learned that sending infantry against the Mongols ended in disappointment. Thereafter the Jin revised their plans and instead of engaging the Mongols in the field they began to depend on the defense of their fortresses and cities. They hoped that the Mongols' efforts to reduce the cities would overextend and exhaust them, thereby exposing them to sudden attacks. This change in strategy may have also been due to the diminishing number of cavalry that the Jin could produce as a result of casualties, desertions, and a lack of horses. In the end all the Jin strategies failed, as the Mongols captured their cities one by one despite the Jin's possession of a significant technological advantage: gunpowder weapons.

While firearms in the modern sense did not exist for another hundred years, particularly in a useful form such as cannons, the Jin did use explosives and firelances. Generally known as 'thunder crash bombs', these were primitive yet effective. The Jin lit fuses on metal containers filled with gunpowder and then delivered them in a variety of ways, such as in the form of trebuchet missiles. Bombs were also lowered via chains against besieging Mongol troops at the base of fortress walls. The explosive, while strong enough to annihilate the enemy as well as any protective device (such as a skin-covered shelter), did little damage to the thick walls. At times such bombs were also used as mines: not terribly efficient ones, as lit fuses ignited them, but if properly placed in ambushes or areas where the Jin thought the enemy would approach, they proved effective at causing both physical and psychological damage. The Jin used another gunpowder recipe in their firelances, which were bamboo tubes affixed to spears and operated rather like a primitive flamethrower. These had a range of ten yards.[4]

Mongol adaptation

During the Mongol conquest of the Jin Empire, various commanders of all ethnicities deserted to their side. Jurchen and Khitan troops were incorporated into the Mongol army, often as *cerik*, and typically served as heavy cavalry. In general the Mongols had little use for infantry in most of their campaigns, but the Han infantry proved useful in the numerous sieges and battles in the mountainous terrain of both northern and southern China. The Han engineers who provided them with both siege engines and technical expertise were perhaps the most significant addition to the Mongol military.

The Mongols adapted to fighting the Jin in a number of ways. First and foremost, they exploited the internal divisions amongst them. The Jüyin quickly joined the Mongols, primarily due to their poor treatment by the Jin and the imposition of increasing restrictions on their movements as the Jin attempted to curtail the Jüyin's contact with nomads north of the Gobi. To enforce this policy, the Jin had established garrisons north of the Jüyin. The Khitan also joined the Mongols in large numbers. Indeed, the Khitans initiated the contact and the Mongols allowed a client Khitan kingdom to emerge in the early years of the war.

The Mongols also realized that the ability of the Jin to support their cavalry was an area of concern, and therefore seized the Empire's pastureland and stud areas. Furthermore, since the Jin elected to fight a defensive war the Mongols seized the opportunity to prevent the Jin cavalry from having the room to maneuver to match their own mobility. When the Jin revised their strategy in the hope of simply waiting out the invaders, the Mongol generals complied and attacked their cities; but rather than exhausting themselves against those that were well-defended, they bypassed strongly defended cities and attacked the weaker ones. However, the Mongols left forces in the vicinity of those cities they ignored, in order to deal with any troops they might send in pursuit and with other Jin groups that might emerge from sheltered areas.

Defending against the 'thunder crash bombs' and firelances proved to be the most difficult challenge for the Mongols. It does not appear that they developed any particularly effective defenses against them. For the Mongols, perseverance in their sieges proved to be the most effective counter. This included starving the opposition as well as pummeling them with trebuchets and flaming arrows. Of course, once the technology was made available to them the Mongols used explosives against the Jin in turn. However, it is not clear if the Mongols used 'thunder crash bombs' in sieges west of China. One reason may be that whereas the necessary materials and facilities to manufacture gunpowder were easily available and properly stored in China, the volatile nature of gunpowder and the logistics of transporting it may have discouraged the Mongols from taking significant amounts with them on campaign, even though they were accompanied by Chinese engineers of their own.

The Khwarazmian Empire

The Khwarazmian Empire had the misfortune of reaching its peak at the same time as Chinggis Khan ascended to power. Sultan Muhammad II, the Khwarazmshah, conquered an empire that stretched from the Syr Darya to the Indus River in the north and east, and to the Zagros Mountains in the west. Possessing an army of 400,000 men, the Khwarazmian state had the potential to be a dominant force in Central Asia. However, the greed of the governor of the border town of Otrar and Sultan Muhammad's own arrogance ultimately reduced this vast empire to ruins.

Organization

The army of the Khwarazmian Empire was a polyglot entity. Comprising a multitude of ethnicities, organization was a major issue. With each group led by its own *amirs* or commanders, who theoretically owed fealty to the Sultan, the military was hampered by the empire's very youth. As the empire had not yet coalesced into a distinct entity, regional ties transcended imperial goals.

Qangli and Kipchak Turks from modern Kazakhstan comprised an important element within the army. Indeed, these nomadic horse-archers were possibly its best soldiers. However, their service to the Khwarazmians resulted from marriage ties, and Sultan Muhammad's Qangli mother had more influence over them than he did. This sort of problem existed throughout the empire and, indeed, contributed to its downfall. Unity between the army's disparate elements, whether Qangli, Kipchak or Khalaj Turk, Pashtun tribesmen from Afghanistan, or Iranian infantry, was ephemeral. Even with an invading force such as the Mongols in the field against them, unity could not be assured.

Turks comprised the cavalry. The nomads primarily served as light cavalry, with semi-nomadic and sedentary *amirs* leading the heavy and medium cavalry. Additionally some *ghulam* or *mamluk* regiments existed. Infantry were numerous but served primarily as garrisons.

Though Turkic cavalry was the most significant factor on the battlefield in the eastern Islamic world, another small but powerful element consisted of war elephants carrying towers filled with archers and javelin throwers. Their presence and smell alone was often enough to unnerve the enemy's horses.

Methods of warfare

When the Mongols invaded, the Sultan adopted a defensive position, relegating his army to defending the cities despite its superior strength. This allowed the Mongols to roam the empire unimpeded. When sieges occurred, the Khwarazmian cavalry often realized that the situation was untenable and sallied forth, in many cases with the simple intention of either breaking through the besiegers and escaping or else deserting to the Mongols. Usually this led to their destruction, either by the Mongols hunting them down after they broke through their lines, or by the Mongols executing them for desertion. (While the Mongols often welcomed deserters, if it was clear that they had deserted in the middle of a battle or at an inopportune time the Mongols had good reason to wonder if such deserters would subsequently abandon them under similar circumstances.)

Mongol adaptation

As the Khwarazmians fought a defensive war, the Mongols quickly adapted to siege tactics. One of the Mongols' primary methods of conducting sieges during this particular campaign was by the use of captives to serve as labor and arrow fodder. There is no evidence to suggest that the Mongols learned any new methods of warfare while fighting the Khwarazmian forces. However, this campaign proved to be a masterpiece of Mongol strategy, as they used their mobility and psychological warfare to gain the submission of a number of cities without resistance. In addition, they manipulated the tensions within the Khwarazmian army to their advantage. In short, it represented the Mongol art of war at its perfection.

The Rus' principalities

Although the Mongols conquered the Rus' principalities in a relatively short time (two years), the Rus' attempted a spirited defense. It was the lack of unity between their princes that contributed to their downfall. Several years had passed between the Battle of the Khalkha River in 1223 and the Mongol invasion of 1238, yet the Rus' had not resolved the differences between their various principalities. Although this disunity hastened their conquest, one must also consider if the Rus' could have defeated the Mongols.

Organization

Each principality possessed its own army, led by its respective prince. The *druzhina*, the prince's corps of retainers, was the most effective unit of the army. Professional warriors, the *druzhina* fought as heavy cavalry but could also serve as infantry. The bulk of the army consisted of the city's militia and *smerdy* or peasants, supplemented by mercenaries. Nomads, typically Kipchak Turks who often formed alliances with the princes, served as auxiliaries and ranked close to the *druzhina* in terms of effectiveness.

Methods of warfare

At the time of the Mongol invasions the Rus' used the sword and spear as their primary weapons. The common levy typically possessed a few self-bows, the occasional crossbow, and of course axes, spears and shields. Only the *druzhina* regularly possessed armor, usually of scale, mail, or lamellar. On the battle-field, the infantry formed a shield wall from behind which the archers fired, while the cavalry, often in conjunction with nomadic horsemen, protected the flanks.[5]

In the open field, the Rus' offered very little challenge to the Mongols. The infantry, whether *smerdy* or militia, possessed little armor and were thus vulnerable to Mongol arrows. Furthermore they lacked the discipline to face a Mongol charge. The Mongols rode in complete silence, breaking into a horrific scream just before making contact. The eerie quality of this action would be sufficient to unnerve most troops lacking discipline or training.

The *druzhina*, on the other hand, could and did present some complications in close combat. When they successfully made contact in a charge, they per-formed admirably. While not always the most disciplined of fighters, they were tough and exceedingly tenacious. Ultimately, the Mongols preferred to simply destroy them from a distance with arrows rather than engage them in close combat.

Mongol adaptation

The Mongols gained little from their exposure to the Rus' military or their defensive tactics. By the late 1230s the Mongols were masters of siege warfare while the Rus' appeared to lack many siege engines. Perhaps more than in any other region since the Khwarazmian War, Russia served as a testing ground for the Mongol armies. Not even its winter weather hindered them, as they used the frozen rivers as highways.

This is not to say that no transfer of military knowledge occurred – it just happened in reverse. After the Mongol conquest, the Rus' abandoned their traditional form of warfare. Daniel of Galicia-Volynia began equipping his army in Mongol fashion after leaving the *orda* of Batu at Sarai in 1246. Even though he secretly plotted against the Mongols, his visit to Sarai clearly convinced him not only of the superiority of Mongol military strategy but also of their armaments in comparison with his own.[6]

The Hungarians

The Mongols carried out their invasion of Europe in 1241 on a wide front, striking both Hungary and Poland. Poland, however, was a secondary target, while the main force drove into Hungary. This was for a number of reasons. The fact that over 40,000 Kipchak Turks fled to Hungary from the Mongols played an important part in the decision. In addition, the Hungarians possessed a very strong army and in recent years had slowly begun extending their influence into the Kipchak Steppe, thus posing a potential threat to the Mongols.

Organization

Like virtually all European armies, the Hungarian army was raised by means of the feudal system. Benefiting from the Alföld Plain – that part of the Eurasian Steppe that extends into Hungary – they possessed an exceptionally large cavalry. Their elite troops were mail armored knights, who relied on a massive and virtually unstoppable charge as their primary offensive maneuver; but due to their country's proximity to the steppe the Hungarians also possessed a number of nomadic or nomadic-influenced light cavalry, who served as scouts and skirmishers.

In addition the nobility and the king fielded retinues of sergeants who fought on horseback and on foot. Those on horseback were, typically, professional soldiers who could not become knights due to their low-born origins. Those who served as infantry were shock troops and provided a stable core for the rest of the infantry, who varied in ability and at times consisted of conscripted peasants using a variety of weapons, typically farming implements or spears.

Despite the preponderance of horsemen in Hungarian armies, they still traveled relatively slowly. This was partially because they were accompanied by infantry but was also due to the army's wagons, which as well as carrying supplies were also integral to the army's defense. At night, the troops chained the wagons together to form a laager to protect the army – a wise precaution for a country bordering the steppe.

In feudal states, the control of a king over his vassals varied greatly, and it was in an attempt to strengthen his own position that Bela IV – the ruler of Hungary at the time of the Mongol invasions – decided to strengthen his hand militarily by agreeing to allow a large number of Kipchaks to settle within the kingdom. The Kipchak Khan, Koten, fleeing from the Mongols, accepted the pre-condition of baptism and entered Bela's service. The addition of a large number of Kipchak warriors strengthened Bela's position not only against the Mongols, but also against his own recalcitrant vassals. Unfortunately the vassals, who already opposed Bela's attempts to increase royal prerogatives, resented the Kipchak presence.[7] Furthermore, the pastoral nomadic lifestyle of the Kipchaks did not mesh well with the sedentary lives of Hungary's peasants and nobles. Clashes became inevitable and the nobility lynched Koten. The Kipchaks reacted by rampaging through Hungary until they entered Bulgaria and even the Byzantine Empire, where many found refuge. Thus the Hungarians lost a valuable contingent of veteran nomadic warriors on the very eve of the Mongol invasion.

Methods of warfare

As with most Western armies, the charge of the knights was irresistible. If timed properly, it swept all opposition from the field. After the charge, fighting devolved into a chaotic mêlée. The infantry served as a base for the cavalry. If discipline was maintained, its packed formations could resist enemy cavalry charges. The infantry followed the knights into battle if the latter's charge broke the enemy, and served as a rallying point. Light cavalry archers and archers on foot served to soften the enemy's ranks and to deter charges. Not until the fourteenth century did massed firepower play an increased role on the battlefield, and it was the knights who were expected to deliver the crushing blow that would defeat the enemy.

The wagon-laager played a fundamental role in Hungarian armies. Although the wagons did not go onto the battlefield, they were in close proximity and

served as a mobile fortress should the army be forced back. The chained
wagons prevented easy access by enemy cavalry and provided shelter from
which archers could fend off the enemy until the Hungarian knights launched a
sally or until help arrived.

Mongol adaptation

The Hungarian knights proved to be worthy adversaries for the Mongols.
Their armor did much to protect them from arrows. However, the Mongols
countered this by using rolling barrages of trebuchet and ballistae fire to
force them from a bridge. The wagon laager, while providing shelter for the
Hungarian army, also became a deathtrap. Realizing that storming the wagons
would be suicidal, the Mongols simply treated it as another stronghold to
besiege.

Their encounters with the Hungarian knights reinforced the Mongols'
determination to choose their own battlefields. Only by using their superior
mobility could they take advantage of the knights. Even with their powerful
bows the Mongols had difficulty in bringing the knights down. Thus only by
flanking operations, feigned retreats, and other steppe tactics, with which the
knights had some familiarity, could the Mongols outmaneuver the Hungarians
and avoid their great charge.

The Mamluks

The Mamluks were among the very few enemies to defeat the Mongols
in combat, and they were never conquered. The Mamluk institution had
appeared in Islamic civilization in the eighth century as the Caliphs sought to
create a military force that was loyal only to the Caliph and not to regional,
tribal, or other personal ties. Most Mamluks were of Turkic origin, primarily
because the Turks were viewed as better, or at least more natural, warriors than
Persians and Arabs. Turks of nomadic origins possessed riding and archery
skills from an early age, so that after purchasing them as slaves one only had to
refine those skills. The Mamluks therefore became perhaps the most highly
trained warriors in the medieval world. They seized power in Egypt in 1250
during the ill-fated Crusade of Louis IX (Saint Louis) and created a Sultanate
that dominated Egypt and then Syria until the sixteenth century.

Organization

Mamluks formed the core of the Sultanate's army, although non-Mamluk
forces also existed. The army consisted of three parts. The first, and typically
the center of their army, consisted of the Royal Mamluks. Known as
mustarawat, ajlab, or *julban*, Royal Mamluks were those directly purchased and

trained by the Sultan. The Sultan also possessed other Mamluks that he gained from other masters, including those of the previous sultan and deceased or dismissed *amirs*. These were known as *mustakhdamun*. The Mamluks of the *amirs* comprised the second part of the Mamluk army, while the *halqa* or non-Mamluk cavalry formed the third.[8] The *halqa* were the forces of non-Mamluk *amirs*. Generally they were inferior to the Mamluks, if not in ability then in terms of social status, at least in the eyes of the Mamluks. Beduins served as ancillary forces and as scouts.

At their peak, in the late thirteenth century, the Royal Mamluks numbered around 10,000 men. They were the elite of the Mamluk forces and carried out most of the fighting. Virtually all were stationed in Cairo, whereas the forces of the various Mamluk and non-Mamluk *amirs* were stationed in the provinces. Compared to most of the enemies of the Mongols, the Mamluk Sultanate was relatively weak in numbers. In the late thirteenth century they could muster almost 75,000 men, including 29,000 Mamluks, and 44,000 *halqa*. Theoretically the Mamluks could muster additional Beduin, Kurd, and Turcomen auxiliaries.[9] Normal Mamluk armies were considerably smaller (30,000 men at the most) due to the need to garrison the dozens of fortresses in Syria.

A subgroup among the *halqa* were the *wadifiyya*, or Mongol refugees and deserters. Several thousand entered Mamluk service during the war between the Golden Horde and the Il-Khanate. Initially, when the Mongol prince Hülegü invaded the Middle East to conquer Baghdad and then Syria, his army included troops from all of the Mongol princely families. After the civil war began, many of these attempted to leave his service and return to their own prince. Those that could not make it back to the Golden Horde fled to the Mamluks, who became allies with the Golden Horde against Hülegü.

Methods of warfare

As medium or heavy cavalry the Mamluks wore mail armor and helmets, and carried shields, lances, and mêlée weapons such as sword and mace. They all carried bows and were extremely proficient in their use. As their primary opponents were the Mongols and the Franks of the Crusader states, they were adept at fighting both types of foe. Against the Mongols, they typically remained on the defensive until a strategic opening came. The Mamluks did not have sufficient horses to maintain the constant movement that the Mongols enjoyed. However, as they were all archers they could maintain a steady rate of fire to deter them. In addition, the Mamluks maintained the utmost discipline and rarely succumbed to Mongol feigned retreats, and executed this tactic just as well themselves. As they were well armored and carried lances, they served as a shock force and could deliver devastating charges like European knights.

Since they lacked the numbers that the Mongols could bring to the field, the Mamluks attempted to ensure that the Mongols could not take advantage of this. Man for man the Mamluks were better soldiers, so that being slightly outnumbered was not a major concern. However, to prevent the Mongols' numbers from becoming a factor the Mamluks used scorched earth policies on the frontier to eliminate potential pasturelands. The Mongols therefore had to choose between bringing more men with fewer spare mounts, or fewer men with more spare mounts. In either case, the strategy worked well in either denying the Mongols the mobility that allowed them to dominate the battle-field, or by preventing them from having an appropriate number of men to compensate for the Mamluks' superior military skills.

In addition the Mamluks realized the limitations of their military. Having fewer men, they rarely invaded Mongol territory. Typically they struck at Mongol allies such as the Crusader lord Bohemund, Prince of Antioch and Count of Tripoli, and Cilicia, also known as Lesser Armenia. The Mamluks timed such attacks to occur when Mongol troops were not in the vicinity or were occupied in the civil wars that wracked the Mongol Empire after 1260.

In actual combat the Mamluk forces usually maintained a defensive arrow shower and sought to lure their opponent closer. Due to their fighting skills they had no fear of close combat. Indeed, only the Knights Templar and Hospitallers were regarded as their equals in mêlée situations. Of course, they used flanking movements and attempted to seize strategically important terrain before a battle.

Mongol adaptation

The Mamluks successfully thwarted several Mongol invasions. Initially, the Mongols did very little to alter their mode of warfare – indeed, they viewed the Mamluks as a minor nuisance to be eliminated once the incessant warfare between the Il-Khans and their cousins ceased. However, the reality, as the Il-Khanid Mongols came to realize, was that the lack of pasture in Syria severely hampered Mongol operations. Even when they defeated the Mamluk forces, they could not maintain a large enough presence to hold the region against counter-attack.

Under Ghazan, the Mongols restructured their military. Part of this was due to economic considerations within the Il-Khanid state. The army became dependent on *iqta* and *timars*, essentially land grants where soldiers used the taxes from the land as their income. Thus the Mongol troops gradually transformed into more traditional Middle-Eastern warriors – some became heavier cavalry, relying on a single, or perhaps two, stabled horses. While nomadic horsemen remained useful, they became auxiliaries.

The Song Empire
The conquest of the Song dynasty proved to be the Mongols' most difficult endeavor. Their war here lasted from 1235 to 1276, when the Song state finally fell to Khubilai Khan. At first glance the Song army does not appear likely to have posed a difficult obstacle to the Mongols. Indeed, infantry comprised the bulk of it, with very few horsemen. The Song primarily fought a defensive war, like the Khwarazmians, Rus', and Jin. However, while the Song struggled valiantly to hold the Mongols back, the primary obstacles to Mongol success proved to be the region's mountainous geography and the Song navy. Until these challenges could be overcome, the Mongols could not defeat the Song.

Organization
Song defensive strategy concentrated on defending places that directly faced the Mongols. It is clear that the Song knew the war would be a protracted struggle, and ensured the protection of nearby agricultural areas. Thus they could better survive Mongol attempts to blockade their fortresses. Finally, the Song relocated local governments to the mountain fortresses so they could securely maintain order.[10]

As most of the army consisted of infantry, the Song stood little chance against the Mongols in the open field. Rather than keeping them in large divisions, their infantry began to operate in smaller units more suited for guerrilla operations. Infantry also played an important role as marines in the navy. The navy primarily operated on the rivers and was instrumental in defending cities and fortresses against the Mongols.

Methods of warfare
The key elements in Song resistance to the Mongols were the topography and mountain forts. These influenced how the Mongols approached a targeted region. The mountains and valleys forced them to take circuitous routes that exposed them to guerrilla attacks. This was particularly true in Sichuan, which was virtually the last region to succumb to the Mongols.[11] The mountain fortresses were generally located atop cliffs, but possessed agricultural land and springs. Being adjacent to rivers, they were better protected against cavalry and enabled the Song navy to assist in their defense. Those located near metropolitan areas helped to defend the cities with sallies and provided an additional source of refuge. As K'uan-chung noted, the mountain fortresses were also close together, thus preventing the Mongols from engaging a single fortress with their full strength.

The combination of the fortress network and the agricultural lands behind the forts allowed logistics to be maintained. It also prevented Mongol armies from dividing and attacking in multiple directions, and enabled the Song to fight a guerrilla war using the fortresses as bases.[12] Like the Jin, the Song also used gunpowder weapons such as 'thunder crash bombs' and firelances. Both of them also used 'fire arrows', or arrows fired from small bronze vessels by a gunpowder explosion. Although not very accurate, such devices could launch an arrow to a range of several hundred yards.[13]

Mongol adaptation

The Mongols' favorite form of warfare, that of high mobility, was not very practical in southern China. The fortresses of the Song as well as the mountainous terrain placed severe limitations on the Mongols' movement. Even after they got over the mountains the terrain did not improve, as the Mongols then entered a region of large and heavily defended cities surrounded by villages and rice paddies, all of which hampered their cavalry. In addition, the Mongols' lack of a navy allowed the Song to reinforce and supply their cities via the rivers. This also enabled them to flank the Mongols in some instances and to prevent them from crossing the major rivers. It is no wonder that some of Möngke's generals were opposed to his campaign against the Song in the 1250s.[14]

While conditions in southern China slowed them, the Mongols took a pragmatic course and sought the aid of those more familiar with this form of fighting. This came from two sources. The first was Song deserters and soldiers from northern China, veterans from the many wars that the Jin had waged against the Song. The second source was Korea, which before its surrender had also utilized virtually impregnable mountain fortresses to resist the Mongols. The Mongols' reliance on Korean and Han Chinese assistance against the Song also affected the organization of the Mongol army, as it enabled Koreans and Chinese to be promoted, whereas previously the Mongols had ensured that Han officers had few opportunities for advancement.[15] The Han Chinese also became increasingly important as infantry, due to the lack of suitable cavalry terrain.

The Mongols attempted to invade from multiple directions in order to find a weak spot. Although this was not a new idea, in the case of the Song it involved taking a wide detour past the mountains and conquering the small kingdom of Da-li west of the Song Empire en route, much as in 1939 the Wehrmacht had to invade Belgium in order to bypass the Maginot Line. However, while the Mongols hoped that this plan would stretch the defenders, the Song continued to build new fortresses.

From the onset of their war with the Song, the Mongols incorporated 'thunder crash bombs' into their arsenal. For the most part these were launched by trebuchets. Initially these were traction trebuchets, powered by men pulling on ropes in order to hurl missiles. Though effective for hurling missiles over the walls, these lacked the power to batter down the walls themselves. Then in 1273, at the siege of Xiangyang, Muslim engineers introduced the counter-weight trebuchet, which possessed greater power and range and allowed the Mongols to crush city walls. Interestingly, the Song devised their own counterweight trebuchets after witnessing their effectiveness.

Another adaptation for the Mongols, and essential to the conquest of the Song, was the creation of a navy. The Mongol navy effectively outmaneuvered the Song, although its operations were carried out and its ships were manned by Chinese and Koreans serving under the Mongols. With their fleet, the Mongols were able to position themselves behind Song defenses and blockade the Song navy until, eventually, it ran out of room to maneuver and was defeated.[16]

Top: The Mongolian steppes in winter when the temperature averages -20 Celsius (-4 Fahrenheit) but may drop to -50 Celsius (-58 Fahrenheit). Bottom: The Mongolian steppes in summer. With the endless sky, there is little wonder why the Mongols worshiped *Möngke Köke Tengri*, or the Eternal Blue Sky. (*Author*)

Top: Mongolian soldiers reenact the advance of a Mongol *jaghun* unit. The black *tuq* or standard indicating a period of war in the center. A white *tuq* was used in times of peace. Middle: Mongolian reenactors of a *jaghun*. An *arban*, or unit of ten, comprises each file, marked by a banner. Bottom: Mongolian soldiers reenact a cavalry charge. (*Author*)

Top: Reenactors shooting composite bows in an archery contest. Middle: The beast of burden for the Mongols, the Bactrian camel is able to carry approximately 200-240 kilograms as a pack animal and pull 400-600 kilograms as a draught animal. Bottom: Each *yam* station maintained several horses for messengers. The modern Mongolian horses are of similar size and proportion to those used in the thirteenth century. (*Author*)

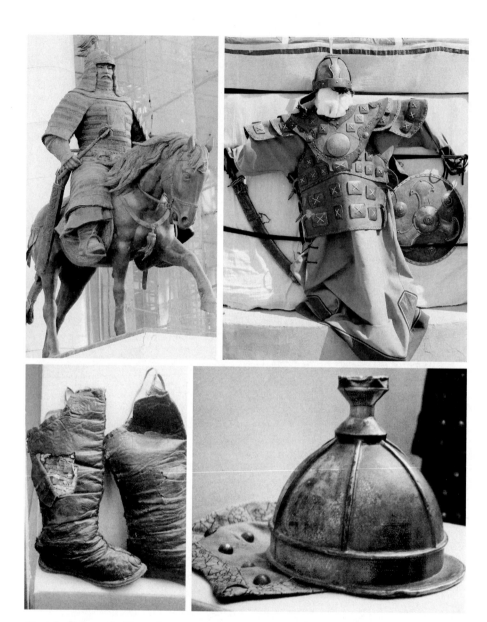

Top left: A statue of a Mongolian warrior in Sukhbaatar Square, Ulaanbaatar. The statue is based on thirteenth-century armor and weaponry. Top right: Mongol leather armor, over a felt *deel* or *degel*, the traditional Mongol robe. Note the large metal disc over the chest to enhance its protection. Bottom left: Thirteenth-century Mongolian boots at the National History Museum, Ulaanbaatar. The torn section reveals that the boots were interlined with scale mail. Bottom right: A Mongolian helmet at the National History Museum in Ulaanbaatar. The leather flap not only protected the neck, but could be fastened in the front to shield the face from dust. (*Author*)

Top left: Close up of the Mongol leather studded armor from the Mongolian National Museum of History located in Ulaanbaatar. Top right: Mongolian fourteenth-century chainmail on display at the National History Museum, Ulaanbaatar. Bottom: Three prisoners in locks being lead away by horsemen in a fourteenth-century illuminated manuscript page from a Saray album. Inv. Diez A fol.70, page 19, detail. (*Bildarchiv Preussischer Kulturbesitz / Art Resource*)

Top left: Ajlun castle. The position of the castle made attacks near impossible beyond frontal assaults. Top right: A castle in northern Jordan. Hülegü's general Ket-Buqa captured it through diplomacy as it is rather unassailable. The castle surrendered in 1260 on the orders of King al-Nasir, ruler of Damascus, who had recently been captured by the Mongols at Nablus. The Mongols dismantled most of the fortifications. Bottom left: The walls and entrance to the citadel of Aleppo. In 1259 the city fell after a 5 day siege. The Mongols massed 20 catapults against the Bab al-Iraq (The Iraq Gate) and stormed the city despite a valiant defense led by Turanshah, the governor of the city. Bottom right: Aleppo citadel. Despite the impressive fortifications, the citadel still fell to a Mongol assault. (*Author*)

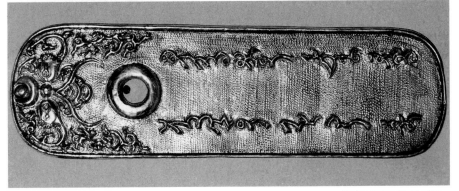

Top: Letter from Guyuk to Pope Urban IV at the National History Museum in Ulaanbaatar. It tells the Pope to come before the Mongol khan with the princes of Europe and submit or face the consequences. Middle: The *gerege* or *paiza* was a passport travelers using the *yam* system carried. The material used—gold, silver, bronze, and wood—indicated the importance and privileges of the bearer. Bottom: The skyline of Kiev as viewed from the Monastery of the Caves, or Pecherskii Monastery, where many Kievans took refuge from the Mongol attack in 1240. (*Author*)

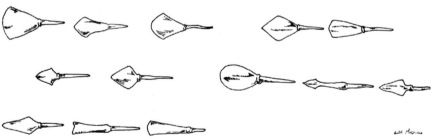

Top: Mongolian horsemen pursuing enemies. From a Saray Album. Inv. Diez A Fol. 71. Oriental Division. Staatsbibliothek zu Berlin, Berlin, Germany (*Bildarchiv Preussischer Kulturbesitz/Art Resource*) Bottom: The Mongols used a wide variety of arrowhead, each with specific purposes. These included narrow points for armor piercing arrows, wide blades for slicing, and blunt arrows for stunning opponents, as well as normal arrowheads for general purposes. (*Lee Modlin*)

Chapter 8

At war with the Mongols

Only through an examination of their military actions can one truly appreciate the Mongol art of war. The following are examples of the Mongols at war, and include a campaign, specific battles, and an example of their siege warfare.

Campaigns

The Khwarazmian War

Mongol expansion into western Siberia and the eastern Dasht-i Kipchak altered the balance of power in Central Asia. With the flight of the Naiman khan, Güchülüg, into the Kara Khitai Empire the region was thrown into turmoil as the Kara Khitan Empire disintegrated. While the Mongols eliminated Güchülüg, the Khwarazmian power to the south continued to grow. Although it dominated much of modern Iran, Afghanistan, Pakistan, Central Asia, and even parts of Iraq, Muhammad Khwarazmshah II's consolidation of Mawarannahr – the land between the Amu Darya and Syr Darya rivers – was less than secure. Thus the prospect of having a powerful neighbor such as the Mongols did not sit comfortably with him. Indeed, after one early encounter with the Mongols it was said that 'fear and dread of them took possession of his heart and mind, and he never again came against them: this was one of the causes of the miseries and troubles which befell the people of Islam'.[1]

In addition to the events that took place just beyond his frontier, Muhammad Khwarazmshah collected intelligence concerning Chinggis Khan's activities, which did little to comfort him. When Muhammad heard about Chinggis Khan's victories in the East, he sent envoys to gather information. They reported seeing a white mountain that, from a distance, they thought was snow, but as they came closer they saw it was a pile of bones. One envoy commented that on part of the road, the 'ground had become so greasy and dark from human fat, that it was necessary for us to advance another three stages on the same road until we came to dry ground again.'[2] They also reported that at one city 60,000 virgins and girls leapt to their deaths to avoid capture by the Mongols.

Despite this grim news, Chinggis Khan did not seek confrontation with the Khwarazmian Empire. Having recently expanded into Central Asia, as well as fighting the Jin Empire in Northern China, his resources were stretched between Korea and the Syr Darya. Consequently, rather than instigating conflict he recognized the potential of trade relations with Khwarazm. When a Khwarazmian caravan reached him, Chinggis Khan greeted the merchants, and said:

> Say ye unto Khwarazm Shah, 'I am the sovereign of the sunrise, and thou the sovereign of the sunset. Let there be between us a fair treaty of friendship, amity, and peace, and let traders and caravans on both sides come and go, and let precious products and ordinary commodities which may be in my territory be conveyed into thine, and those of thine, the same manner, let them bring into mine.[3]

Chinggis Khan sent his own caravan to accompany the merchants back to Muhammad, along with gifts for the Sultan such as a gold nugget the size of a camel neck, and 500 camels with gold, silver, silks, a variety of furs, raw silk, and other goods.

When this caravan reached the Khwarazmian border city of Otrar, its governor, Inal Khan, ended any possibility of peace. He massacred the Mongol-sponsored caravan, believing them to be spies. While it is probable that the merchants *were* spies, Inal Khan's greed influenced him and he probably acted with Muhammad's consent. Chinggis Khan did not immediately declare war; he sought the extradition of Inal Khan and attempted to maintain commercial ties. Chinggis Khan, ever an astute military leader, may have been wary about initiating another campaign while still consolidating his territories in Central Asia and fighting the Jin.

After all attempts to settle the Otrar incident peacefully had failed, Chinggis Khan prepared for war and informed Sultan Muhammad of his intent.[4] In 1219, he gathered an army and moved west from northern China. In preparation for the campaign he ordered mares and geldings to be collected for remounts and milk. He also ordered men to prepare their rations, with every *arban* taking three dried sheep and a cauldron.[5]

The generals Sübedei, Jebe, and Toquchar led the vanguard and avoided attacking towns, while Chinggis Khan crossed the Altai Mountains and began his march on Khwarazm. Temüge Otchigin, Chinggis Khan's youngest brother, remained in Mongolia to maintain order. The Mongols summered on the Irtysh River in 1219 to allow their horses to fatten before advancing on Otrar in the autumn. The speed of the Mongols' preparation and march impressed contemporary observers, as they arrived on the borders in just three months, rather than the estimated four.[6]

Aware that Mongol retribution seemed certain after the failure of negotiations, Muhammad prepared for war. He ordered a wall to be built around his capital of Samarqand and gave it a considerable garrison. To cover the cost of this and new units of archers, he raised taxes for the third time that year. To defend his empire, he garrisoned his army in the cities, believing that the Mongols would be unable to take them by siegecraft.

This decision was only reached after lengthy debate. Some advisors had suggested that the Sultan should give up Mawarannahr, as it was untenable. They advised him to retreat south of the Amu Darya and use the river as a moat while gathering armies to defend the regions of Khwarazm and Khurasan. Another faction advised that they should withdraw to Ghazna in Afghanistan, using the mountains to gather their forces: with India serving as a rampart, his commanders believed that they could then hold their ground more effectively. Muhammad liked this idea the best and even proceeded to Balkh. His son Jalal al-Din, however, wanted to gather the armies and lead them against the Mongols, while the Sultan went to their western territories to raise more troops. The final option was to abandon not only Mawarannahr, but essentially the entire eastern portion of the empire, and take refuge in the western regions. This would buy them the time and space to gather troops and then attack the overextended Mongols.[7] By the time they reached an agreement, however, the Mongols had arrived. According to his critics, if Sultan Muhammad had fought the Mongols before dividing his forces he would have easily annihilated them.[8] Of course, hindsight is always perfect.

Mawarannahr

The sources are divided on what happened when the Mongols reached Otrar. Some state that Chinggis Khan left Chaghatay and Ögödei there while he and Tolui went to Bukhara by marching through the Kyzyl Kum desert. Meanwhile Jochi marched towards Jand.[9] Other contemporary writers who endured the invasion wrote that the Mongols reached Otrar and attacked day and night until the city fell. After capturing the governor Inal Khan, Chinggis Khan ordered that his ears and eyes be filled with molten silver as retribution for the massacre of the caravan.[10]

Afterwards, Badr al-Din al-Amid, a Khwarazmian official, came to the Mongol emperor and offered his services. He advised Chinggis Khan to undermine Sultan Muhammad's trust in his army by exploiting tensions within the royal family. Chinggis Khan agreed and ordered letters to be forged and addressed to *amirs* related to the Sultan's mother, Terken Khatun, who was a member of the nomadic Qangli Turk tribe. Chinggis Khan then used a deserter to pass the letters to Muhammad, who was shocked by their content. The letters said:

> We came from the land of the Turks with our clients and our vassals because we desired to give service to his [Muhammad's] mother; we have lent him assistance against all the princes of the earth, also to him, thanks to us, conquered countries, crushed the pride of princes and maintain the people under his yoke. But today, that the sentiments of the sultan in regard to his mother had changed, that he show rebellion and ingratitude toward her, she asks you to abandon her son. In consequence, we will wait your coming for us to place your orders and follow your instructions.[11]

In addition, Chinggis Khan sent an envoy to Terken Khatun with this message and further sowed dissension. In response, Terken Khatun evacuated in haste from Khwarazm, abandoning its defense. Meanwhile, at Otrar the Mongol army divided and began to attack the Khwarazmian Empire from multiple directions.

After Otrar, the main Mongol army under Chinggis Khan's command arrived at Bukhara in February 1220 as discussed in the prologue. Although concerned about the fate of Mawarannahr, after hearing of the fall of Bukhara Muhammad slowly crossed the Amu Darya. With this indication that he had little confidence in holding the region, his authority began to erode and 7,000 troops deserted him to join Chinggis Khan.

Meanwhile, Chinggis Khan moved against Samarqand, taking with him a levy of captives from Bukhara. They proceeded to capture the outlying regions of Samarqand. If a place resisted, Chinggis Khan left a blockade and moved to the next location, while additional forces joined him at Samarqand.

Possessing a garrison of 60,000 soldiers and several war elephants, the defenders of Samarqand may have outnumbered the army that Chinggis Khan led against them. They successfully conducted a sortie against the Mongols and returned with a few prisoners, who were tortured. Afterwards the Mongols set an ambush, presumably luring part of the garrison out, although both sides suffered heavy casualties in the ensuing sortie. Following this measure of retaliation, the Mongols surrounded the city and bombarded it incessantly with catapult missiles and arrows. Furthermore, Chinggis Khan stationed men at all the gates to prevent the Khwarazmian cavalry from sallying forth, which enabled the Mongols to withstand the attacks of the unsupported Khwarazmian elephant corps and infantry.[12]

Due to his concern regarding what the Mongols would do to avenge the tortured prisoners once the city walls were breached, Samarqand's Shaykh al-Islam, or highest-ranking religious leader, secretly opened negotiations with Chinggis Khan.[13] The Mongols and the Shaykh concluded an agreement. As a result the siege ended quickly, lasting no more than ten days.

Fulfilling his part of the deal, the Shaykh al-Islam opened the gates for the Mongols on 17 March 1220. The Mongols then allegedly killed and plundered all but 50,000 people under the protection of the *qadi* or judge and the Shaykh al-Islam. As with many such episodes, several sources imply that the Mongols massacred the entire population. However, a year later, the report of a party of Chinese Taoist monks traveling to meet Chinggis Khan indicates that Samarqand's population consisted of 125,000 people. This, of course, is well below the pre-invasion figure of 500,000, and the magnitude of the massacre should not be diminished, but it is important to remember that the Mongols were not interested in ruling a desert devoid of life.[14]

As at Bukhara, Samarqand may have submitted but its citadel remained defiant. The Mongols attacked this in a familiar fashion, using levies from the city itself and previously conquered cities and bombarding it with siege weapons until it submitted. The Mongols then razed the fortifications and divided most of the population and garrison – with the exception of the protected 50,000 – into units of tens and hundreds. They also separated Turks from Tajiks and pressed the Turks into military service, as they were nomads whereas the Tajiks were sedentary townspeople and peasants. The Turks were given the tonsure that the Mongols wore, thus indicating that they were Mongol soldiers.[15] Others were pressed into the general levy, presumably to serve as laborers and arrow fodder in future sieges. In addition, Chinggis Khan took 30,000 artisans and craftsmen from the population and sent them to Mongolia. Finally, Mongol *shahnas* or *daruqacin* (civil administrators) were put in charge of the city.

After the capture of Samarqand, the Mongol army dispersed into smaller units and struck other regions of the empire. During the siege Chinggis Khan had already dispatched units into surrounding regions, including 30,000 men under Jebe, Sübedei, and Toquchar sent after Sultan Muhammad. Meanwhile, the commanders Alaq Noyan and Yasa'ur were sent to Wakhsh and Talaqan in modern Afghanistan. Chinggis Khan himself moved to the region of Nakhseb to summer, and then captured Tirmid in the early autumn. From here, he further divided his army by sending additional units to Khurasan, Ghur, and Ghazna, and wintered in present day Tajikistan in 1220–21.[16]

In 1220, Jochi had received orders to invade the Khwarazmian homeland when the Mongols reached Otrar, and after the fall of Otrar he was joined by the armies of Chaghatay and Ögödei. En route to Urganj, the principal city of Khwarazm, Jochi attacked several strongholds along the Syr Darya. He also sent an envoy to negotiate the surrender of the city of Suqnaq, but its citizens executed him. As the violation of an envoy's immunity was considered an act of war, Jochi proceeded against the city and captured it after a brief siege. He then moved against the city of Jand and other border strongholds.[17] Jand fell through a surprise attack, although its residents maintained a stubborn resistance. The Mongols filled the moat and attacked with rams, catapults, and ladders. After storming the city, the Mongols divided up the craftsmen, artisans, and keepers of hunting animals. The rest were placed in the levy.

Urganj remained Jochi's primary target. The commander of the region, Arzala Shah, felt he could not resist the Mongols, so he and the royal household fled to Tabaristan and Mazandaran in northern Iran, and Jochi captured Urganj in 1221 after a siege that lasted five months. He attempted to capture it peacefully, as it was to be part of his domain, but it refused to surrender and he was forced to take action. Nonetheless, he proceeded cautiously, perhaps to minimize damage to the city. The Mongols approached in *nerge* fashion and destroyed the outer fortifications, filled the moat, and maintained a barrage from their siege weapons. The siege weapons, including catapults, were constructed on site and used mulberry wood soaked in water as missiles because of a shortage of stone, the citizens having cleared the region of usable material. The Mongols also constructed battering rams on wheels and a tortoise to facilitate storming the city.[18]

Much of Urganj was razed, despite Jochi's efforts to spare it. This resulted in part from the fact that he, Chaghatai, and Ögödei quarreled over what approach to take to its capture. Jochi, of course wished to spare it, but the other brothers wanted to plunder it as quickly as possible. Frustrated by their indecisiveness, Chinggis Khan sent Tolui to settle the matter.[19] In addition to attacking Urganj, Jochi's men also pursued and captured the family of Arzala Shah. Once the region had submitted to Jochi, he and Chaghatai turned north against the Qangli tribes and subdued them one by one.

The flight of Muhammad

With the fall of Bukhara and Samarqand, Muhammad Khwarazmshah II fled across the Amu Darya towards Nishapur, but ordered his commanders to hold their positions. Disorder and tumult arose throughout the empire. When Chinggis Khan learned of Muhammad's flight and the general disorder throughout the empire, he sent an army under Jebe and Sübedei to pursue Muhammad in May 1220. (As mentioned on page 95, Toquchar had been recalled after disobeying his orders.) Hearing that the two Mongol generals had crossed the Amu Darya, Muhammad fled from Nishapur towards Mazandaran.

While pursuing Muhammad, Jebe and Sübedei captured the city of Balkh. Initially it submitted without a struggle and they left a *daruqaci* or Mongol representative to govern it, but later it rebelled by not providing fodder and supplies when requested, which resulted in a later Mongol attack. When they reached Nishapur, the Mongols did not attack but instead managed to negotiate its surrender. Meanwhile, Sultan Muhammad fled on towards Mazandaran, south of the Caspian Sea. Surprised by a Mongol attack, he left his chamberlain Utsuz with orders to move to Damghan and Iraq and fled to an island in the Caspian Sea. His boat had barely left the shore when the pursuing Mongol horsemen arrived and fired arrows at him. Nonetheless, he escaped the Mongols only to die in hiding from dysentery, in late 1220 or early 1221.[20]

During their pursuit of Muhammad, the Mongols avoided heavily fortified towns, as their task was to destroy the enemy leader, not to reduce cities. However, with their quarry beyond reach Sübedei went to Isfarayin and Jebe entered Mazandaran. Sübedei also attacked Damghan, Simnan, and the city of Rayy, where he rendezvoused with Jebe before they divided their forces again. Jebe then attacked Hamadhan, while Sübedei raided Qazvin and Zanjan in 1221. Hamadhan submitted to Jebe and sent horses, clothing, provisions, and prisoners. In addition, they accepted a *daruqaci*. Then Jebe defeated a Khwarazmian army commanded by Beg Tegin Silahdar and Küch Bugha Khan at Sujas.[21] Although they did not capture Muhammad, the Mongols devastated Mazandaran. In addition Jebe left troops to blockade fortresses where Muhammad's harem hid, while Sübedei captured the fortress of Ilal, where Terken Khatun, Muhammad's mother, had taken refuge. Sübedei forwarded the royal prisoner to Chinggis Khan.

Following Muhammad's death Jebe and Sübedei's expeditionary force moved on into Transcaucasia, gaining the submission of several towns as well as defeating the Georgians. They then passed over the Caucasus Mountains through Derbend before entering the Dasht-i Kipchak and ultimately joining Jochi's forces, then located in modern Kazakhstan. Considering their lack of significant reinforcements, modern maps or communication systems, and that they marched thousands of miles through hostile and unfamiliar territory, this remains, despite Jebe's death along the way, a truly astonishing feat.

Khurasan and Ghur

After taking Tirmid, Chinggis Khan and his son Tolui divided their army into smaller units to invade Khurasan. One was led by his son-in-law Tifjar Noyan and the general Yerka Noyan, at the head of a *tümen*. One commander of this army, Il-Kouch, was killed when he came to the city of Nesa, and the Mongols vowed vengeance and laid siege to the city with 20 mangonels while also attacking other towns. The Mongols sent captives against the walls with battering rams, protected by screens constructed from donkey skins. If the captives did not complete their attack, the Mongols slew them.[22]

The main target in Khurasan was the city of Nishapur, which had rebelled after submitting to Jebe and Sübedei. However, much as in the campaign against Samarqand, the Mongols did not attack Nishapur until they had destroyed its dependencies and moved against other regional cities. After this they reunited their forces at Nishapur. Tifjar Noyan was killed in a sortie by the garrison, and when Yerka sent news of his death to Chinggis Khan he also asked for reinforcements. In response Chinggis Khan sent 50,000 men and Tolui, his youngest son and perhaps the most talented in the arts of war.[23]

Tolui attacked Merv in 1221 before moving against Nishapur. In one account, he massacred the entire populations of Merv and Nishapur because of Tifjar's death. In a scene reminiscent of Rome's destruction of Carthage, he razed the walls and killed everyone after taking Nishapur in the winter of 1221–2. He then had the city ploughed into the ground by yoked oxen. Other authors contradict this, indicating that a massacre took place but only after the Mongols had performed their routine sorting of the population according to their usefulness.[24] After Nishapur, Tolui marched on Harat in modern Afghanistan and pitched camp, placing catapults on all sides of the city. Despite a stiff resistance that lasted eight months, Harat too fell before the Mongol onslaught.[25]

Afterwards the Mongols once again divided up their forces, some of which rampaged across Khurasan and Sistan while others marched towards Ghazna in Afghanistan. Throughout the campaign in Khurasan, the Mongol units followed a standard operating procedure. Each time a *minqan* invaded a province, the peasants were forced to construct mangonels and dig tunnels until their towns were taken. Similar procedures were carried out in Sistan.

As Jochi attacked Khwarazm and Chinggis Khan struck at Tirmid, another Mongol army, led by Tulan Cherbi and Arslan Khan of the Qarluq, laid siege to Walkh for eight months. Only one approach led to the fortress, which forced the Mongols to try to fill a surrounding defile with debris. However, the son of the chief of Walkh came to the Mongols and showed them another path, which took the Mongols three nights to traverse. At dawn on the fourth day they attacked and captured Walkh, before going on to capture other cities in the region of Ghur.

The major task for the Mongols in Khurasan was not so much the conquest of territory as the destruction of the remaining Khwarazmian threat. Jalal al-Din, the son of Muhammad Khwarazmshah II, embodied this challenge to Mongol supremacy. After the death of his father, he went from Khwarazm to Nishapur and then to Ghazna via the desert between Khurasan and Kirman. In the winter of 1221–2 he arrived at Ghazna and was joined by Malik Khan of Harat, who had previously submitted to the Mongols but had joined Jalal al-Din after Toquchar disobeyed Chinggis Khan's orders and plundered his territory.[26]

At Bost, Jalal al-Din learned Chinggis Khan had besieged Talaqan with a very large army. The Khwarazmians therefore decided to attack a smaller Mongol force laying siege to Kandahar while he was occupied. In their surprise attack, the allies wiped out all but a few Mongol troops, who escaped to Chinggis Khan at Talaqan. After Jalal al-Din reached Ghazna, Chinggis Khan sent another force after him led by a *güregen* named Fiku Noyan and his stepbrother, Shiqi Qutuqtu.[27] Fiku set out from Harat but was defeated at Parwan in 1221–2.

Upon learning of Fiku Noyan's defeat, Chinggis Khan left Talaqan and rode towards Ghazna. Jalal al-Din fled upon hearing of his approach. He had little choice, as his army had disintegrated, losing roughly half of its men, after quarrelling over booty from the victory over Fiku Noyan.

Chinggis Khan finally caught the Khwarazmian prince near the Indus River in late 1221. Jalal al-Din made a strong attack against the Mongol center, but a *tümen* that had been ordered to move round behind the Khwarazmians hit his right wing, commanded by Amin Malik. As a result the right wing crumbled and Jalal al-Din's son was captured. With his army in disorder, Jalal al-Din retreated to the Indus and escaped. However, Chinggis Khan sent a detachment to pursue him across the Indus. This force raided several cities and besieged Multan for 42 days, although it is uncertain if they captured it.[28] Meanwhile, Chinggis Khan mopped up the remnants of Jalal al-Din's army, then proceeded towards Badakhshan and captured its fortress.

Jalal al-Din's defeat initiated the Mongol campaign against Ghur, which consisted of a number of sieges. The conquest of Ghur provided the Mongols with a possible launching point for operations in India. Chinggis Khan stayed in Gibari for three months and sent envoys to the Sultan of Delhi, Iyaltimish Shams-al-Danya wa-al-Din. While in Gibari, he considered attacking India and then returning to Mongolia via the Himalayas, as he realized that this would allow him to attack the Jin from the rear. However, when his shamans burned the shoulder blades of sheep to determine if this was an opportune route they did not receive a favorable sign. In addition, he received news of the revolt of the Tangut against Muqali, the general overseeing operations against the Jin Empire.[29] This brought the campaign against Khwarazm to an end, with the Mongols only occupying the regions of Khwarazm (south of the Aral Sea) and Mawarannahr and the Amu Darya serving as a suitable frontier. Nonetheless, the once powerful sultanate lay in ruins, and with its ruling house dead or in hiding it no longer posed a major threat. Although Jalal al-Din had escaped, the only territory that he or any of his relatives could claim excluded their homeland, and thus the Khwarazmian Empire could never rise again. Without a firm base of support, it was difficult for the Sultan to establish a new kingdom.

Battles

Chakirma'ut

The pinnacle of the Mongols' wars with the Naiman occurred in 1204/5 at Chakirma'ut, which was a battle for control of the Mongolian steppes. After the defeat of the Kereit tribes in 1204, the Naiman – who lived in western Mongolia – viewed themselves, with good reason, to be the dominant power in

The Battle of Chakirma'ut 1204

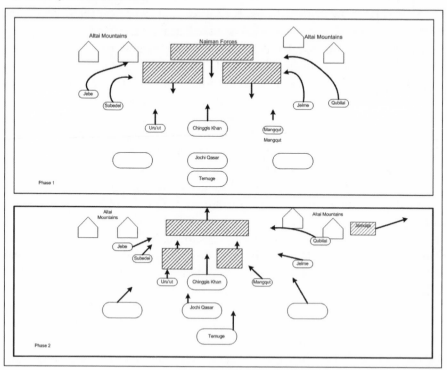

the steppes. Consequently they saw the Mongols, who now controlled central and eastern Mongolia, as a threat.

Tayang Khan, the ruler of the Naiman, said:

> I am told that yonder east are a few Mongols. These people with their quivers frightened the old Ong-qan of former days, caused him to abandon his companions and made him perish. Do they now want to be rulers themselves? Even if there are two shining lights, the sun and the moon, in the sky above – both the sun and moon are indeed there – yet how can there be two rulers on earth? Let us go and bring here those few Mongols![30]

Although a pre-eminent power, the Naiman augmented their forces by rallying other tribes against the Mongols. However, Alaqush, the leader of the Önggüt tribe, successfully extricated himself from making any commitment to the Naiman and instead warned Chinggis Khan of their impending attack.[31] Despite the fact that it was an inopportune season for war, as winter had only recently ended and the Mongol horses were extremely lean, the Mongol army assembled in readiness, and in the middle of May 1204, Chinggis Khan marched against the Naiman, his vanguard under Jebe and Qubilai encountering them on the Sa'ari steppe.[32]

To confuse the Naiman, Jebe and Qubilai lit numerous campfires at night, hoping to convince them that a considerable Mongol force was present.[33] In addition, this deception served as a delaying tactic to give the Mongols time to rest and fatten their horses. However, Tayang Khan was aware of the weakened condition of the Mongols' horses, and desired to lure their army across the Altai Mountains so that he could ambush it after their horses had been further exhausted. He was also concerned that if the Naiman opted for direct combat and the Mongols gained the upper hand, it would be difficult to extricate his forces and regroup with the mountains to their back. His son Güchülüg, however, saw this as cowardly. He preferred a more direct attack, depending on the Naiman's superior numbers rather than strategy and tactics. Güchülüg's opinion eventually prevailed and the Naiman took the offensive,[34] supported by other steppe tribes whose leaders included Jamuqa, Chinggis Khan's sometime *anda* and rival, who served as a military advisor to Tayang Khan – a not unreasonable position, since he was the only leader in Mongolia who had ever defeated Chinggis Khan in battle.

Chinggis Khan did not wait passively once his scouts spotted the Naiman advancing out of the mountains near the Naqu Cliffs. He understood the importance of seizing strategic terrain, which in this case was not the highlands: as his army was the smaller, he wanted to keep the Naiman pinned against the

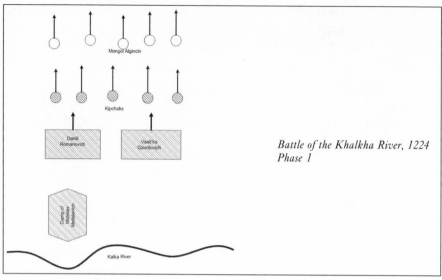

*Battle of the Khalkha River, 1224
Phase 1*

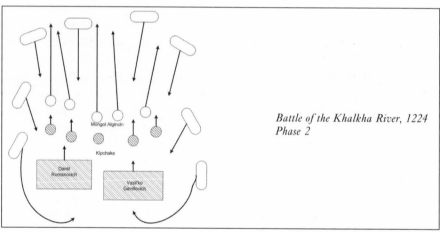

*Battle of the Khalkha River, 1224
Phase 2*

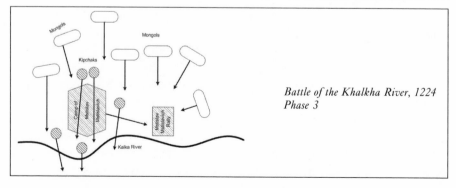

*Battle of the Khalkha River, 1224
Phase 3*

mountains so that they could not bring their full strength against him. It is also at this battle that we first gain an understanding of Mongol battle formations. Chinggis Khan ordered his men to advance in *caragana* marching order, to stand in *nagur* formation, and to fight in chisel formation.[35] In the meantime, skirmishes between the scouts of both armies occurred, with the Mongols gaining the upper hand.

Chinggis Khan advanced, leading the *algincin* or vanguard in person while his brother Jochi Qasar commanded the *qol jasa'ulba* or main body. His youngest brother, Temüge Otchigan, commanded the reserve force, which included extra horses so that when the Mongols' mounts became exhausted they could be easily replaced.

In the forefront of the *algincin* were the *dörben noqas*, or Chinggis Khan's 'four hounds': Jebe, Qubilai, Jelme, and Sübedei. They forced the Naiman back and also began to encircle their flanks. The *dorben noqas* received support in this from two elite forces within Chinggis Khan's army, the Uru'ut and Manqut. These two tribes served as his shock troops during the wars of unification in Mongolia and more than once dominated the battlefield.

Forced to retreat lest they become completely encircled, the Naiman withdrew to the mountains. Meanwhile, Chinggis Khan pressed home his attack. From the account of the battle in *The Secret History of the Mongols* it is not clear if he attacked as the Naiman retreated, or if his force surprised the Naiman's rearguard before they had fully begun their withdrawal from the plain.

From their vantage point, the Naiman could see the approach of Jochi Qasar and the reserve force under Temuge. However, Tayang Khan could do little to prevent their approach, as the *algincin* were pressing his forces and preventing him from deploying them. Gradually, the Mongols hemmed the Naiman in and completed their encirclement, trapping them on a mountain top. During the retreat to the top of the mountain, Jamuqa broke away from Tayang Khan, deserted the Naiman, and fled north. According to legend he sent a message to Chinggis Khan as he went, informing him that the Naiman, and particularly Tayang Khan, were demoralized.

Nightfall prevented further action, but under the cover of darkness the Naiman attempted to escape. This resulted in many falling over the cliffs until 'they piled on top of each other; they fell breaking their bones and died crushing each other till they were like heaps of rotten logs'.[36]

The following morning the Mongols pressed home their advantage and defeated the Naiman. Tayang Khan attempted to flee but was captured. His son Güchülüg escaped and established a fortified camp that resisted the Mongols' attacks for a brief time, before he retreated to the Irtysh River. The remaining Naiman and the tribes who had accompanied Jamuqa submitted to Chinggis Khan on the southern slopes of the Altai Mountains.

Jamuqa himself was also captured, being turned over to Chinggis Khan by his own men, who were tired of living on the run and hoped for a reward. The Mongol ruler executed them for their disloyalty. Jamuqa, at his own request, was executed, but with due honor. He was rolled in a carpet and trampled by horses, the significance of this form of execution being that his blood would not spill on to the ground. As the Mongols believed that the blood also carried the soul, it was important that it did not become trapped in one location and was able to enter the spirit world.

Ultimately, the Battle of Chakirma'ut in 1204 gave Chinggis Khan supremacy in the steppes and allowed him to create a Mongol state.

Khalkha River

The first encounter between the Mongols and the Rus' occurred in 1224 at the Khalkha River. This resulted from a reconnaissance expedition by the Mongol generals Sübedei and Jebe, which had begun with their pursuit of the Sultan Muhammad II during Chinggis Khan's invasion of the Khwarazmian Empire in 1219–23. The Mongol reconnaissance westward took them across the Caucasus Mountains and into the Kipchak steppe. After defeating an army of Alans and Kipchaks, the Mongols continued to pursue the fleeing Kipchaks. These, under Koten Khan, turned for aid to the Rus' princes with whom they shared political and marital ties, especially Koten's brother-in-law, Prince Mstislav Mstislavich of Galicia.[37] The Rus' joined the Kipchaks after the nomads convinced them that if they did not form an alliance now, the Rus' would surely be the Mongols' next target. Mstislav also recognized that if the Mongols did defeat the Kipchaks, they would most likely be incorporated into the Mongol forces.[38]

The Mongols were apparently not interested in the Rus' at this time, and told them so.[39] However, the Rus' ignored this message, killed the Mongol envoys, and gathered their forces, which included Grand Prince Mstislav Romanovich of Kiev, Prince Mikhail of Chernigov, Mstislav Mstislavich of Galich, Daniil Romanovich, the grandson of Mstislav of Kiev, and others.

Setting out against the Mongols, they met another embassy, which warned the Rus' that since they had killed the previous envoys war was guaranteed. Since the Rus' had not encountered the Mongols previously, their murder of the envoys was a bold move, especially since they had heard that the Mongols – whose origins were a mystery to them – had conquered many peoples, including the Alans, Abkhazians, and Cherkess. Furthermore, the Kipchaks feared the Mongols, and their opinion was not to be taken lightly.

The Rus' armies joined the Kipchaks near Varangian Island in the Dnepr River, where the allied forces received word that the Mongols were in sight and were surveying the Russian boats. This prompted Daniil Romanovich to conduct his own intelligence-gathering mission and he pushed ahead with a sizable number of troops. Daniil confirmed that the Mongols were in the vicinity and reported his findings to Prince Mstislav Mstislavich. He and several of the younger princes then decided to attack the enemy and crossed the Dnepr. They defeated the Mongols and pursued them, after which other princes also joined the chase. Although the Mongols fled before them, they always remained in view, and in this way the Rus' and Kipchak forces followed the Mongols for eight days until they reached the Khalkha river. On the ninth day, Prince Mstislav Mstislavich ordered Prince Daniil Romanovich to cross the Khalkha River and continue in pursuit of the Mongols. Meanwhile, Prince Mstislav Mstislavich established a base camp along the banks of the Khalkha.

The pursuing force used the more lightly armed Kipchaks for its scouts and vanguard, and prepared for battle as reports came in of skirmishing between the Mongols and the Kipchaks. As the Rus' caught up with their vanguard, the Mongols took flight and the Rus' cavalry charged after them for the kill. But when other Mongol forces emerged from hiding it slowly occurred to the Rus' that the retreat had been a trap. As the Mongols enveloped their flanks, the Rus' were hit by volleys of arrows.

The Kipchaks broke and fled, pursued by Mongol troops. Princes Vasil'ko Gavrilovich and Daniil Romanovich attempted to withstand the attack but both were struck down by Mongol lances. Shaken by the sudden Mongol attack, the Kipchaks continued their retreat to and through the Rus' camp on the Khalkha, trampling the Russian tents in their flight 'so that the princes had no time to muster their troops'.[40]

The Kipchaks fled for good reason, as the Mongols were following them closely. Unfortunately for the Rus', however, the Mongols did not continue their pursuit of the Kipchaks but attacked the camp instead, which was still in chaos after the Kipchak stampede. A massacre ensued, as the Rus' had little opportunity to organize a defense. Many attempted to flee, but Prince Mstislav Romanovich of Kiev, his son-in-law Prince Andrei, and Prince Aleksandr Dubrovich rallied a force along the river. Here they had fortified a rocky area on the banks, from which they resisted several Mongol attacks. Meanwhile a portion of the Mongols pursued the rest of the Kipchaks and Russians to the banks of the Dnepr.

After three days of siege, Prince Mstislav Romanovich and the other princes finally surrendered after negotiations with one Ploskinia, a Brodniki (the predecessors of the Cossacks). Whether the Brodniki had joined the Mongols of their own free will is unknown, but, knowing the Kipchak and Rus' languages, they proved useful to the Mongols. Ploskinia secured Mstislav's surrender and the Mongols captured the fort.

The Mongols then celebrated their victory with a feast. They built a platform on which they sat, ate, and drank. They probably sang raucous songs, stomped their feet, and perhaps even danced. The captive Rus' princes, however, did not enjoy the festivities, for the Mongols had used them as part of the construction of the platform and they were crushed beneath its boards during the banquet.[41]

Of the important Russian leaders, only Prince Mstislav Mstislavich escaped by crossing the Dnepr.[42] Only one in ten of the Rus' who set out is said to have returned home. A chronicler recorded that after their victory, the Mongols 'turned back from the Dnepr, and we know neither from whence they came nor whither they have now gone'.[43]

The Mongols at this time were not interested in conquest, only reconnaissance, and they did not attempt to seize any lands after defeating the Rus'. They only made sure that the Rus' and the Kipchaks could not interfere with their return east. Yet the Mongols did learn valuable information from the experience: approximate troop strengths, the tactics of their opponents, the fact that the Kipchaks and the Rus' were allies, and knowledge of the terrain. The Rus' evidently were not worried about the Mongols coming back. In fact, the Mongols would not be a threat to the Rus' for another 14 years, when they returned in unprecedented numbers intent on conquest.

Sieges

Baghdad

Although Baghdad and the Abbasid Caliphate had withstood several years of Mongol attacks since the 1230s, they remained independent and defiant of the Mongols. The Caliphate maintained a sizeable army and the defenses of the city.[44] However, when, after ruling for 17 years, Caliph al-Mustansir died at the age of 52 in 1242, Baghdad's days of independence began to wane, and its demise was hastened by the ascension of Mustasim ibn Mustansir to the throne. One chronicler wrote:

> After Mustanser [sic], Musta'sen [sic] his son [ruled] sixteen years.
> This man possessed a childish understanding, and was incapable of
> distinguishing good from bad; and he occupied all his time in playing
> with doves, and in amusing himself with games with birds. And

ɔinting out that companions of Muhammad had been martyred and
killed without resulting in catastrophe, Nasir al-Din Tusi advised
to proceed with his invasion.[49]

258, Hülegü marched on Baghdad with an army that included
ns, Armenians, and the garrison of Mosul. When Hülegü was 20 miles
e Abbasid military leaders, Sulaiman Shah and Malik Izz al-Din ibn
Din (the Kurdish champion of the Caliph and commander of the right
d the *Sar-Damatdar*, Mujahid al-Din, attempted to motivate the
nto taking action, but he chose to leave matters in the hands of his
n Alqami, who naturally did nothing.[50]

Mongol prince approached the city from the east, the *tammaci* of the
ast, Baiju, moved towards Baghdad from the northwest. The prefect
lace, Rukn al-Din, attempted to intercept Baiju's vanguard, but was
approximately 30 miles from the city. Initially Rukn al-Din forced
gols back to the Dujayl district, but then Baiju arrived and secured a
victory.

a bridge of boats constructed by Badr-al-Din Lu'lu's engineers,
my, which included Armenians and Georgians, crossed the Tigris.
hate forces stationed at Takrit attempted to prevent the crossing by
he bridge, but the Mongols rebuilt it. They then proceeded to capture
holds of Kufa, Hillah, and Karkh, although Baiju suffered a setback
attempted to approach closer to Baghdad's western side.[51]

ng to one account, Malik Izz al-Din and Mujahid al-Din led 20,000
across the Tigris reinforced by troops from nearby towns such as
ongol troops engaged them, but the Abbasid forces defeated them.
wanted to pursue them but Mujahid al-Din held back, fearing that
igned retreat. Thus they made camp near the Nahr-i-sher stream, a
he Euphrates. At night, the *wazir* Alqami had saboteurs destroy the
flood the plain, and the Mongols took advantage of the sabotage to
flooded Abbasid camp at dawn.[52]

h this account should not be dismissed out of hand, since it is
, its recorder, the Persian refugee Juzjani, was prone to credit
ccess to the treachery of others rather than their own efforts. Thus
porting evidence the exact role of the *wazir* in military engagements
ble. But Alqami certainly played a significant role in the diplomatic

s defeat the Muslims withdrew to Baghdad and defended Sanjari
Kasr Sulaiman Shah. Baiju, meanwhile, moved to the western side
on 22 January 1258, while Ket Buqa arrived from Najasiyya and
Hülegü, arrived from the east a few days later. The siege began

when it was said unto him, 'The Tatars are pr
Baghdad, even as they have captured the famous
destroyed [them],' he replied, 'This is our thron
give them permission they cannot come in.' And
end of the kingdom of the 'Abbasides in the
man.[45]

Under his administration, the authority of the
1250–1 Mustasim abolished the appanages of th
recruited by his father, thus dismantling the army a
Then in 1258 an increase in inter-religious violence
Muslims demonstrated his inability to maintain co
These events motivated the *wazir*, Ibn Alqami, a S
pondence with the Mongols and seek to overthrow t
disbanded units of Kurdish troops, as well as other
of making peace with the Mongols. Of course, Cali
with less serious matters, remained unaware of th
even though some of Hülegü's messengers fell int
government, Mustasim failed to believe that the M
and no one could persuade him otherwise. Baghda
for the coming onslaught.[46]

After conquering the Assassins of Alamut in
Möngke and Khubilai Khan, headed from Qazvin
to prepare for war against Baghdad.[47] He plan
Baghdad first and its environs in the mountains.
governor of Dartang, Husam al-Din Akka, who
Mustasim, and Husam submitted to the Mongols
but, apparently overwhelmed by the upturn in h
he commanded the army of Baghdad he could
for him, his fortunes now took another turn, as h
promptly ordered him to destroy all of his fort

Before marching against Baghdad, Hülegü
astrologers to determine when he should attac
attack Baghdad at all, or else a series of catastro
including all of their horses dying, the men be
and a drought followed by cold destructive win
this would mean that the plants would cease
turn into desert. Finally, they said, a great r
Meanwhile all of his commanders were advisin
to resolve this conflicting advice he referred t

After
Caliph
Hülegi
In
Georgi
away, t
Fath al-
wing)
Caliph
wazir,

As th
Middle
of the p
defeated
the Mor
Mongol

Using
Baiju's a
The Cal
burning
the stron
when he

Accor
horsemer
Karkh. M
Izz-al-Di
it was a f
branch of
dykes and
attack the

Althou
conceivab
Mongol s
without su
is question
process.

After th
Masjid and
of the city
Sarsar, wi

on 29 January. The city authorities attempted to negotiate, but the time for diplomacy had passed, and the Mongol prince detained their ambassadors and continued the siege, though he continued with the negotiations in order to undermine Abbasid resistance, stating that clergy and non-combatants would be spared.

The Mongols focused their catapult fire on a single point, the Ajami tower, and had reduced it to rubble by 1 February. Despite this, they were unable to break into the city until the next day, and negotiations continued even after the Mongols had seized a portion of the walls.

Izz al-Din and Mujahid al-Din counseled the Caliph to abandon the city and flee downriver to Basra, but Ibn Alqami proposed to the Caliph that he would personally negotiate with the Mongols. The terms that Hülegü offered consisted of taking al-Mustasim's daughter as a wife, and the Caliph's recognition of Hülegü's authority much as the Abbasids had recognized the Sultan's authority during the Saljuq era. If the Caliph accepted these terms, then Hülegü would halt his attack. The Caliph had no choice, and he and his leading notables left the city to conclude the treaty. Hülegü then executed most of the notables and eventually ordered the execution of the Caliph himself, having him rolled in a carpet and trampled to death after first berating him for hoarding his wealth rather than spending it on the city's defense.[53]

The army of Baghdad was also to surrender, but when a Mongol commander was wounded in the eye by an arrow during this process Hülegü hastened the assault. In addition a Mongol force was sent against Basra, which it sacked. Baghdad finally surrendered on 10 February. The Mongols then completed the massacre of the army.

Thus in 1258 the Abbasid Caliphate came to an end, and after a sporadic conflict that raged for roughly 20 years Baghdad entered Mongol hands. Hülegü gave his consent for a general pillaging of the city that lasted 34 days, beginning on 13 February.[54]

Although the Mongols had conquered Baghdad, resistance did not immediately come to an end. Ten thousand Abbasid troops hid in a *wadi* and continued their struggle against the Mongols rather effectively by guerrilla warfare. They targeted many of the Christians in Baghdad in retaliation for the city's destruction, probably because of the participation of Georgian and Armenian troops in its capture. They also successfully captured the *wazir* and the *daruqaci* of Baghdad. Although Mongols forces attempted to destroy them, the insurgents found it more expedient to flee than to engage in open combat against the Mongols. However, they were eventually captured and executed. Afterwards, Hülegü asked the now liberated *wazir* Ibn Alqami what the source of his former prosperity had been, to which he responded that it came from the Caliph. The *wazir* was then executed, Hülegü retorting that 'Since thou didst not observe the rights of gratitude towards thy benefactors, thou art, indeed, not worthy of being in my service'.[55]

The siege of Caizhou

Although the Mongol sieges of Zhongdu and Kaifeng are good examples of siege warfare, the Jin Empire's last stand at the town of Caizhou is the ideal example of their siege techniques and of their ruthless approach. Using the *nerge*, the Mongols isolated the city and over-stretched its food supply by herding the local population inside. Their tactics during this operation show how effectively they spread fear among the local people. Although the great general Sübedei captured Kaifeng, a less well-known general, Tachar, commanded the Mongol army at Caizhou.

By 1231 the Mongols had reduced the Jin Empire to eastern Honan and the Jin capital of Kaifeng. Knowing that the Mongols would lay siege to Kaifeng, the Jin Emperor, Ai-Tsung, decided to move to Caizhou. Realizing that this was not the most defensible location he could have chosen, the supreme commander of the Jin army, a Khitan named Kuan-nu, urged the Emperor to go to Sui-yang instead, which was better protected. The Emperor, however, perceived this as a slight on his abilities and ordered Kuan-nu's execution. Thus, when another commander, Puxian, arrived at Caizhou and found in turn that the city was not strong enough to withstand a prolonged siege, it was too late to go elsewhere, as by that time the Emperor was on his way. Later even the Emperor regretted his decision.[56] Nonetheless, the move extended the life of the Jin Empire for a few months, as Kaifeng fell to Sübedei in 1233.

Others also attempted to persuade the Emperor to abandon his plan to go to Caizhou. In August 1233 the Prince of Yen, Yung-An, wrote a letter suggesting to the Emperor that he should go instead to Shang-Tung at Kuei-te, for a number of reasons. The first was because Kuei-te was surrounded by water which would hinder Mongol attacks. Secondly, although short of grain, Kuei-te was self-sufficient due to ample local supplies of fish and vegetables. The third reason was because 'the fact that the enemy left Kuei-te was not for our own sake. It was like letting people leave and following them from behind, or staying away from the hard spot and attacking the vulnerable'.[57] A fourth reason was that Caizhou was only 100 li away from the frontier with the Song, who could supply the Mongols with troops and grain – which did indeed occur after the Mongols entered an alliance with the Song dynasty.[58] Prince Yung-An, unwittingly foreseeing the future, noted that the Emperor could not avoid catastrophe this way. The prince's fifth reason was that even if Kuei-te fell, the Emperor could flee by water to Caizhou, but if Caizhou fell, then there would be no escape, as he would have to fight his way to the sea. As a sixth reason, Prince Yung-An noted that the season was hot and rainy. Furthermore, the land had been flooded, and therefore, reinforcements would have difficulty reaching Caizhou, whereas they could get to Kuei-te by water. Despite his sound strategic reasons, the Emperor and his counselors rejected Yung-An's pleas out of distrust of his loyalty.[59]

As the Mongols continued their conquest of North China, the Jin armies suffered from desertion, not only by their soldiers, but also among their generals. In addition the Jin had overextended their armies to defend their territory, so that when called upon their generals could not come to the aid of the Emperor.[60] Thus the Mongols commanded by Tachar Noyan progressed quickly and attacked the Emperor at Caizhou in October 1233. Wa Kang, the Jurchen court astrologer, predicted that the Jin would win but that the siege would last until the thirteenth day of the following year, 'When there would not be a single person or horse in the city'.[61] Naturally this prediction pleased the Emperor, who nonetheless checked the grain supply. Unfortunately for the Jin this prediction was not quite accurate, as the city fell on 9 February 1234 – the tenth day of the new year in the Chinese calendar. However, the Mongols did leave on the thirteenth day.[62]

Despite the forecast of victory, some Jin officials attempted to thwart the Mongol attack, not relying on magic and astrology for their salvation. A retired general named Nei-tsu A-hu-tai urged the Emperor to seek an alliance with the Song in order to acquire grain and to prevent the Song from joining the Mongols.[63] His advice went unheeded, however, and on 18 September 1233 the Song captured the Tang Prefecture. Furthermore Song forces massed at the border and the Jin forces there required reinforcement. The Emperor sent 3,300 men in addition to words of encouragement:

> The fact that the Tatars [i.e. the Mongols] unleash their forces and often win battles is because they rely on their northern style and use the tricks of the Chinese. It is very difficult to fight against them. As to the Song, they are really not our match! They are weak and not martial, just like women. If I had 3,000 armored soldiers, we could march into Chiang and Huai provinces. Take courage![64]

Indeed, the Jin were victorious over the Song at Chang-tu Tien. Yet against the Mongols they remained less stalwart, as by 28 September 1233 the latter had taken or were already past the Chün and Xü prefectures.[65] By October the Jin commanders were all aware that Caizhou was the Mongols' target. The Mongols approached Caizhou in late October in the *nerge* fashion, taking other cities and isolating it. The Commander of Lu Shan, Yüan Chih, arrived with reinforcements for Caizhou, but he had to fight a running battle to reach the city. Meanwhile, many commanders withheld their troops in order to protect their own territories.[66] The Mongol forces operated in many columns, forcing the Jin to react to their attacks and preventing them from consolidating their efforts.

As the Mongols arrived, Jin officials began to requisition grain, and those who acquired more grain received promotions and increased stipends. But such was the widespread sense of fear that currency devalued overnight, and even members of the Jin Imperial Guard deserted to the Mongols shortly after their attack began on 19 November.

As the siege continued, the situation of the Caizhou grew desperate. By December food prices in Caizhou had reached astronomical figures and cannibalism resulted. Even hanging the culprits failed to end this. Yet although food for the general population was scarce, the Emperor still ate well, as one of his men, Wen-Tun Ch'ang Sun, led a small army out daily to Lien Chiang, west of the city, to catch fish. However, in November even the Emperor felt hunger pangs, as Tachar ordered his *algincin* to ambush and destroy this force. Ch'ang Sun died in the encounter.

Other signs of desperation included one faction amongst the Jurchen developing plans to have their soldiers drink a magic potion that would protect them. Another involved equipping their horses with lion masks and big bells round their necks to frighten the Mongol horses. Even the Emperor saw the folly of this plan and dismissed it.[67] Caizhou's situation worsened further when the Song joined the Mongol besiegers with 10,000 men. They even breached a wall, though the Jin drove them back.

As 1234 approached, the city had high hopes of relief, as the Emperor had sent messengers to all towns and forts still held by the Jin, requesting that they mount a coordinated attack on the first day of the Chinese New Year. However, no one came. The Mongols had intercepted some of the messengers, and those Jin commanders who the others had reached realized that any attempt to rescue Caizhou was doomed. Many of the commanders preferred to sit and wait and then submit to the Mongols on favorable terms. As the Mongols abhorred disloyalty, to desert the Emperor at a crucial moment could result in execution by them. However, if their submission took place after the fall of Caizhou they would be received favorably.

On 8 January 1234 the Mongols had burst the embankment of the Lien River in conjunction with Song efforts to flood the Ju River, which protected the western and southern approaches to Caizhou. The flooding allowed the Mongols to penetrate to the western edge of the city, and by 20 January they had captured its western portion. To preserve their gains from counter-attacks, the Mongols erected a palisade. Tachar did not rush his attack in pursuit of glory, but secured his position first to ensure victory. The Jin continued to resist, slaughtering their horses for rations and destroying civilian houses to build inner defensive works. In a last ditch effort, the Emperor even sent the court eunuchs and courtiers to man the walls. Needless to say, these last reinforcements did little to stem the Mongol tide. Failing to halt the Mongols, on 8 February Emperor Ai-Tsung abdicated to Nei-tsu Ch'eng-lin, and the following day Caizhou fell to the Mongols.[68]

The siege of Caizhou is a vivid example of not just the fall of a city but of the last struggles of a proud dynasty. The Mongols had been at war with the Jin for over 20 years. Although other campaigns often diverted the Mongols' attention, the fact that the Jin continued to resist them for so long demonstrates the extraordinary efforts the Jin made to defend themselves. It also shows the depth of ability among the Mongol commanders. Sübedei, the leading Mongol general at the time, initiated the destruction of the Jin, but before the war was over he was reassigned to lead the campaign against the Kipchaks and the Rus' and on into Europe. The fact that the Mongols could switch commanders in the midst of a war demonstrates the confidence they had in their generals. It was some time before the Jin collapsed, and yet a younger, less experienced general was capable of finishing the campaign. Ögödei Khan was confident his army would accomplish its task without the guidance of his senior commander.

Chapter 9

Legacy of the Mongols

The extraordinary capabilities of the Mongol military are clearly demonstrated by a study of their campaigns, but their impact on military history is less well understood. To properly assess this, the strengths and weaknesses of their military system need to be explored and the distinctive character of their method of warfare needs to be set in context. Also, their influence on the development of warfare from the medieval period to the present day must be considered.

Strengths of the Mongols
The greatest assets of the Mongol military system were the mobility of their troops and their discipline. Horse-archer armies have a long history; often they have dominated their opponents through their astounding firepower and speed of movement. However, nomadic armies could be their own worst enemies as they often lacked discipline. They preferred to pillage and plunder rather than fulfilling their objectives, and in defeat they were liable to disintegrate rather than regroup.

The Mongols overcame these weaknesses. They refined traditional steppe tactics and combined them with an iron and, at times, draconian discipline. This, in turn, enhanced their mobility, as Mongol commanders could operate more independently than ever before with a more effective force. Thus the Mongol khans enjoyed the advantage of being able to set a number of objectives for their commanders while on campaign, and could trust their commanders to follow their instructions. Strong discipline allowed the Mongols to carry out deep, penetrating attacks during invasions, and made it easy for them to concentrate their firepower quickly against important targets.

Weaknesses of the Mongols
Despite their overwhelming martial abilities, the Mongols also possessed weaknesses. Although they are often popularly portrayed as an unstoppable force of nature, the Mongols did suffer a number of setbacks and outright defeats. However, as they possessed an amazing ability and willingness to learn

new forms of warfare, as well as a strong urge to avenge prior losses, the Mongols viewed defeats as only momentary setbacks.

Although their mobility in warfare was a key strength, it was also a factor in their major weakness. In order to maintain their tactical speed in combat, as well as on the march, the Mongol military system was dependent on each warrior having several horses. As their horses were pasture fed, the Mongols needed to secure grazing lands. Usually the Mongols made arrangements to ensure that pastures were available. However, the amount of pasture on hand dictated how many men could be stationed in an area.

Another weakness, although it rarely surfaced in comparison with other contemporary armies, was the quality of the soldiers. In general, the Mongols were good soldiers. Due to the harsh conditions of the steppe, nomads could endure the elements and became good warriors exceptionally skilled in horsemanship and archery. However, even at the height of the Mongol Empire its army was not on a par with select units in the rest of the medieval world. Groups such as the Mamluks and the Japanese samurai were all–military elites whose lives centered on the art of war. Certainly, some Mongol warriors possessed skills that paralleled the best of these elite groups, but as a whole the Mongol army had good soldiers, but not elite forces. When the Mongols first invaded Japan in the 1270s, the samurai suffered greatly but adjusted. The Mamluks were rarely bested by the Mongols, although it did happen on occasion, as in Ghazan Khan's invasion in 1299–1300.

Both of these elite forces gave the Mongols considerable problems. The samurai attempted to engage them in the accustomed manner of warfare in Japan, with an emphasis on single combat. Unfortunately for the samurai, the Mongols viewed warfare as a team sport. But once they realized that trying to fight the Mongols and their Korean and Chinese infantry in single combat was futile, the Japanese began to gain the upper hand. As talented archers and brilliant swordsmen, they could battle the Mongols both from a distance and in close combat.

A similar story can be told about the Mamluks, who first defeated the Mongols at Gaza and then in the climactic battle of Ayn Jalut in 1260. They were slaves of steppe origins – often Kipchak Turks, the very people that the Mongols had defeated and incorporated into their own armies – who after being purchased in the slave markets of Egypt and Syria spent years honing their skills with lance, sword, bow, and horse. Although they lacked the mobility of the Mongols due to their heavier armor and fewer horses – typically just one horse per man – the Mamluks were highly trained in all areas of war, unlike the average Mongol warrior.

The samurai and the Mamluks were the elite of the medieval world. The Mongols could defeat them if the conditions were ideal, including the possession of superior numbers, but man for man the Mamluk and the samurai were superior warriors simply because their whole lives were devoted to war. Unlike the knights of Europe who had similar martial virtues, they also mastered archery and could compete with the Mongols in that area of military expertise, whereas the Mongols simply avoided closing for combat when fighting against knights. Yet at the same time, to compare the Mongols with the Mamluks or samurai is like comparing a regular modern infantry soldier with a US Navy SEAL, a Green Beret, or a British SAS trooper. When compared with other average soldiers, they were without peer.

Overall legacy to warfare
The overall impact of the Mongols on the art of war is hard to gauge. Indeed, the Mongols continued the dominance of steppe warfare in Eurasia. That is to say, highly mobile horse-archers remained dominant, although some permutations developed. The steppe and areas on its periphery continued to be influenced by horse archers to some degree. Even the Ming Dynasty (1368–1644) retained a large number of Mongol cavalry because of their value. Yet to understand the influence of the Mongol art of war it needs to be examined in areas removed from the steppe.

Mongol influence on Eastern European warfare
Although Eastern Europe is some distance from the steppe, the influence of the Mongols can be traced in the development of the region's armies. Its Slavic principalities had always had frequent contact with steppe nomads, but did not readily adopt the techniques of steppe warfare. They fought according to their own traditions, using the nomads as allies and auxiliaries. It was not until the Mongol period that steppe warfare began to have an impact on military thinking in the region. Previously there had been no need to fight like the nomads; while the Kipchaks and Pechenegs who had preceded the Mongols were worthy adversaries, they could be countered. The Mongol style of warfare was unlike anything the Rus' had encountered before, and they had no answer to it. To cling to their old military system in the face of such overwhelming power would have been the height of folly.

The Muscovites, for instance, chose to emulate the Mongols in many ways; they followed a trend that other Rus' cities had started, adopting the Mongol military system. The transition was assisted by the fact that Russian warriors were incorporated into the Mongol military. The Muscovites organized their army along similar lines and used steppe nomad tactics and weapons.[1] They also adopted aspects of Mongol administration. Prince Ivan III (the Great) instituted the *yam* system and applied it in much the same way as the Mongols.

For Moscow, the transition made sense, as the primary threats to its security came from the various offshoots of the Golden Horde plus the Lithuanians, who fought in a similar manner. The Russian nobility fought as horse-archers, rather than as shock cavalry as their pre-Mongol ancestors had. Although Ivan IV created the *streltsy* or musketeers in the sixteenth century, one of their primary roles was to defend the string of forts on the southern frontier against nomadic incursions. Indeed, the growing importance of the Cossacks as well as the use of Tatar light cavalry by Muscovy emphasized the need for troops experienced in steppe warfare. It was not until Peter the Great that Russia's military focus began to shift from the steppe as European powers became its primary enemies.

Despite the efforts of Peter and his successors, Mongol influence persisted, albeit with dwindling importance. For instance, Kalmyks or western Mongols, who migrated to the Volga River in the early 1600s, served an important role in the defense of Russia's southern frontier. The conquest of Central Asia during the nineteenth century renewed Russian interest in steppe tactics. Mikhail Ivanin (1801–74), who gained an appreciation of steppe warfare when he served against the Khanate of Khiva, saw some benefits in it even if it was no longer the dominant form of fighting, and in 1846 wrote *The Art of War of the Mongols and the Central Asian Peoples*.[2] Russia's military academies soon incorporated this into their curriculum, where it remained in use until World War II, as will be discussed later in this chapter.

Gunpowder and the end of steppe warfare?
The spread of gunpowder is directly related to the rise of the Mongols. Although gunpowder recipes had been slowly making their way across Asia from China, the *Pax Mongolica* accelerated their spread. Although they may have used catapult-launched bombs in siege warfare beyond China, unfortunately there is no definite documentary evidence to confirm it, as the terms later used for gunpowder weapons are synonymous with catapults. Considering that the Mongols rarely met a weapon they did not like, we can be certain that if they found a way to transport it safely, it would have been incorporated into their arsenal for campaigns outside China. Nonetheless, its use remains speculation.[3]

It is known, however, that the Mongol Empire was the primary transmitter of the knowledge of gunpowder, whether directly, through its use in war, or simply because most of the major trade routes ran through it. While it is unlikely that Europe gained its knowledge of gunpowder directly from the

Mongols, we do know that it appeared there only after the Mongol invasion. Most likely merchants, perhaps even the Polo family, traveling through the Mongol Empire carried the recipe back. This eventually led to European dominance over much of the world after the year 1500.

As Kenneth Chase demonstrated in his study on the spread of firearms, the Mongols are linked to the rise of European hegemony by more than the spread of gunpowder. The Mongols' tactics and weapons also impacted on neighboring areas. As the nomads' composite bow outcompeted muskets and other early firearms in terms of range and accuracy, not to mention rate of fire, nomadic armies could decimate firearm-equipped infantry. In addition, the nomads were too mobile for early cannons; not until the sixteenth and seventeenth centuries did cannon-manufacturing techniques advance to the point of producing easily maneuverable artillery pieces.

Meanwhile, in order to increase their power and control Western European kings were virtually the only people who could afford the expense of producing cannons. As the resistance of castles continually improved against traditional siege weapons, rulers became dependent on cannon to smash forts in order to defeat their enemies and to bring recalcitrant vassals into line. In addition Western European armies fought steppe nomads less often, so mobility was less of an issue than protection against more powerful weapons. Knights consequently continued to increase the strength of their armor to protect them against crossbows, longbows, and early firearms. As a result the knight became less mobile. Early cannons and firearms, however, could be effective against knights and infantry in a way that they could not be against steppe nomads. Of course, the knights eventually disappeared, while light and medium cavalry evolved to counter the artillery.

A similar effect occurred in China, where cannons were used extensively by the Ming dynasty, which drove the Mongols out in 1368. However, cannons played only a small role in the defeat of the Mongols – indeed, Ming use of cannons was primarily limited to siege warfare and battles in South China. For the reasons described above, the Ming did not use cannons extensively on their northern frontier with the Mongolian tribes.

The ramifications of this use were great. Countries sharing borders with steppe nomads saw less development in gunpowder weaponry until their prime military focus shifted to sedentary states. Only then did the technology improve. Towards the end of the seventeenth century field artillery pieces became more mobile, thus providing support for musket-armed infantry. The cannons easily disrupted steppe cavalry formations and possessed a greater range than the composite bow. Only then did dominance of steppe warfare decline. Yet it should be noted that only one state developed a truly effective method of dealing with horse-archers prior to the 1600s: Ottoman Turkey. This may have been because of its need to deal with both the strongly fortified cities of Habsburg Europe and the horse-archers on the Sultanate's eastern border, ranging from the Aq Qoyunlu and the Safavids (defeated at Chaldiran in 1514) to the Mamluk Sultanate (conquered in 1516–17).

Influence on tank warfare
Considering the Mongols' success and their emphasis on fast-moving units and firepower, it is not surprising that a re-evaluation of Mongols tactics occurred when armies became mechanized in the twentieth century. What is surprising is that very few military experts made the connection. The British scholar B.H. Liddell Hart saw combined formations of tanks and mechanized infantry as the modern equivalent to the Mongols. Liddell Hart's basic premise of mechanized warfare was that a highly mobile tank force could operate independently and in advance of the main army. In doing so, it could cut enemy communications and supply lines, thus paralyzing the enemy's army;[4] one's adversary would, at best, only be able to react, and would be unable to formulate any offensive action. While correct in this interpretation, Liddell Hart missed a key objective of Mongol strategy, which was the annihilation of the enemy's field armies. Of course, having witnessed the senseless trench warfare of World War I, Liddell Hart hoped to avoid such large death tolls in the future.

Liddell Hart's idea of using the Mongol emphasis of mobility and firepower came to fruition in the training of Britain's first experimental tank brigade. Its successful performance in exercises, along with Liddell Hart's chapter on Chinggis Khan and Sübedei in *Great Captains Unveiled*, also played a key role in the proposal by General Douglas MacArthur, then Army Chief of Staff, in 1935 to establish a similar unit in the American army. MacArthur also recommended that the Mongol campaigns should be studied for future use.[5] Unfortunately his advice went unheeded until World War II; his suggestion having been made at the end of his term of office, it was not pursued both because of the more conservative nature of his successors and because of the lack of resources to do so at the time.

Francis Gabriel's view is that while Liddell Hart made these observations, he did not fully appreciate other aspects of Mongol military thinking, such as the use of both light and heavy cavalry, or the use of infantry and preparatory fire before an assault.[6] However, Gabriel's interpretation is not quite accurate, as in Liddell Hart's own writings after World War II he advocated a return to lighter tanks. He saw a tendency amongst NATO countries to use heavily armored tanks that were less mobile and called for a return to mobility by an increase in the use of light tanks, whilst still maintaining a sufficient number of heavy tanks to provide power. One of the factors in his coming to this decision was that he noted the Mongols operated most effectively when they combined light and heavy cavalry rather than deploying just one type.[7] Indeed, he wrote: 'The basic factors, and most distinctive features in tank operations are speed and flexibility. These twin qualities are of more fundamental importance than the armour of the tank'.[8] This was very true of Mongol warfare. Furthermore, in his classic work *Great Captains Unveiled*, Liddell Hart dubs the Mongols the inventors of artillery preparation.[9]

Another British military theoretician, J.F.C. Fuller, also viewed tanks as being modern 'Mongols', and encouraged the use of self-propelled artillery. However, he emphasized the role of airplanes. Despite advocating the adoption of Mongol tactics, Liddell Hart's and Fuller's ideas were not immediately accepted in Western military circles.[10] Farther to the east, though, others made practical use of similar, yet distinctively different ideas.

Blitzkrieg

The style of warfare known as *Blitzkrieg*, made famous by the German Wehrmacht during World War II, bears remarkable similarities to the Mongol art of war, and this is not by accident. In part the evolution of the *Blitzkrieg* owed its origins to information gained from the Soviets as a result of the Rapallo Pact of 1923. It emerged from the operational doctrine of the Soviet General Mikhail Nikolayevich Tukhachevsky (1893–1937), who emphasized 'employment of forward aviation in concert with rapidly moving tank columns.'[11] Tukhachevsky's view was that Soviet warfare should be concerned with the 'seizure and maintenance of the offensive over a long period of time'.[12] This is what modern military strategists refer to as the 'deep battle'. Meanwhile, during the same period after World War I, military leaders in France, Britain, and America focused instead on developing tactics and strategies aimed at forcing the enemy into peace talks, rather than crushing him. Traditional methods of steppe warfare were familiar to military theorists in Russian and Soviet academies, and Liddell Hart's ideas about how to combine Mongol techniques with modern tank tactics had also filtered into the Soviet Union. Indeed, while they had independent origins the strategies of Liddell Hart and Tukhachevsky are virtually identical and owe much to the Mongol system.

The Soviet concept of 'deep battle' shares the Mongols' goals of hampering the enemy's ability to concentrate his armies and forcing him to react to the attackers' movements rather than executing his own offensive plans. Thus by 1937, according to Francis Gabriel, the Soviets possessed an army that was Mongol in doctrine and tactical sense due to the work of Marshal Tukhachevsky and Mikhail Vasilyevich Frunze (1885–1925) in developing the 'deep battle' strategy.[13] Unfortunately for the Soviets, in the very same year Stalin purged most of the Red Army's officers and executed Tukhachevsky. Thus when Germany invaded, the Red Army was in disarray, Tukhachevsky's tank armies – the centerpiece of his 'deep battle' strategy – having been broken up. Serving as infantry support rather than the main battle force, they could do little to stop the Wehrmacht during the early part of World War II.

The Wehrmacht's devastating *Blitzkrieg* strategy drew upon other influences besides those of the Soviets. Two German officers in particular played a significant role in the development of the German military and thus created a force designed specifically for executing the *Blitzkrieg*. The first of them was General Hans von Seeckt, who organized the Reichswehr (the German army between WWI and the establishment of the Wehrmacht). One of the critical elements in its structure and training was that subordinate officers were trained to quickly assume command positions and replace their superiors should the need arise, such as if they were killed, incapacitated, or removed from command. Thus a major was expected to effectively command a division should his general die. Even privates were trained in command and leadership situations so that they could assume the leadership of their unit.[14] This was very similar to the Mongols' own view of command and leadership, although it was probably coincidental as a more likely antecedent was Napoleon's adage that every soldier carried a marshal's baton in his knapsack, meaning that anyone in his army could advance to the highest rank.

The Mongol influence in Seeckt's system appears more in Reichswehr operational strategy. His writings from 1921, before the Rapallo Pact, state that 'what would matter in future warfare was the use of relatively small, but highly skilled mobile armies in co-operation with aircraft'.[15] There does not appear to be any direct link between Seeckt and the Mongols, rather he came to this conclusion based on his experience in World War I as well as by listening to his subordinates in the Reichswehr. Ultimately, what he desired was to avoid the static warfare of World War I, and, much like the Soviets, focus on mobility that would facilitate operations that would overwhelm the enemy and force him to react. Furthermore, the purpose of the attack was to annihilate the enemy before he could counter the attack.[16]

One of Seeckt's subordinates was General Heinz Guderian. Guderian, like other German tank commanders, studied the works of Fuller, Liddell Hart, and Martel, all of whom emphasized the tank as an offensive weapon supported by other units (whether artillery, infantry, or air power), and not vice versa.[17] Guderian, like Seeckt, believed that tanks would restore mobility to warfare.

As has been discussed, Fuller and Liddell Hart were greatly influenced by the Mongols, and thus Guderian, at least indirectly, carried these ideas into the German *Blitzkrieg*.

Indeed, Guderian's concept of warfare greatly resembles a Mongol operation. He believed that tanks were best used en masse and for striking quickly, so that they hit the enemy's defenses before the enemy could intervene or deploy effectively. Much like the Mongol practice of using auxiliaries or *cerik* troops to finish off isolated fortresses, Guderian indicated that once the defenses had been penetrated by the *panzers*, then other units could carry out the mop-up duties, particularly of any static defenses.[18]

Mongol influence in modern warfare remains very apparent, albeit indirect. Indeed, many commanders of the 2003 Iraq War may have realized that their actions reflected the theories of Liddell Hart, but probably not that their ultimate roots lay with the Mongols. Considering the abilities of the Mongol army and the skill of its generals, including Chinggis Khan himself, who formulated the underlying principles of the Mongol art of war, it would not be surprising for a modern-day military commander, when confronted by a tactical or strategic dilemma, to consider the question: What would Chinggis do?

Glossary

Airagh – Mongolian term for fermented mare's milk, the preferred drink of most steppe nomads. The alcoholic content was fairly low, although more potent drinks could be made. See also *kumiss*.

Ajlab – The Royal Mamluks (see *mamluk*), or those recruited and trained by the Sultan. See also *mustarawat* or *julban*.

Alginci (pl. *algincin*) – The vanguard and scouts of the *tamma*. Typically they were stationed closer to cities than the main *tamma* force.

Amir – Arabic term for commander. Most of the Islamic sources use this term in place of *noyan*.

Anda – A blood brother. The blood-brother relationship bonded two men together for life, and was often considered stronger than normal familial ties. During the bonding ritual, the two men or boys drank a little of their blood and exchanged gifts. Chinggis Khan's *anda* Jamuqa became his greatest rival.

Arban (pl. *arbat*) – A military unit of ten men or an economic unit of ten households.

Arban-u noyan – Commander of an *arban*.

Aurug – Units created by Chinggis Khan to supply his army. Originally an *aurug* was an extended family unit. After the assimilation and dispersal of conquered tribes, Chinggis Khan created new *aurugs* to better integrate his state. In addition, the *aurug* helped provide for the needs of the military.

Ba'adur – The braves or warriors who members of the *keshik* should strive to emulate. Also to be found rendered as *bahadur* and *baatar*.

Balaghci (pl. *balaghcin*) – Members of the *keshik* in charge of the palace gates or approaches to the camp of the khan.

Baojun – Chinese term for the catapult corps within the Mongol army. It is unclear if the Mongols had a specific name for this part of their siege train.

Baraghun ghar – Right wing (literally 'west hand') of the Mongol army. The Mongols typically drew up facing south, and used the terms north, south, east and west to describe directions, rather than the more usual left and right.

Biceci (pl. *bicecin*) – Those who recorded annals for the khan. Often a duty of a member of the *keshik*. The *biceci* also served in the civil governments in the provinces, essentially as secretaries.

Bilig – A maxim or saying of Chinggis Khan. While not officially a law, the maxims of Chinggis Khan carried great weight in the minds of the Mongols.

Bombog kharvaa – The modern Mongolian name for a training exercise similar to the Mamluk training technique known as *qabaq*. *Bombog kharvaa* or ball shooting consisted of placing three leather balls on poles. The mounted archer attempted to hit the first one while advancing upon it, then the second as he rode by it. The final ball was targeted after the archer had ridden past it, using the Parthian shot.

Borici (pl. *boricin*) – One who cooked and served drink. A very important position in the *keshik*, as such men had close contact with the khan. Only the most trusted men would be appointed *boricin*.

Caracole – A modern military term referring to a body of horsemen advancing and firing, and then retiring while another body came forward to repeat the maneuver. This form of attack required regular practice to be performed successfully. It is best known for its use in sixteenth- and seventeenth-century Europe by pistol-armed cavalry. The Mongol *nagur* or 'lake' formation was most likely a caracole attack.

Caragana – A Mongol military formation, named after a thorny shrub. The only problem is that no one really knows how these formations operated. The *caragana* has been interpreted as a close formation and also a more open formation of clumps.

Cerik – A military force composed of the sedentary population, used by the Mongols to garrison certain locations. In many ways it mirrored the *tamma*, which consisted of nomads.

Chevauchée – A military term used in fourteenth- and fifteenth-century Europe to describe a method of living off the land whilst intentionally laying waste the surrounding region. In addition to obtaining food, the raiders also acquired plunder. An added benefit might include luring the enemy out of his fortresses, thus avoiding lengthy sieges.

Ch'i-tan chün – Chinese term for the Khitan *cerik*.

Daraci (pl. *daracin*) – Member of the *keshik* in charge of wine and other alcoholic beverages. A position of importance, considering the great consumption of alcoholic beverages (especially *kumiss*) at court functions.

Daruqaci (pl. *daruqacin*) – A governor assigned to a town or district, who would also have some military authority over a small body of troops. The *daruqaci* could be a Mongol, often from the *keshik*, or a local official. (Persian equivalent: *shahna*.)

Dasht-i Kipchak – The Kipchak Steppe, which dominated much of modern Southern Russia and Ukraine and stretched into Kazakstan, covering the area roughly from the Carpathian mountains to north of the Aral Sea. It was the homeland of the Kipchak Turks, a nomadic group conquered by the Mongols. It was subsequently the core of the Jochid Ulus or Golden Horde khanate.

Deel or *degel* – The traditional knee-length steppe coat that fastened on one side. It could be treated to make it somewhat waterproof and was often lined to protect its wearer against the cold.

Dörben külü'üt – See *külü'üd*.

Dörben noqas – The 'Four Hounds' of Chinggis Khan, consisting of four of his most talented generals: Jebe, Sübedei, Jelme, and Qubilai. The *dörben noqas* and their units served as an elite brigade known for its tenacious pursuit of fleeing opponents.

Druzhina – The companions and retainers of a Rus' prince. They formed the core of the prince's army and typically fought as heavy cavalry.

Faris – Arabic term for a cavalryman or one who had knowledge of the *furisiyya*, the arts of horsemanship, archery, fencing, and wielding a lance from horseback.

Ghulam – Persian term for slave. The general term used for household slaves as well as military slaves. See also *Mamluk*.

Güregen – A son-in-law of Chinggis Khan. This was a very prestigious title. It was later used by any non-Chinggisid who married a Chinggisid wife.

Halqa – Non-Mamluk cavalry in the armies of the Mamluk Sultanate.

Han – Ethnic Chinese. During the thirteenth century, what is now modern China consisted of several ethnic groups, much as it does today. However, it had often been ruled by non-Han dynasties.

Hei Chün – 'Black Army', as the pre-1235 *cerik* of Han troops were known. In Mongolian and steppe nomadic culture, the color black has the symbolic meaning of 'commoner' or 'subordinate'.

Hoy-in Irgen – Literally 'the people of the Forest', who lived in the wooded areas around Lake Baikal, north of the Mongolian steppes and west to the Yenesei river valley. Tribes included the Oyirad, Buriyad, and Kirghiz. They submitted to the Mongols in 1207–8 but rebelled in 1218.

Hsin Chün – 'New Army' in Chinese. This *cerik* resulted from the conscriptions of 1236 and 1241 that increased the *Hei Chün* to over 95,000 men and led to its reorganization as the *Hsin Chün*.

Iqta – Arabic term for a land grant. Unlike a European fief, the recipient of an *iqta* did not enjoy ownership of the land or control the people working it, but only received income from the grant. This was a fairly common practice throughout the Islamic world. See also *timar*.

Jadaci (pl. *jadacin*) – A shaman who specialized in weather magic. He used special stones in an attempt to summon storms during the course of battle.

Jaghun (pl. *jaghut*) – A military unit of 100 men, comprising ten *arbat*, or an economic unit of 100 households.

Jaghun-u noyan – Commander of a *jaghun*.

Jarlighci (pl. *jarlighcin*) – One who wrote sacred decrees or the laws mandated by Chinggis Khan or other khans. Often an additional position held by a member of the *keshik*.

Je'ün ghar – Left wing (literally 'east hand') of the Mongol army. The Mongols typically drew up facing south, and used the terms north, south, east and west to describe directions, rather than the more usual left and right.

Julban – The Royal Mamluks (see *Mamluk*), or those recruited and trained by the Sultan. See also *mustarawat* or *ajlab*.

Jurched – The ethnicity of the Jin dynasty that ruled northern China and Manchuria from 1125 to 1234. The Jurched were Manchurian in origin, and were semi-nomadic before becoming assimilated into Chinese culture. Many were recruited into the Mongol armies, where they often served in their own formations.

Kebte'ül – The night-guards of the *keshik*. Originally consisted of 80 men but gradually increased to 1,000.

Keshik – The bodyguard of the khan. Composed of 10,000 men in three distinct units of day guards (*turqa'ud*), night guards (*kebte'ül*), and quiver bearers (*qorcin*).

Keshikten – Members of the *keshik*.

Khitans – A people who at one time ruled northern China and much of Mongolia as the Liao dynasty (945–1125). After being overthrown by the Jurched, one group established a new kingdom in Central Asia known as the Kara Khitai. The Khitans were ethnically and linguistically similar to the Mongols. Many served not only in the main Mongol army, but also in special Khitan armies.

Köldölci – See *üldüci*.

Külü'üd – Chinggis Khan's four heroes. These were four companions of Chinggis Khan who became his most trusted generals during the wars in Mongolia. They were Boroghul, Bo'orchu, Muqali, and Chila'un.

Kumiss – Turkic term for fermented mare's milk. Slightly alcoholic and the preferred beverage of most Mongols.

Laager – A fort made by forming wagons into a circle. Typically the wagons were also chained together to prevent their removal. The Hungarians tended to use laagers on campaign.

Li – A Chinese unit of measurement. Although its exact size varied throughout history, the *li* remained close to half a kilometer, or quarter of a mile.

Mamluk – A slave-soldier in the Islamic world. The majority were Turks taken from the steppe. After purchase, their masters had them trained to be *faris*. In the process they converted to Islam and were then manumitted. Mamluks were the elite warriors of the Islamic world. In 1250 they took over Egypt, and went on to defeat the Mongols at Ayn Jalut in 1260, thus expanding the Mamluk Sultanate into Syria.

Meng-ku chün – Chinese term for the regular Mongol army, as opposed to a *tamma*.

Minqan (pl. *minqat*) – A military unit of 1,000 men or an economic unit of 1,000 households. The *minqan* was the essential tactical and strategic unit of the Mongol army.

Minqan-u noyan – Commander of a *minqan*.

Moira – A Byzantine military unit. A *moira* consisted of three or more *tagmas*, which were units of 200 to 400 horsemen.

Morinci (pl. *morincin*) – Member of the *keshik* in charge of the imperial wagons and horses. See also *ula'aci*.

Mustakhdamun – Mamluks that a sultan gained from other masters, including those of the previous sultan and deceased or dismissed *amirs*. See *amir* and *Mamluk*.

Mustarawat – The Royal Mamluks (see *Mamluk*), or those recruited and trained by the Sultan. See also *ajlab*, or *julban*.

Nagur – Literally 'lake', a Mongol military formation. It has been interpreted as an open formation, but also as an attack in waves, like the caracole.

Nasij – A gold brocade cloth in great demand by the Mongol elite. Skilled textile workers were often sent to production centers to weave it.

Nerge – A hunting technique used by the Mongols that also became a training technique and common tactical and strategic practice. In the *nerge*, the Mongols would fan out over several miles, forming a circle. Then they would gradually close and contract the circle, trapping their prey within a ring of men and horses.

Noyan (pl. *noyad*) – Lord or commander. This title initially referred to a military commander, but eventually also referred to members of the nobility, typically not from the Chinggisid family. The noble *noyad* were usually commanders of *tümen*.

Nü-chih chün – Chinese terms for the Jurched *cerik*.

Orda or *ordu* – A Mongolian and Turkic term referring to the camp of a prince or general. It also served as the root of the English word 'horde'.

Örlüg – Marshal of an army. This term was generally applied to nine specific companions of Chinggis Khan, the *yisün örlüg*. These were Muqali, Bo'orchu, Boroghul, Chila'un, Jebe, Qubilai, Jelme, Sübedei, and Shiqi Qutuqtu.

Ortaq – A merchant. Merchants, typically Muslims, could and often did wield considerable influence within the Mongol Empire. As the Mongols strongly supported trade, this is not surprising. In return *ortaqs* often provided intelligence to the Mongol generals about regions they passed through. They were also valued for their administrative and fiscal talents. Unfortunately, much of the administrative corruption found during the regencies of Töregene and Oghal-Qaimish was due to the avarice of *ortaqs* placed in tax-gathering positions. Möngke Khan rooted out most of these individuals.

Parthian shot – Refers to a horse-archer turning in his saddle as he retreats and firing backwards at the enemy. The Parthians defeated the Roman army of Crassus at Carrhae in 53 BC.

Qabaq – Arabic term for a gourd. Also the name of a Mamluk archery drill in which a gourd was affixed to a post and horse-archers shot at it while they rode past it. The poles were typically set in a line and at varying heights to challenge the archer with a variety of angles and situations. Similar training exercises were conducted in the steppe under the name *bombog kharvaa*.

Qadi – A judge of religious law in the Islamic world. Typically the *qadi* was government-appointed.

Qamuq Monggol Ulus – The name of Chinggis Khan's new state or nation following his unification of the steppes of Mongolia. The name means the Whole or All of the Mongol nation. It included all of the various tribes of Mongolia, including Turkic groups, but now lacking their original tribal leaders. The focus of its tribal leadership was Chinggis Khan, his family, and his military commanders. It eventually became known as the *Yeke Monggol Ulus* or Great Mongol State.

Qighaj – Arabic military drill, also known as *qipaj*. This was similar to the *qabaq*, but involved the rider shooting downward at a target as he rode by, often rising in his stirrups to give him a better vantage point.

Qipaj – See *qighaj*.

Qol – Center or pivot, also to be found rendered as *ghol*. Refers to the center of the army.

Qoninci (pl. *qonincin*) – One who tended sheep. Members of the *keshik* also performed this task by serving as shepherds for the imperial flocks.

Qorci (pl. *qorcin*) – A quiver bearer or archer in the *keshik*. The *qorcin* consisted of 1,000 men, and was one of the three major divisions of the khan's bodyguard.

Qulaghanci (pl. *qulaghancin*) – Men who captured thieves and seem to have acted as police. Members of the *keshik* also served in this capacity.

Qurci (pl. *qurcin*) – Someone who played music. Often a position within the *keshik*. Not to be confused with the *qorci*.

Quriltai – An assembly of Mongol leaders, including nobility and army commanders, where they discussed issues of state, elected new leaders, assigned commanders, and discussed invasion plans.

Qurut – A Mongol ration and a staple item of their diet. Typically a powdered milk or paste made from milk. It was reconstituted in boiling water or in waterskins placed on the horse's saddle, the natural motion of the horse mixing the *qurut* with the water.

Shahna – See *daruqaci*.

Siba'uci or *siba'ucin* – Falconer. Often one of the additional duties of a member of the keshik.

Siyah (pl. *siyat*) – A rigid endpiece on the tip of a composite bow. These acted as levers so that the bow could be drawn with less weight, working in a similar way to the modern pulley system used in compound bows.

Smerdy – The militia of a Rus' city.

Sügürci (pl. *sügürcin*) – Member of the *keshik* in charge of garments for imperial use.

Tamma – A military force of selected units sent to control the borders between the steppe and sedentary lands. It was also expected to extend Mongol control and influence into territory surrounding its camps.

Tammaci (pl. *tammacin*) – Member of a *tamma*. The term could refer not only to the soldiers comprising a *tamma*, but also to its commander.

Tan-ma-ch'ih chün – Chinese term for the *tammaci* army.

Temeci (pl. *temecin*) – One who tended camels. Members of the *keshik* also performed this task by taking care of the imperial herds.

Timar – A land grant in the Islamic world, usually assigned to a warrior in lieu of a salary. Unlike a European fief, the recipient of a *timar* did not enjoy ownership of the land or control the people working it, but only received income from the grant. This was a fairly common practice throughout the Islamic world. See also *iqta*.

Töb – Center. Typically used to refer to the center of the army.

Tümen (pl. *tümet*) – A military unit of 10,000 men or an economic unit of 10,000 households.

Tümen-ü noyan – Commander of a *tümen*.

Tuq – Mongol standard or banner, typically a drum and nine horsetails on top of a pole. This would usually be erected outside the khan's tent and showed the condition of the day: during times of peace the horsetails were white, but during wartime they were black.

Turqa'ut – The day-guards in the *keshik*. Grew from 70 men to 8,000.

Ughurgh-a – A pole-lasso used by Mongolian nomads. The lasso was attached to a long shaft that enabled the lassoed animal to be controlled and directed. It is uncertain if it was used in warfare.

Ula'aci – Member of the *keshik* in charge of the imperial wagons and horses. See also *morinci*.

Üldüci – Member of the *keshik* who assisted the emperor with his sword and bow. Also to be found rendered as *köldölci*.

Ulus (pl. *ulsyn*) – A Mongolian term generally used to refer to a state, nation, possessions, or patrimony. The Mongol Empire was often referred to as the *Yeke Monggol Ulus* or Great Mongol State or Nation. After the empire broke apart it divided into four separate *ulsyn*, consisting of the Great Khan's in China and Tibet; the Chaghatayid in Central Asia; the Jochid in Russia and the southern steppes of Eurasia, extending into modern Kazakhstan; and the Il-Khanid, extending from Afghanistan and the Amu Darya river to the Euphrates and modern Turkey.

Wadifiyya – Mongol refugees who took shelter in the Mamluk sultanate. Typically they had deserted from the Il-Khanid state. They often served as *halqa* forces for the Mamluks.

Wazir – An Arabic term referring to a Caliph's or Sultan's chamberlain. The *wazir* often handled the daily affairs of state. In some instances he was the power behind the throne. Often found rendered as 'vizier'.

Yam – A Mongol post station. These were placed at 20–30 mile intervals to provide messengers and dignitaries with spare horses, food, and shelter.

Yamci – An individual who maintained a *yam*.

Yasa – The ordinances of Chinggis Khan. Many of these laws were customary while the rest were developed by Chinggis Khan and later khans. They were maintained and enforced by the *jarlighcin*, who often came from the *keshik*.

Yisun örlüg – The Nine Paladins, a term applied to nine companions of Chinggis Khan: Muqali, Bo'orchu, Boroghul, Chila'un, Jebe, Qubilai, Jelme, Sübedei, and Shigi-Qutuqtu.

List of abbreviations used in the notes

Abu Shamah   Abu Shamah, Shihab al-Din Abd al-Rahman ibn Ismail al-Shafi, *Tarajim rijal, al-qarnayn al-sadis wa'l-sabi al-ma'ruf bi-dhayl al-rawdatayn*, edited by Muhammad Kawthari. Cairo: Izzat al-Attar al-Susayni, 1947.

Al-Athir   Ibn al-Athir. *Al Kamil fi al-Tarikh*, vol. XII. Beirut: Dar Sadr, 1979.

Dhahabi   al-Dhahabi. *Kitab Duwal al-Islam (Les Dynasties de L'Islam)*, translated by Arlette Negre. Damascus: Institut Français de Damas, 1979.

EL   *Ermonlinskaia Letopis'*, edited by A.I. Tsepkovym. Russkie Letopis'. Ryazan': Naste Vremia, 2000.

Grigor   Grigor of Akanc. 'The History of the Nation of the Archers by Grigor of Akanc', translated and edited by R.P. Blake and R.N. Frye, *Harvard Journal of Asiatic Studies* 12 (1949): 269–399.

IL   *Ipat'evskaia Letopis'*, edited by A.I. Tsepkovym. Russkie Letopis', vol. 1. Ryazan': Aleksandriya, 2001.

IWR   Guillelmus de Rubruc. 'Itinerarium Willelmi de Rubruc', in *Sinica Franciscana: Itinera et Relationes Fratrum Minorum Saeculi XIII et XIV*, edited by P. Anastasius Van Den Wyngaert, 164–332. Sinica Franciscana, vol. 1. Firenze: Apud Collegium S. Bonaventurae, 1929.

JPC/Dawson   John de Plano Carpini, in Christopher Dawson, ed., *The Mongol Mission: Narratives and Letters of the Franciscan Missionaries in Mongolia and China in the Thirteenth and Fourteenth Centuries*, translated by a nun of Stanbrook Abbey. London: Sheed and Ward, 1955.

Juvaini/Boyle   Juvaini, Ala-ad-Din Ata-Malik. *Genghis Khan: The History of the World-Conqueror*, edited and translated by J.A. Boyle. Seattle: University of Washington Press, 1997.

Juvaini/Qazvini   Juvaini, Ala al-Din Ata Malik ibn Muhammad. *Tarikh-i-Jahan-Gusha*, edited by Mirza Muhammad Qazvini. E.J.W. Gibb Memorial Series (3 vols). Leiden/London: Brill, 1912, 1916, 1937.

Juzjani   Juzjani, Minhaj Siraj. *Tabaqat-i-Nasiri* (2 vols). Lahore: Markazi Urdu Bord, 1975.

Juzjani/Habibi   Juzjani, Minhaj Siraj. *Tabaqat-i-Nasiri* (2 vols), edited by Abd al-Hayy Habibi. Kabul: Anjuman-i Tarikh-i Afghanistan, 1964–5.

Juzjani/Raverty	Juzjani, Minhaj Siraj. *Tabakat-i-Nasiri (A general history of the Muhammadan dynasties of Asia)* (2 vols), translated by Major H.G. Raverty. New Delhi: Oriental Books Reprint Corp, 1970.
Kiracos	Kiracos de Gantzac. 'Histoire d'Armenie'. *Deux Historiens Arméniens: Kiracos de Gantzax, XIII S, 'Histoire d'Arménie'; Oukhtanès d'Ourha, X S, 'Histoire en Trois Parties'*, translated by M. Brousset. St Petersburg: Imperial Academy of Sciences, 1870.
Liao Shi	'Liao Shi' in *History of Chinese Society: Liao 907–1125*, edited and translated by Karl A. Wittfogel and Feng Chia-Sheng. Philadelphia: The American Philosophical Society, 1949.
Maqrizi	al-Maqrizi, Ahmad ibn Ali. *Kitab al-Suluk Li-Marifat Fi Dul al-Muluk*, edited by Ziyardah Muhammad Mustafi. Cairo: Lajnat al-Talif wa al-Tarjamah wa al-Nashr, 1956.
Maqrizi/Quatremère	al-Maqrizi, Ahmad ibn Ali. *Histoire des Sultans Mamlouks de l'Egypte*, translated by Etienne Quatremère. Paris: Oriental Translation Fund of Great Britain and Ireland, 1837, 1845.
MNT	Gaadamba, Sh., ed. *Mongolyn Nuuts Tovchoo*. Ulaanbaatar: Ulsiin Khevleliin Gazar, 1990.
Nasawi	Nasawi, Muhammad ibn Ahmad. *Sirah al-Sultan Jalal al-Din Mankubirti*. Cairo: Dar al-Fikr al-Arabi, 1953.
Nasawi/Houdas	en-Nasawi, Mohammed. *Histoire du Sultan Djelal ed-din Mankobirti*, translated by O. Houdas. Paris: l'École des Langues Orientale Vivantes, 1895.
Nuwayri	al-Nuwayri, Ahmad ibn Abd al-Wahhab. *Nihayat al-Arab Fi Funun al-Adab*. Edited by Said Ashur. Cairo: Al-hayat al Misriyyat al-ammat lil-kitab, 1975.
RD/Karimi	Rashid al-Din. *Jami al-tawarikh*, edited by B. Karimi (2 vols). Teheran: Iqbal, 1983.
RD/Musavi	Rashid al-Din. *Jami al-tawarikh*, edited by Muhammad Rushn Mustafi Musavi, Teheran: Nashr al-Buruz, 1995.
RD/Thackston	Rashiduddin Fazlullah. *Jami'u't-tawarikh: Compendium of Chronicles*, translated by W.M. Thackston, Parts 1–3. Sources of Oriental Languages and Literatures, vol. 45, edited by Sinasi Tekin and Gönül Alpay Tekin. Central Asian Sources IV. Cambridge, Harvard University: Department of Near Eastern Languages and Civilizations, 1998.
Rubruck/Dawson	William of Rubruck in Christopher Dawson, ed., *The Mongol Mission: Narratives and Letters of the Franciscan Missionaries in Mongolia and China in the Thirteenth and Fourteenth Centuries*, translated by a nun of Stanbrook Abbey. London: Sheed and Ward, 1955.
Rubruck/Jackson	William of Rubruck. *The Mission of Friar William of Rubruck: His Journey to the Court of the Great Khan Mongke, 1253–1255*, translated by Peter Jackson, edited by Peter Jackson and David Morgan.

	Works Issued by the Hakluyt Society, 2nd Series, vol. 173. London: The Hakluyt Society, 1990.
SHM	Rachewiltz, Igor de, trans., *The Secret History of the Mongols*. Leiden: Brill, 2004.
SHM-C	*The Secret History of the Mongols*, translated by F.W. Cleaves. Cambridge: Harvard University Press, 1982.
SHM-O	*The Secret History of the Mongols: The Life and Times of Chinggis Khan*, translated by Urgunge Onon. Richmond, Surrey: Curzon Press, 2001.
SHM-R	*The Secret History of the Mongols*, translated by Igor de Rachewiltz, in *Papers on Far Eastern History* 4 (September 1971): 115–63; 5 (March 1972): 149–75; 10 (September 1974): 55–82; 13 (March 1976): 41–75; 16 (September 1977): 27–65; 18 (September 1978): 43–80; 21 (March 1980): 17–57; 23 (March 1981): 111–46; 26 (September 1982): 39–84; 30 (September 1984): 81–160; 31 (March 1985): 21–93; 33 (March 1986): 129–37.
SNB	Ibn Abi al-Hadid, Abd al-Hamid ibn Hibat Allah. *Sharh Nahi al-Balaghah*. Beirut: Dar Maktabah al-Hayat, 1963.
SWQZL	He Qiutao. 'Sheng Wu Qin Zheng Lu (Bogda Bagatur Bey-e-Ber Tayilagsan Temdeglel)', in *Bogda Bagatur Bey-e-Ber Tayilagsan Temdeglel*, edited by Asaraltu. Monggol Tulgur Bicig-un Cubural, 3–94. Qayilar: Obor Monggol-un Soyul-un Keblel-un Qoriy-a: Kolun Boyir Ayimag-un Sinquva Bicig-un Delgegur tarqagaba, 1985.
Thomas of Spalato	Thomas of Spalato. *Istoriye Arxiyepiskopov Saloni i Splita*, translated by A.I. Solopov, edited by O.A. Akumovoi. Moscow: Indrik, 1997. (L = Latin text; R = Russian text.)
TMEN	Doerfer, Gerhard. *Türkische und Mongolische Elemente Im Neupersischen, Unter Besonderer Berücksichtigung Älterer Neupersischer Geschichtsquellen, vor Allem der Mongolen- und Timuridenzeit*. Veröffentlichungen der Orientalischen Kommission, vol. 16. Wiesbaden: F. Steiner, 1963–75.
TR	De Bridia, C. 'The Tartar Relation', in *The Vinland Map and the Tartar Relation*, edited by R.A. Skelton et al. New Haven: Yale University Press, 1965.
Wang O	*The Fall of the Jurchen Chin: Wang O's Memoir on the Ts'ai-Chou Under the Mongol Siege (1233–1234)*, translated by Hok-lam Chan. Münchener Ostasiactiche Studien, vol. 66. Stuttgart: F. Steiner Verlag, 1993.
YM	Iohannes de Plano Carpini. 'Ystoria Mongalorum', in *Sinica Franciscana: Itinera et Relationes Fratrum Minorum Saeculi XIII et XIV*, edited by P. Anastasius Van Den Wyngaert. Sinica Franciscana, vol. 1, 27–130. Firenze: Apud Collegium S. Bonaventurae, 1929.

YS chapter 98   *Yuan Shi*, translated by Ch'i-ch'ing Hsiao. Chapter 98 in *The Military Establishment of the Yuan Dynasty*, 72–91. Cambridge: Harvard University Press, 1978.

YS chapter 99   *Yuan Shi*, translated by Ch'i-ch'ing Hsiao. Chapter 99 in *The Military Establishment of the Yuan Dynasty*, 92–124. Cambridge: Harvard University Press, 1978.

Zenkovsky/NC   Zenkovsky, Serge A., ed. *The Nikonian Chronicle* (5 vols), translated by Serge A. and Betty Jean Zenkovsky. Princeton: The Kingston Press, 1984.

Zhao Hong   Zhao Hong. *Meng-Da Bei-Lu: Polnoe Opisanie Mongolo-Tatar*, translated by Nikolai Ts. Munkuev. Moscow: Academy of Sciences (Nauka), 1975.

Notes

Prologue

1 Ata Malik Juvaini, *Genghis Khan: The History of the World Conqueror*, translated by J.A. Boyle (Seattle: University of Washington Press, 1997), p. 105.
2 Juvaini, p. 107.
3 Matthew Paris, *English History*, vol. I, translated by J.A. Giles (New York: AMS Press Inc., 1968), p. 312.

Chapter One

1 Paul Ratchnevsky, *Genghis Khan: His Life and Legacy*, translated by Thomas Nivison Haining (Cambridge, Mass., 1992), pp. 15–16.
2 *The Secret History of the Mongols*, translated by Igor de Rachewiltz (Leiden: Brill, 2004) (henceforth SHM), p. 14.
3 SHM, p. 14.
4 SHM, p. 20. Temüjin and Jochi-Kasar had successfully caught a fish in a stream. This was a major accomplishment, not only in terms of securing food but also because the Mongols typically do not catch or eat fish. Bekhter and Belgütei then took the fish from the children of Hö'elün. Despite their protestations, Hö'elün did not intervene, telling them essentially to learn to get along. This was the last straw, as only a few days before Temüjin and Jochi-Kasar had brought down a lark only to have Bekhter take it away. Thus the two conspired to kill Bekhter, but allowed Belgütei (the younger of the two) to live.
5 Ratchnevsky, pp. 24–8; SHM, pp. 22–6. There are no clear dates for how long Temüjin was imprisoned, or exactly when it happened, other than that it was after Bekhter's death. It is quite possible that Temüjin was captured several times, as *The Secret History of the Mongols* indicates that in his youth he suffered at the hands of his relatives on multiple occasions.
6 Ratchnevsky, pp. 34–7; Timothy May, *The Mechanics of Conquest and Governance: The Rise and Expansion of the Mongol Empire, 1185–1265*, PhD dissertation (The University of Wisconsin-Madison, 2004), pp. 169–76.
7 May, pp. 169–76.
8 Ratchnevsky, pp. 45–7, 49–50.
9 SHM, p. 76.
10 SHM, pp. 84–6.
11 SHM, pp. 111–12.

12 SHM-R (1984), p. 44; SWQZL, pp. 39–40; RD/Musavi, pp. 422–3; RD/Karimi, pp. 308–9; RD/Thackston, vol. 1, p. 204. Rashid al-Din noted that Quduqa-Beki submitted in AH604/1208 while Chinggis Khan, after conquering Xi-Xia, led his army to the Irtysh to deal with Güchülüg and Toqto'a Beki of the Merkit. It is possible that Jochi's actions were as a wing of the army that defeated the Merkits and Naimans at the Irtysh.

13 SHM-R (1984), pp. 44–5. This included the Buriyad, Barqut, Ursut, Qabqanas, Tubas, Shibir, Kesdiyim, Tuqas, Bayid, Tenleg, Tö'eles, Tas, and the Bajigid. The Buriyad dwelt on the eastern side of Lake Baikal, with the Barqut north of them. The locations of the Ursut and Qabqanas are uncertain but were probably to the west of Baikal. The Tubas dwelt in the modern region of Tannu Tuva.

14 SHM-R (1984), p. 44; RD/Thackston, vol. 1, p. 204; Martin, *Rise of Chinggis Khan*, p. 102. Rashid al-Din noted that the Kirgiz submitted to Chinggis Khan's envoys, Atlan and Bu'ura.

15 Martin, *Rise of Chinggis Khan*, p. 102.

16 Xi-Xia consisted of a Tangut, Tibetan, and Chinese population with a mixture of nomadic pastoralist and sedentary cultures.

17 David Morgan, *The Mongols* (Oxford: Basil Blackwell, 1986), pp. 64–5. Like many scholars, Morgan viewed the attack on the Xi-Xia as a practise run for an attack against the Jin, being 'against a state which was organised largely on Chinese lines, and if successful it would open a western route into China to add to the more direct northern path of invasion. No doubt the Mongols, always alive to the importance of commerce, were also interested in control of the major trade routes that passed through Xi-Xia.'

18 Isenbike Togan, *Flexibility and Limitation in Steppe Formations: The Kerait Khanate and Chinggis Khan* (vol. 15 of the Ottoman Empire and Its Heritage Series, edited by Suraiya Faroqhi and Halil Inalcik), (Leiden: Brill, 1998), p. 70. Xi-Xia always served as a refuge for the steppes. Toghril Ong-Qan's uncle, Gur Qan (not the Gur Qan of Kara Khitai), took refuge there after Toghril and Yisügei defeated him. There may have also been some clan relationship between the Kerait Tübe'en and the Tangut T'o-pa clans.

19 Ruth Dunnell, 'The Hsi Hsia', pp. 154–214, in *The Cambridge History of China vol. 6: Alien Regimes and Border States, 907–1368*, edited by Herbert Franke and Denis Twitchett (Cambridge: Cambridge University Press, 1994), p. 164. It is not clear whether or not he had actually found refuge in Xi-Xia or simply attempted to establish himself there. In any case, he then moved into Northeastern Tibet before being driven into the Tarim Basin.

20 Martin, *The Rise of Chingis Khan*, p. 112.

21 SHM-R (chapter 11), p. 84; SHM-C, pp. 185–6, SHM-O, pp. 236–7; MNT, pp. 221–2. Also see RD/Musavi, p. 572; RD/Karimi, p. 427; RD/Thackston, vol. 2, pp. 289–90, Martin, *The Rise of Chingis Khan*, p. 119. Martin sees the Tangut as vassals, whereas the SHM states that the Tangut king actually submitted and offered to serve as the right wing of the Mongol forces. The treaty that resulted from the negotiations stipulated that Chinggis Khan would receive Chaqa, a daughter of Li An-Chuan, and tribute of camels, woolen cloth, and falcons, and that the Tangut would be vassals of Chinggis Khan and contribute troops.

22 Paul D. Buell, *Tribe, Qan, and Ulus in Early Mongol China, Some Prolegomena to Yüan History, Dissertation* (The University of Washington, 1977), p. 47. H. Desmond Martin, *The Rise of Chingis Khan and his Conquest of North China* (Baltimore: The Johns Hopkins Press, 1950), pp. 101, 149; Thomas Allsen, 'The Rise of the Mongolian Empire and Mongolian rule in North China', pp. 321–413, in *The Cambridge History of China vol. 6: Alien Regimes and Border States, 907–1368*, edited by Herbert Franke and Denis Twitchett (Cambridge: Cambridge University Press, 1994), pp. 348–9. The Önggüd tribes switched their loyalty to the Mongols. It is unclear if the Jüyin also sought Mongol protection. Thomas Allsen describes the Jüyins as an 'ethnically mixed people inhabiting the sensitive Jin-Tangut-Önggüd border regions, who frequently served the Jin as military auxillaries'.

23 SHM, pp. 177–8; He Quiutao, *Sheng Wu Qin Zheng Lu*, edited by Asaraltu (Qayilar: Obor Monggol-un Soyul-un Keblel-un Qoriy-a, 1985), p. 45. Chinggis Khan agreed to peace and accepted the Jin princess Gungju as a wife, while the Jin Emperor sent gold, silver, satin, and other goods.

24 Nasawi, pp. 44–5; Nasawi/Houdas, pp. 19–20.

25 Serge A. Zenkovsky, ed., *Medieval Russia's Epics, Chronicles, and Tales* (New York: Meridian, 1974), p. 193.

26 IWR, p. 286; Rubruck/Dawson, p. 184; Rubruck/Jackson, p. 222.

27 Dhahabi, pp. 266–7; Grigor, pp. 333–5; Juzjani/Habibi, vol. 2, p. 708; Juzjani/Raverty, pp. 1252–3. Grigor of Akanc wrote that before the execution, Hülegü berated the Caliph for having hoarded his wealth rather than spending it on the defence of Baghdad.

28 Juvaini/Boyle, p. 607; Juvaini/Qazvini, vol.3, p. 90.

29 Huang K'uan-chung, 'Mountain Fortress Defence: The Experience of the Southern Sung and Korea in Resisting the Mongol Invasions', in *Warfare in Chinese History*, edited by Hans Van de Ven, Sinica Leidensia Series, vol. 47 (Leiden: Brill, 2000), p. 237; Rossabi, *Khubilai Khan*, p. 45.

30 RD/Musavi, pp. 851–2 ; RD/Karimi, pp. 602–3; RD/Thackston, vol. 2, p. 415.

31 RD/Musavi, pp. 851–2; RD/Karimi, pp. 602–3; RD/Thackston, vol. 2, p. 415.

32 K'uan-chung, 'Mountain Fortress Defence', p. 238.

33 RD/Musavi, p. 853; RD/Karimi, p. 604; RD/Thackston, vol. 2, p. 416.

Chapter Two

1 Thomas T. Allsen, *Mongol Imperialism* (Berkeley: University of California Press, 1987), pp. 198, 201, 204. The Jochid Ulus ranged from the Carpathian Mountains bordering Hungary in the west to modern Kazakhstan in the east, encompassing virtually all of the territory in between. It was the part of the Mongol lands bequeathed to Jochi, the eldest son of Chinggis Khan. Twenty-seven of the forty-three were positioned in the portion east of the Rus' principalities and west of the Volga. Sixteen *tümet* were situated in the western part of the Jochid Ulus. An additional, but unknown, number of *tümet* also existed in the portion of the Jochid Ulus ruled by Orda, east of the Volga River.

2 The Chaghatayid Ulus was the territory given to Chaghatayid, the second son of Chinggis Khan. It consisted roughly of the former Soviet Central Asian republics, sharing some of this territory with the Jochid Ulus. Also it extended into modern China's Xinjiang Autonomous Region, and took in most of Afghanistan.

3 John Masson Smith Jr, 'Mongol Society and Military in the Middle East: Antecedents and Adaptations', in *War and Society in the Eastern Mediterranean, 7th and 15th Centuries*, edited by Yaacov Lev (Leiden: Brill, 1996), p. 249; Valery Alexeev, 'Some Aspects of the Study of Productive Forces in the Empire of Chenghiz Khan', in *The Rulers From the Steppe: State Formation on the Eurasian Periphery*, edited by Gary Seaman and Daniel Marks (Los Angeles: University of Southern California Press, 1991), pp. 189–90.

4 SHM, 25–6. This figure did not include the Forest People. Considering the source, these may be the only credible figures we have for the initial Mongol troop strength. The author of *The Secret History of the Mongols* had no reason to inflate them as a chronicler of an invaded country would.

5 YS chapter 98, p. 75.

6 YS chapter 98, pp. 73, 75; Ch'i-ch'ing Hsiao, *The Military Establishment*, pp. 17–18.

7 Zhao Hong, *Meng-Da Bei-Lu: Polnoe Opisanie Mongolo-Tatar*, translated by Nikolai Ts. Munkuev (Moscow: Academy of Sciences [Nauka], 1975), p. 67.

8 Marco Polo, *The Travels of Marco Polo*, vol. 1, edited by Henri Cordier, translated by Henry Yule (New York: Dover Publications, 1993), pp. 260–1; Juvani/Boyle, p. 30; Juvaini/Qazvini, p. 22.

9 Grigor of Akanc, 'The History of the Nation of the Archers by Grigor of Akanc', edited and translated by R.P. Blake and R.N. Frye, *Harvard Journal of Asiatic Studies* 12 (1949), p. 325; YS chapter 98, p. 74.

10 YS chapter 98, p. 74.

11 YS chapter 98, p. 75.

12 Hsiao, *The Military Establishment*, p. 18.

13 Ch'en Yuan, *Western and Central Asians in China under the Mongols: Their Transformation into Chinese*, translated by Ch'ien Hsing-hai and L. Carrington Goodrich, Monumenta Serica Monograph 15 (Los Angeles: University of California Press, 1966), p. 73.

14 William of Rubruck, 'The Journey of William of Rubruck', in *The Mongol Mission: Narratives and Letters of the Franciscan Missionaries in Mongolia and China in the Thirteenth and Fourteenth Centuries*, edited by Christopher Dawson, translated by a nun of Stanbrook Abbey (London: Sheed and Ward, 1955), pp. 101–2; William of Rubruck, *The Mission of Friar William of Rubruck: His Journey to the Court of the Great Khan Mongke, 1253–1255*, translated by Peter Jackson, edited by Peter Jackson and David Morgan, Works Issued by the Hakluyt Society, 2nd Series, vol. 173 (London: The Hakluyt Society, 1990), p. 88; Guillelmus de Rubruc, 'Itinerarium Willelmi de Rubruc' in *Sinica Franciscana: Itinera et Relationes Fratrum Minorum Saeculi XIII et XIV*, edited by P. Anastasius Van Den Wyngaert, *Sinica Franciscana*, vol. 1 (Firenze: Apud Collegium S. Bonaventurae, 1929), pp. 183–4.

15 YM, pp. 64–5; JPC/Dawson, p. 26.

16 Hsiao, *The Military Establishment*, p. 10; Isenbike Togan, *Flexibility and Limitation in Steppe Formations: The Kerait Khanate and Chinggis Khan*, The Ottoman Empire and Its Heritage Series, edited by Suraiya Faroqhi and Halil Inalcik, vol. 15 (Leiden: Brill, 1998), pp. 132–6. Isenbike Togan provides a lucid explanation of the formation of tribal units from segments of other tribes.

17 Juvaini/Qazvini, vol. 1, p. 24; Juvaini/Boyle, p. 32.
18 Polo, vol. 1, p. 261; Juvaini/Boyle, p. 31. Juvaini noted this as well. The higher-ranking officer passed orders to his immediate subordinates and they in turn did the same.
19 SHM, pp. 160–1.
20 SHM, pp. 152–4.
21 SHM, pp. 152–3. Assuming that every commander sent a son, then the maximum amount of recruits for the *keshik* greatly exceeded the size of a full-strength *tümen* with a sum of 55,290 men, not including any recruits from the commoners. The sons of the *minqan-u noyad* would result in 95 *aqa* (elder brothers), 95 *degü* (younger brothers), and 950 companions. The sons of the *jaqun-u noyad* would produce 950 *aqa* and 950 *degü* along with 4,750 companions. Finally the *arban-u noyad* would contribute 9,500 *aqa*, 9,500 *degü* and 28,500 companions. If only the *aqa* came, then Chinggis Khan would have acquired 10,545 men.
22 Allsen, *Mongol Imperialism*, pp. 73–4.
23 SHM, p. 161.
24 SHM, pp. 161–2. After Boroghul died, another member of the Besüd tribe replaced him.
25 SHM, pp. 161–2.
26 Paul D. Buell, 'Kalmyk Tanggaci People: Thoughts on the Mechanics and impact of Mongol Expansion', *Mongolian Studies* 6 (1980), p. 45. For more on the *tamma* see also Jean Aubin, 'L'Ethogenese Des Qaraunas', *Turcica* 1 (1969), pp. 74–5; Donald Ostrowski, 'The *tamma* and the dual-administrative structure of the Mongol Empire', *Bulletin of the School of Oriental and African Studies* 61 (1998), 264.
27 Paul D. Buell, *Tribe, Qan, and Ulus in Early Mongol China, Some Prolegomena to Yüan History*, PhD dissertation (The University of Washington, 1977), p. 70; YS chapter 98, p. 73; Grigor, p. 333; Ostrowski, p. 264.
28 YS chapter 98, p. 73.
29 YS chapter 98, p. 74.
30 Li Chih-Ch'ang, *The Travels of an Alchemist: The Journey of the Taoist, Ch'ang-Ch'un, from China to the Hindukush at the Summons of Chingiz Khan, Recorded by His Disciple, Li Chih-Ch'ang*, edited by Arthur Waley (London: G. Routledge & Sons, 1963), p. 85. Chaghatai had a road constructed near the Sairam Lake during the Khwarazm war. It went through a defile with 48 bridges wide enough for two carts. It is unclear whether the road was actually paved or just a route cleared of obstructions.
31 Buell, *Tribe, Qan, and Ulus*, pp. 73–4; Allsen, *Mongol Imperialism*, pp. 192–3.
32 Buell, *Tribe, Qan, and Ulus*, pp. 74–6.
33 Hsiao, *The Military Establishment*, pp. 12–13.
34 Allsen, *Mongol Imperialism*, p. 195.
35 YS chapter 98, p. 74. Other units were the *Kao-li chün* or Korean army; the *Ts'un-po chün* or Yunnan army; the *She Chün* or Fuchien army; and the *Xin-fu-chün* or 'newly adhered army' comprising Sung troops.

Chapter Three

1 RD/Thackston, vol. 2, p. 297; RD/Karimi, p. 437; RD/Musavi, p. 585. For more information on the *ortaqs* or merchants please refer to Thomas T. Allsen, 'Mongolian Princes and Their Merchant Partners, 1200–1260', *Asia Major* 2 (1989), pp. 83–126;

Elizabeth Endicott-West, 'Merchant Associations in Yüan China: The Ortogh', *Asia Major* 2 (1989), pp. 127–54.

2 Ssu-ma Chien, *Records of the Grand Historian*, vol. 2, translated by Burton Watson (New York: Columbia University Press, 1961), p. 153.

3 YM, pp. 49–50; JPC/Dawson, p. 18.

4 Zhao Hong, *Meng-Da Bei-Lu: Polnoe Opisanie Mongolo-Tatar*, translated by Nikolai Ts. Munkuev (Moscow: Academy of Sciences [Nauka], 1975), pp. 65–6.

5 J.D. Latham and W.F. Paterson, *Saracen Archery: An English Version and Exposition of a Mameluke Work on Archery* (London: The Holland Press, 1970), p. xxv.

6 R.P. Blake and R.N Frye, 'The History of the Nation of the Archers by Grigor of Akanc', *Harvard Journal of Asiatic Studies* 12 (1949), pp. 269–399.

7 One performed the 'Parthian shot' by riding away from the intended target while twisting one's torso round towards the target and firing. Although this technique was performed by all horse-archers from the steppe, its devastating use against the Roman armies of Crassus at Carrhae in 53BC by the horse-archers of the Parthian empire appears to be the origin of the term.

8 J.D. Latham, 'Notes on Mamluk Horse-Archers', *Bulletin of the School of Oriental and African Studies* 32 (1969), pp. 258, 261. *Qabaq* is a Turkic word meaning 'gourd'.

9 'Old Songs of Arrows', *Mongolia Today* 7 (2002), http://www.mongoliatoday.com/issue/7/archery.html.

10 *History of Chinese Society: Liao (907–1125)*, translated and edited by Karl A. Wittfogel and Feng Chia-Sheng (Philadelphia: The American Philosophical Society, 1949), p. 533.

11 '*Liao Shih*' in Wittfogel and Feng, *History of Chinese Society: Liao (907–1125)*, p. 567. During these, not only did the ethnic Khitans conduct military drills, but the Chinese soldiers in their armies also practised with catapults, crossbows, swords and spears.

12 Herbert Franke, 'Chinese Texts on the Jurchen (1) A Translation of the Jurchen Monograph in the San-Ch'ao Pei-Meng Hui-Pien', *Zentralasiatische Studien* 9 (1975), p. 180.

13 Maurikos, *Maurice's Strategikon: Handbook of Byzantine Military Strategy*, translated by George T. Dennis (Philadelphia: University of Pennsylvania Press, 1984), p. 62. A *moira* consisted of three or more *tagmas*, which were units of 200 to 400 horsemen.

14 Ronald S. Love, ' "All the King's Horsemen": The Equestrian Army of Henri IV, 1585–1598', *Sixteenth Century Journal* 22, no. 3 (1991), p. 519.

15 John Masson Smith Jr has written two articles that deal with this issue as well as other issues concerning Mongol military, which will be discussed elsewhere at length: 'Ayn Jalut: Mamluk Success or Mongol Failure?' *Harvard Journal of Asiatic Studies* 44 (1984), pp. 307–45; and 'Mongol Society and Military in the Middle East: Antecedents and Adaptations', *War and Society in the Eastern Mediterranean, 7th and 15th Centuries*, edited by Yaacov Lev, in The Medieval Mediterranean Peoples, Economies, and Cultures, 400–1453, vol. 9 (Leiden: Brill, 1996).

16 Smith, 'Mongol Society', p. 256.

17 Juvaini/Boyle, pp. 27–8; Juvaini/Qazvini, pp. 19–20. The *nerge* is also referred to as the *jerge* in the Mongolian and Muslim sources. The primary meaning of *nerge* appears to be rank, row, or perhaps even a military column.

18 Wittfogel and Feng, *History of Chinese Society: Liao (907–1125)* (Philadelphia: The American Philosophical Society, 1949), pp. 119, 126–9, 565. The importance of the hunt in military training was so great that Chinese inhabitants of the empire were forbidden to hunt. See Wittfogel and Feng, p. 568.

19 *Umar Ibn Ibrahim al-Ansi al-Ansari, Tafrij al-Kurub fi Tadbir al-hurub* (Cairo: American University at Cairo Press, 1961), p. 103.

20 SHM, p. 76.

21 Juzjani/Raverty, pp. 952–3; Juzjani, p. 117. Juzjani, of course, was not present. Furthermore, considering that he wrote his chronicle from the safety of Delhi, one must question how accurate this statement is. Nevertheless, it does demonstrate that outsiders or non-Mongols recognized that the discipline of the Mongols, and the expectations of their leaders, were quite high. This anecdote is similarly told about Motun, a Xiong-nu prince who directed his bodyguard to shoot whoever he singled out, without hesitation. He first pointed at his favorite horse and then his wife. Those who failed to carry out the order were executed. After he felt confident in their obedience and discipline, he eventually pointed out his father, Tumen, the *Shan-yü* or ruler of the Xiong-nu. Without hesitation, Motun's bodyguard fired, killing the old Khan and thus effectively raising Motun to the throne. Refer to E.H. Parker, *A Thousand Years of the Tartars* (New York: Dorset Press, 1987), p. 9, and Ying-Shih Yü, 'The Xiong-nu', pp. 118–50, *The Cambridge History of Early Inner Asia*, edited by Denis Sinor (Cambridge: Cambridge University Press, 1990), p. 120.

22 SHM, p. 127.

23 JPC/Dawson, p. 17; YM, p. 49.

24 YM, p. 77; JPC/Dawson, p. 33.

25 Valery Alexeev, 'Some Aspects of the Study of Productive Forces in the Empire of Chenghiz Khan', pp. 186–7, in *The Rulers From the Steppe: State Formation on the Eurasian Periphery*, edited by Gary Seaman and Daniel Marks (Los Angeles: University of Southern California Press, 1991), p. 194.

26 The ideology of world conquest will be discussed in the conclusion of chapter 6.

27 Marco Polo, *The Travels of Marco Polo*, vol. 1, edited by Henri Cordier, translated by Henry Yule (New York: Dover Publications, 1993), pp. 260–1.

28 Liao Shih, pp. 559–60. Michal Biran, ' "Like a Mighty Wall": The Armies of the Kara Khitai (1124–1218)', *Jerusalem Studies in Arabic and Islam*, 25 (2001), p. 64. Michal Biran, in her study of the Kara Khitai, thought it was doubtful if that kingdom actually fulfilled these standards, as the warriors purchased their own equipment. However, there were several mines in that region (see p. 65). The Tangut, neighbors of the Kara Khitai Empire, and an enemy then ally and later subject kingdom of Chinggis Khan, produced high quality weapons. The Tangut themselves tended to use swords, bows, lances, and daggers, as well as catapults during sieges.

29 YM, pp. 76–7; JPC/Dawson, pp. 32–3.

30 Smith, 'Ayn Jalut', pp. 313–15. See also Smith, 'Mongol Society', pp. 249–50; and Reuven Amitai, 'Whither the Ilkhanid Army? Ghazan's First Campaign into Syria (1299–1300)', in *Warfare in Inner Asian History, 500–1800*, edited by Nicola Di Cosmo, *Handbook of Oriental Studies, Section 8: Central Asia*, vol. 6 (Leiden: Brill, 2002), p. 255. Amitai essentially agrees with Smith, and wrote that even as late as 1300 the Mongols

were poorly equipped, but slowly began to use more equipment made by professionals. Amitai wrote that there is nothing in the sources, either literary or archaeological, to indicate that the Mongols used professional artisans to make weapons. See also J.F. Verbruggen, *The Art of Warfare in Western Europe During the Middle Ages From the Eighth Century to 1340*, 2nd edition, translated by Colonel Sumner Willard and R.W. Southern (Rochester, NY: Boydell Press, 1997), p. 202. He wrote: 'Man for man, the Mongols were poorer and less well armed than most of their enemies, but huge numbers could be gathered – the thrust west involved 150,000 men. Each unit was so co-ordinated by a system of signals, and selected archers could change the direction of fire by using whistling arrows.'

31 Hok-lam Chan, 'Siting by Bowshot: A Mongolian Custom and Its Sociopolitical and Cultural Implications', *Asia Major* 4 (1991), pp. 53–78.

32 Ralph Payne-Gallwey, *The Projectile-Throwing Engines of the Ancients and Turkish and Other Oriental Bows* (Totowa, NJ: Rowman and Littlefield, 1973), p. 12.

33 Latham and Paterson, p. xxv.

34 Latham and Paterson, pp. xxvii–xxix. The force caused by this can be five times greater than the pull weight of the bow at full draw, as the momentary thrust on the string checks the movement of the arms of the bow. But how far did the maximum killing range extend? Killing range is defined as the range of the bow in which an arrow still carried enough force to kill someone. This can be calculated as $K = (M = vw)$. See Charles R. Bowlus, 'Tactical and Strategic Weaknesses of Horse-archers on the Eve of the First Crusade', pp. 149–166, *Autour de la Premiere Croisade*, edited by Michel Balard (Paris: Publications de la Sorbonne, 1996), p. 161.

35 SHM-R (1972), p. 157. During the raid that Temüjin, Ong-Qan, and Jamuqa conducted against the Merkit, Temüjin's half-brother Belgütei shot bone-tipped arrows. Carpini indicated that: 'They also have other arrows for shooting birds and animals and unarmed men; these are three digits wide; in addition they have various other kinds of arrows for shooting birds and animals'. JPC/Dawson, p. 35; YM, p. 80. For the archaeological evidence, refer to Yu. C. Khudyakov, *Vooruzheniye Tsentral'no-Aziatskikh Kochyevnikov v Epokhu Rannyego i Razvitogo Spegnyevekov'ya* (Novosibirsk: Academy of Sciences, 1991), p. 64. The Mongols used seven types of metal arrowheads, their cross-sections being: 1) triangular or Y shaped with three edges, found in two forms; 2) a narrow ellipse, with a variety of points totaling eighteen different styles; 3) oval shaped; 4) triangular, like a pyramid; 5) rhombus shaped like a diamond, found in three styles (one resembles a chisel while the others come to a point); 6) diamond shaped, but different from the rhombus shaped variety (one arrow head possesses a point, the remainder are chisel tipped); and 7) rectangular, with two styles, like chisels; Khudyakov, pp. 118–19. Khudyakov (p.122) has also cataloged five varieties of bone tips: 1) a round cone; 2) triangular, in five forms and shapes; 3) elliptical, found in two varieties; 4) six-sided; and 5) trapezoid.

36 Owen Lattimore, *Nomads and Commissars* (New York: Oxford University Press, 1962), p. 22.

37 SHM, p. 159; Khudyakov, pp. 126–7. The materials for manufacture tended to be ubiquitous. In addition to the manufacture of quivers, birch bark was commonly used

not only in quiver construction but also as a writing material, for which purpose it continued to be used into the early modern period.

38 R.W. Reid, 'Mongolian weaponry in the Secret History', *Mongolian Studies* 15 (1992), p. 88.

39 Bowlus, p. 161.

40 YM, p. 79; JPC/Dawson, p. 34; Zhao Hong, p. 78. See A. Rahman Zaky, 'Introduction to the Study of Islamic Arms and Armour', *Gladius* 1 (1961), p. 17. Zaky wrote that most of the swords in the Middle East tended to be double-edged straight blades, with curved sabres becoming more common around 1500; nevertheless, they did appear more frequently in some Islamic regions during the thirteenth century as a result of the Mongol conquests.

41 Denis Sinor, 'The Inner Asian Warriors', *Journal of the American Oriental Society* 101, no. 2 (1981), p. 142.

42 YM, pp. 77–8; JPC/Dawson, p. 33.

43 David Nicolle, *Medieval Warfare Source Book: Warfare in Western Christendom* (London: Arms and Armour, 1995), p. 136.

44 YM, pp. 78–9, 80; JPC/Dawson, pp. 34–5; David Nicolle, *Arms and Armour of the Crusading Era, 1050–1350*, vol. 1 (White Plains, NY: Kraus International Publications, 1988), p. 18; H. Russell Robinson, *Oriental Armour* (New York: Walker and Co, 1967), p. 7.

45 IWR, p. 182; Rubruck/Jackson, p. 88; Rubruck/Dawson, p. 102. Rubruck also noted that the *degel* of the Mongols differed from similar garments worn by the various Turkic tribes: 'Tartars differ from the Turks, for the Turks tie their tunics on the left, but the Tartars always on the right.'

46 YM, p. 79; JPC/Dawson, p. 34. According to John de Plano Carpini: 'The upper part of the helmet is of iron or steel, but the part affording protection to the neck and throat is of leather.' David Nicolle, *Medieval Warfare Source Book*, p. 196.

47 Zhao Hong, pp. 68–9. It is doubtful if the typical Mongol possessed herds numbering hundreds and thousands, although the nobility certainly did.

48 Juzjani/Raverty, p. 968; Juzjani, p. 128; Zhao Hong, p. 69. Zhao Hong simply indicated that the Mongols took several remounts in order to not wear out their horses. The Mongols rode a different horse every day. Bowlus, p. 161.

49 R.H.C. Davis, *The Medieval Warhorse: Origin, Development, and Redevelopment* (London: Thames and Hudson, 1989), p. 18. Indeed, the warhorse was part of the knight's weaponry as it was expected to kick and bite. The mares were usually kept to stud and used only for women and priests. Unlike the Mongols, Europeans did not use geldings at all in warfare. Zhao Hong noted that the Mongols specifically taught their horses not to bite and kick. Zhao Hong, pp. 68–9.

50 Polo, vol. 1, p. 260.

51 Zhao Hong, pp. 68–9.

52 Smith, 'Ayn Jalut', p. 336.

53 Zhao Hong, pp. 68–9; Polo, vol. 1, p. 260.

54 Juvaini/Qazvini, vol. 3, pp. 97–8; Juvaini/Boyle, p. 612.

55 Bar Hebraeus, pp. 424–5; Juvaini/Boyle, pp. 608–9; Juvaini/Qazvini, p. 93; Claude Cahen, *Pre-Ottoman Turkey*, translated by J. Jones-Williams (New York: Taplinger

Publishing, 1968), p. 275. One such instance occurred in 1256 when Hülegü came to winter in the Mughan plain. Baiju, the chief *noyan* in the Middle East prior to the arrival of Hülegü, was forced to move his camp from the strategically located Mughan plain to pastures in Rum.

56 Polo, vol. 1, p. 262.

57 YM, pp. 50–1; JPC/Dawson, p. 18; Meserve, *Historical Perspective*, p. 32.

58 Ruth Meserve, *An Historical Perspective of Mongol Horse Training, Care and Management: Selected Texts*, PhD dissertation (Department of Uralic and Altaic Studies, Indiana University, 1987), p. 32; B. Bold, *Mongolian Nomadic Society: A Reconstruction of the 'Medieval' History of Mongolia* (New York: St Martin's Press, 2001), p. 38.

59 Zhao Hong, pp. 68–9.

60 Zhao Hong, p. 78, YM, pp. 50–1; JPC/Dawson, p. 18; Meserve, *Historical Perspectives*, p. 34.

Chapter Four

1 Donald W. Engels, *Alexander the Great and the Logistics of the Macedonian Army* (Berkeley: University of California Press, 1978), p. 123.

2 Juzjani, p. 128; Juzjani/Raverty, pp. 273, 968.

3 Martin, *The Rise of Chingis Khan*, p. 28.

4 Engels, pp. 40–1.

5 YM, pp. 47–8; JPC/Dawson, p. 16.

6 IWR, pp. 175–7; Rubruck/Dawson, pp. 96–8; Rubruck/Jackson, pp. 76–9. *Airagh* is the proper Mongolian term for *kumiss*, which is a Turkic term.

7 John Masson Smith Jr, 'Mongol Campaign Rations: Milk, Marmots, and Blood?' *Journal of Turkish Studies* 8 (1984), p. 225.

8 Zhao Hong, pp. 68–9.

9 Polo, vol. 1, p. 262; IWR, p. 179; Rubruck/Jackson, pp. 82–3; Rubruck/Dawson, p. 99.

10 Smith, 'Mongol Campaign Rations', p. 226.

11 Smith, 'Mongol Campaign Rations', p. 226.

12 JPC/Dawson, p. 17; YM, pp. 48–9.

13 IWR, pp. 176–7; Rubruck/Jackson, pp. 79–80; Rubruck/Dawson, pp. 97–8; Smith, 'Mongol Campaign Rations', pp. 226–7.

14 Polo, vol. 1, pp. 261–2.

15 Smith, 'Mongol Campaign Rations', p. 226.

16 Bold, *Mongolian Nomadic Society*, p. 77 (SHM-C, p. 224).

17 Zhao Hong, pp. 69–70.

18 Smith, 'Mongol Campaign Rations', pp. 226–7.

19 Engels, pp. 14–15. See Bold, *Mongolian Nomadic Society*, p. 38.

20 Juvaini/Boyle, p. 30; Juvaini/Qazvini, vol. 1, p. 22.

21 Thomas Allsen, 'The Circulation of Military Technology in the Mongolian Empire', pp. 265–94, *Warfare in Inner Asian History, 500–1800*, edited by Nicola Di Cosmo (*Handbook of Oriental Studies, Section 8: Central Asia*, vol. 6), series editors Denis Sinor and Nicola Di Cosmo (Leiden: Brill, 2002), p. 266; Li Chih-Cha'ng, *The Travels of an Alchemist: The Journey of the Taoist, Ch'ang-Ch'un, from China to the Hindukush at the*

Summons of Chingiz Khan, Recorded by his Disciple, Li Chih-Ch'ang, translated by Arthur Waley (London: G. Routledge & Sons, 1963), p. 72.; Thomas T. Allsen, 'Technician Transfers in the Mongolian Empire', *The Central Eurasian Studies Lectures* 2 (2002), p. 6; Thomas T. Allsen, *Commodity and Exchange in the Mongol Empire: A Cultural History of Islamic Textiles*, Cambridge Studies in Islamic Civilization (Cambridge: Cambridge University Press, 1997), passim. See also Yu. C. Khudyakov, *Vooruzheniye Tsentral'no-Aziatskikh Kochyevnikov v Epokhu Rannyego i razvitogo Spegnyevekov'ya* (Novosibirsk: Academy of Sciences, 1991) for a discussion of the archaeological evidence for Mongol weaponry.

22 Kh. Perlee, 'On Some Place Names in the *Secret History*', translated by L.W. Moses. *Mongolian Studies* 9 (1985–6), pp. 83–102; Idem, 'Xyatan Nar, Tednii Mongolchuddtei Xolbogdson Ni' ('The Khitan and their relations with the Mongols'), *Studia Historica* vol. 1 no. 1 (Ulaanbaatar, 1959); Idem, 'Mongolyn Tuuxen Nutgiin Zarim Uul, Usyg Survalzhilsan' ('On Studying some Place Names of Historical Sites in Mongolia'), SUAM 3 (1962), pp. 78–82; Idem, 'K Istorii Drevnix Gorodev I Poselenii v Mongolii' ('On the History of Ancient Cities and Settlements in Mongolia'), *Sovetskaya Arxeologiya* 10 (1957), pp. 43–52.

23 Juvaini/Qazvini (1912), pp. 169, 173, 177; Juvaini/Boyle, pp. 212, 216, 220. It may be argued that these examples were to demonstrate Ögödei's generosity and munificence. It should not be denied, however, that Juvaini's demonstrations of generosity served another purpose, which was to legitimize the rule of the Mongols. In doing so, Juvaini highlighted favorable and, most importantly, just traits in his otherwise pagan masters, as it was better to be ruled by a just pagan ruler than a corrupt and self-serving Muslim king.

24 Manfred Ullman, *Islamic Medicine* (Edinburgh: Edinburgh University Press, 1978). This remains one of the most comprehensive books on medieval Islamic medicine.

25 Sophia Kaszuba, 'Wounds in Medieval Mongol Warfare: Their Nature and Treatment in *The Secret History*, with some notes on Mongolian Military Medicine and Hygiene', *Mongolian Studies* 19 (1996), p. 64.

26 Francis W. Cleaves, 'A Medical Practice of the Mongols in the Thirteenth Century', *Harvard Journal of Asiatic Studies* 17 no. 3 (1954), passim. Cleaves does not speculate on why this was done. Instead, he suggests that it would be better for medical doctors to determine this, but does not follow up on it.

27 Carpini, p. 12.

28 Carpini, pp. 16–17.

Chapter Five

1 Juvaini/Boyle, p. 25; Juvaini/Qazvini, pp. 17–18.

2 Frances Dvornik, *Origins of Intelligence Services: The Ancient Near East, Persia, Greece, Rome, Byzantium, the Arab Muslim Empires, the Mongol Empire, China, Muscovy* (New Brunswick, NJ: Rutgers University Press, 1974), pp. 275–6.

3 Dvornik, pp. 274–5.

4 SHM–R (1974), p. 65.

5 Polo, vol. 1, p. 261.

6 YM, pp. 81–2; JPC/Dawson, pp. 36–7; R.C. Smail, *Crusading Warfare, 1097–1193* (Cambridge: Cambridge University Press, 1995), pp. 82–3.

7 Denis Sinor, 'The Inner Asian Warriors', *Journal of the American Oriental Society* 101/2 (1981), p. 140. At the battle of Mohi in 1241, the Mongol barrages were described as being like rain.

8 Dalantai, 'Menggu Singxue Yanjiu', p. 286.

9 David Nicolle, *Medieval Warfare Source Book: Warfare in Western Christendom* (London: Arms and Armour, 1995), p. 187.

10 Juvaini/Boyle, p. 176; Juvaini/Qazvini, vol. 1, pp. 138–9.

11 JPC/Dawson, p. 36; YM, p. 81; Smith, 'Mongol Society', pp. 251–2.

12 Polo, vol. 1, p. 262.

13 John A. Lynn, 'Tactical Evolution in the French Army, 1560–1660', *French Historical Studies* 14, no. 2 (1985), p. 182. The ineffectiveness of the *caracole* contrasts with the rolling charge of the Mongols, who could fire more shots and, unlike cavalry in later periods, rarely had to contend with opponents who employed massed fire power. However, as Carpini contended, arming more troops with crossbows would be an effective counter to Mongol attacks. See YM, pp. 96–7; JPC/Dawson, p. 46.

14 SHM, p. 103. The phrasing is '*si'üci qatquldu'a qatqulduya*' or to fight in chisel combat.

15 Dalantai, 'Menggu Singxue Yanjiu', p. 282.

16 IL, pp. 495–7; EL, pp. 98–9; Zenkovsky, pp. 194–5.

17 Polo, vol. 1, p. 262.

18 Dalantai, 'Menggu Singxue Yanjiu', pp. 281–2.

19 Martin, *The Rise of Chingis Khan*, p. 33.

20 Dalantai, 'Menggu Singxue Yanjiu,' p. 286.

21 RD/Thackston, vol. 2, p. 327. Although *nerge* is the term typically used, some manuscripts use *järge*.

22 YM, pp. 81–2; JPC/Dawson, p. 36.

23 Zhao Hong, p. 67; Nasawi, pp. 117–18; Nasawi/Houdas, p. 91. This practice was carried out at Nishapur and in numerous places in the Jin Empire.

24 Nasawi, pp. 95–6; Nasawi/Houdas, p. 68. Translation mine. Ilal was a citadel in Mazandaran where Turkhan Khatun, the mother of Muhammad, Khwarazmshah, took refuge during the Mongol invasion of the Khwarazmian Empire. Carpini confirms this procedure: see YM, pp. 83–4; JPC/Dawson, p. 37.

25 YM, pp. 83–4; JPC/Dawson, pp. 37–8. According to Carpini, 'they even take the fat of the people they kill and, melting it, throw it on to the house, and wherever the fire falls on this fat it is almost inextinguishable.'

26 YM, pp. 83–4; JPC/Dawson, pp. 37–8. It is interesting that Carpini notes this, indicating that he observed much and asked many questions about previous actions by the Mongols.

27 Nasawi, pp. 113–14; Nasawi/Houdas, p. 87.

28 John Masson Smith Jr, 'Demographic Considerations in Mongol Siege Warfare', *Archivum Ottomanicum* 13 (1993–4), p. 333.

29 Zenkovsky NC, vol. 2, pp. 311–12.

30 Thomas Barfield, *The Perilous Frontier: Nomadic Empires and China, 221 BC to AD 1757, Studies in Social Discontinuity* (Oxford: Blackwell, 1989), p. 203.

31 Martin, *The Rise of Chingis Khan*, p. 28.

32 SHM-C, p. 121. *The Secret History of the Mongols* indicates that their campfires became more numerous than the stars in the sky.

33 Juvaini/Qazvini, vol. 2, p. 137; Juvaini/Boyle, p. 406; YM, pp. 81–2; JPC/Dawson, pp. 36–7.

34 Dalantai, 'Menggu Singxue Yanjiu', p. 283.

35 Dalantai, 'Menggu Singxue Yanjiu', p. 287. Dalantai may be referring to the *qara'ana* formations in which Chinggis Khan's army marched against the Naiman in 1204. See SHM-C, p. 124, footnote 49. If this is true, then Francis W. Cleaves' analysis is the opposite of Dalantai's, in that Cleaves views the *qara'ana* formation as its namesake: a thorny shrub that grows in thick clumps. Thus, in his opinion, the Mongols marched in compact formations. However, Cleaves believes that in 'lake' formations the Mongols would spread out over a wide front.

36 *Geoffroi de Villehardouin and Jean Joinville, Chronicles of the Crusades*, edited and translated by Margaret R.B. Shaw (Baltimore: Penguin Books, 1983), pp. 286–7.

37 Bar Hebraeus, p. 397; RD/Karimi, pp. 457–8; RD/Musavi, pp. 638–9; RD/Boyle, p. 36. Rashid al-Din noted that the Mongols carried raincoats and felt coats in their saddles to combat the cold and the rain.

38 RD/Boyle, pp. 36–7; RD/Karimi, pp. 457–8; RD/Musavi, pp. 638–9.

39 RD/Karimi, pp. 457–8; RD/Musavi, pp. 638–9; RD/Boyle, pp. 36–7.

40 D. Sinor, 'On Mongol Strategy', p. 240.

41 SHM-R (1972), p. 155; Thomas T. Allsen, 'Prelude to the Western Campaigns: Mongol Military Operations in the Volga-Ural Region, 1217–1237', *Archivum Eurasiae Medii Aevi* 3 (1983), p. 10. See also Martin, 'The Mongol Army', *Journal of the Royal Asiatic Society* (1943), p. 75. During the operation in which a combined force led by Toghril Ong-Qan, Temüjin, and Jamuqa attacked the Merkit who had kidnapped Börte, the wife of Temüjin, Temüjin did not pursue the leaders. Instead, as the combined army had surprised the Merkits, victory was swift, and the Merkits dispersed. Rather than pursuing them further, he took satisfaction in his victory and the retrieval of his wife. As a consequence, the Merkits remained a nuisance until they were finally annihilated in 1209.

Chapter Six

1 V.V. Bartold, *Turkestan Down to the Mongol Invasion*, 4th edition (Philadelphia: Porcupine Press Inc and E.J.W. Gibb Memorial Trust, 1977), p. 355; Thomas T. Allsen, 'Guard and Government in the Reign of the Grand Qan Mongke, 1251–1259', *Harvard Journal of Asiatic Studies* 46, no. 2 (1986), p. 517.

2 SHM-R (1972), pp. 159–63.

3 SHM-O, p. 87; SHM-R (1972), p. 154; SHM-C, pp. 43–4. Translation from SHM-R (1972), p. 154.

4 The *yisün örlüg* consisted of Muqali, Bo'orchu, Boroghul, Chila'un, Jebe, Qubilai, Jelme, Sübedei, and Shiqi Qutuqtu.

5 YM, p. 68; JPC/Dawson, p. 27; Polo, vol. 1, p. 261.

6 JPC/Dawson, p. 27; YM, pp. 64–5.

7 Rashiduddin Fazlullah, *Jami'u't-tawarikh: Compendium of Chronicles*, vol. 2, translated by W.M. Thackston, Sources of Oriental Languages and Literatures, vol. 45 (Cambridge,

Harvard University: Department of Near Eastern Languages and Civilizations, 1998), p. 299; Rashid al-Din, *Jami' al-tawarikh*, edited by B. Karimi (Teheran: Iqbal, 1983), p. 440; Rashid al-Din, *Jami' al-tawarikh*, edited by Muḥammad Rushn Musṭafi Musavi (Teheran: Nashr al-Buruz, 1995), p. 588.

8 RD/Thackston, vol. 2, p. 295; RD/Karimi, p. 435; RD/Musavi, p. 583.

9 RD/Thackston, vol. 2, p. 296; RD/Karimi, p. 438.

10 Sübedei remains one of the most studied Mongol generals and a number of studies have appeared. The best scholarly treatise is Paul D. Buell, 'Sübötei Ba'atur', in *In the Service of the Khan: Eminent Personalities of the Early Mongol-Yuan Period (1200–1300)*, edited by Igor de Rachewiltz, Hok-lam Chan, Hsiao Ch'i-ch'ing and Peter W. Geier, pp. 13–26 (Wiesbaden: Harrassowitz Verlag, 1993).

11 The most complete study on the career of Chormaqan is Timothy May, *Chormaqan Noyan: The First Mongol Military Governor in the Middle East*, MA thesis, Central Eurasian Studies, Indiana University, 1996.

12 Timothy May, 'A Mongol-Ismaili Alliance? Thoughts on the Mongols and Assassins', *Journal of the Royal Asiatic Society*, 14/3, pp. 1–9.

Chapter Seven

1 Thomas Allsen, 'The Rise of the Mongolian Empire and Mongolian rule in North China', pp. 348–9, in *The Cambridge History of China, vol. 6: Alien Regimes and Border States, 907–1368*, edited by Herbert Franke and Denis Twitchett (Cambridge: Cambridge University Press, 1994).

2 Jing-Shen Tao, *The Jurchen in Twelfth-Century China: A Study in Sinicization* (Seattle: University of Washington Press, 1976), p. 9.

3 Tao, pp. 86–7.

4 Stephen Turnbull, *Genghis Khan and the Mongol Conquests 1190–1400* (Oxford: Osprey Publishing, 2003), p. 33; Kenneth Chase, *Firearms, a Global History to 1700* (New York: Cambridge University Press, 2003), pp. 33–5, 39.

5 David Nicolle, *Arms and Armour of the Crusading Era, 1050–1350* (White Plains, NY: Kraus International Publications, 1988), p. 73.

6 George Vernadsky, *The Mongols and Russia* (New Haven: Yale University Press, 1953), p. 145.

7 Peter Jackson, *The Mongols and the Latin West 1221–1405* (Harlow: Longman, 2005), pp. 61–2.

8 David Ayalon, 'Studies on the Structure of the Mamluk Army I', *Bulletin of the School of Oriental and African Studies* 15 (1953), p. 204.

9 Ayalon, 'Studies on the Structure of the Mamluk Army III', *Bulletin of the School of Oriental and African Studies* 16 (1954), pp. 70–2.

10 Huang K'uan-chung, 'Mountain Fortress Defence: The Experience of the Southern Sung and Korea in resisting the Mongol Invasions', pp. 222–51, in *Warfare in Chinese History*, edited by Hans Van de Ven (Leiden: Brill, 2000), p. 234.

11 K'uan-chung, pp. 222, 238.

12 K'uan-chung, p. 237.

13 Kenneth Chase, pp. 33–5, 39.

14 Morris Rossabi, *Khubilai Khan: His Life and Times* (Berkeley: University of California Press, 1988), p. 43.

15 K'uan-chung, p. 246.

16 Paul D. Buell, *Historical Dictionary of the Mongol World Empire* (Lanham, MD: Scarecrow Press, 2003), p. 201.

Chapter Eight

1 Juzjani/Habibi, vol. 1, p. 366; Juzjani/Raverty, pp. 269–70.

2 Juzjani/Habibi, vol. 2, p. 650; Juzjani/Raverty, 963–5. According to Juzjani, Muhammad wanted to conquer China, and the envoys were sent to gather military intelligence.

3 Juzjani/Habibi, vol. 2, pp. 650–1; Juzjani/Raverty, p. 966.

4 SNB, p. 71; Juvaini/Boyle, pp. 79–81; Juvaini/Qazvini, vol. 1, p. 61.

5 Juzjani/Habibi, vol. 1, p. 367; vol. 2, pp. 751–2; Juzjani/Raverty, pp. 273, 968–9.

6 SNB, vol. 3, p. 70.

7 Juvaini/Boyle, pp. 376–7; Juvaini/Qazvini, vol. 1, pp. 106–8.

8 Nasawi, pp. 89–90; Nasawi/Houdas, pp. 62–3.

9 RD/Karimi, pp. 353, 430–1; RD/Thackston, vol. 2, pp. 241, 291; SWQZL, p. 51.

10 Juzjani/Habibi, pp. 367–8, 652–3; Juzjani/Raverty, pp. 273–4, 969–71; Nasawi, p. 91; Nasawi/Houdas, p. 63.

11 Nasawi, pp. 92–3; Nasawi/Houdas, pp. 64–5.

12 Juzjani/Habibi, vol. 2, p. 653; Juzjani/Raverty, pp. 979–80; Juvaini/Qazvini, vol. 1, p. 92; Juvaini/Boyle, p. 118.

13 RD/Karimi, pp. 363–4; RD/Thackston, vol. 2, pp. 248–9; Bar Hebraeus, p. 381; Juvaini/Qazvini, vol. 1, p. 94; Juvaini/Boyle, p. 120. The sources are inconclusive on the length of the siege. Some put it at five days, others at ten days.

14 Bar Hebraeus, p. 381; RD/Karimi, pp. 362–3; RD/Thackston, vol. 2, pp. 248–9; Juzjani/Habibi, pp. 368, 653; Juzjani/Raverty, pp. 274, 979–80; Li Chih-Ch'ang's *The Travels of the Alchemist*, edited by Arthur Waley, p. 93.

15 RD/Karimi, p. 364; RD/Thackston, vol. 2, pp. 248–9; Juvaini/Qazvini, vol. 1, pp. 94–7; Juvaini/Boyle, pp. 120–2.

16 Juvaini/Qazvini, vol. 1, pp. 101–2; Juvaini/Boyle, pp. 128–9; Juzjani/Raverty, p. 1005; RD/Karimi, pp. 374–5; RD/Thackston, vol. 2, p. 255; SWZQL, p. 51.

17 Juvaini/Qazvini, vol. 1, pp. 67–8; Juvaini/Boyle, pp. 86–8, 124; RD/Karimi, pp. 354–6; RD/Thackston, vol. 2, pp. 242–3; SWQZL, p. 51.

18 Juvaini/Qazvini, vol. 1, p. 100; Juvaini/Boyle, p. 126, Nasawi, pp. 171–2; Nasawi/Houdas, pp. 154–5; Juzjani/Habibi, pp. 370, 678–9; Juzjani/Raverty, pp. 281, 1097–1100; Al-Athir, p. 394; RD/Karimi, pp. 371–4; RD/Thackston, vol. 2, pp. 253–5.

19 RD/Karimi, pp. 371–4; RD/Thackston, vol. 2, pp. 253–5; Juvaini/Qazvini, vol. 1, p. 100; Juvaini/Boyle, p. 126; Nasawi, pp. 170–1; Nasawi/Houdas, p. 154.

20 Juzjani/Habibi, vol. 2, pp. 370, 653–4; Juzjani/Raverty, pp. 279, 992; Al-Athir, p. 370; Nasawi, pp. 106–7; Nasawi/Houdas, pp. 79–80; Dhahabi/Negre, pp. 208–9.

21 Juvaini/Qazvini, vol. 1, pp. 115–16; Juvaini/Boyle, p. 147; Nuwayri, pp. 316–17.

22 Nasawi, p. 113; Nasawi/Houdas, p. 87.

23 Nasawi, pp. 117–18 ; Nasawi/Houdas, pp. 91–2. According to Nasawi, the Mongols quickly built over 200 catapults for the siege, although this number is certainly an exaggeration.

24 Juzjani/Habibi, vol. 2, p. 661; Juzjani/Raverty, pp. 1026–31; Al-Nuwayri, p. 325; Al-Athir, p. 391.

25 Juzjani/Habibi, vol. 2, p. 661; Juzjani/Raverty, pp. 1036–7; Al-Athir, p. 393; SNB, vol. 3, p. 79; SWQZL, pp. 51–2; Nuwayri, pp. 326–7. Approximately 600,000 were killed according to Juzjani, about a quarter of the population. This is rather significant in my mind. Although Juzjani has certainly inflated the number of the dead and the overall population, this is a rare occasion on which he does not accuse the Mongols of slaughtering the entire population of a locale.

26 Juzjani/Habibi, vol. 1, pp. 372–3; Juzjani/Raverty, pp. 287–8; Nuwayri, p. 253; Nasawi, pp. 126–8; Nasawi/Houdas, pp. 102–3, 108; SHM-R (1984), pp. 96–7.

27 Juzjani/Habibi, pp. 372–3, 660; Juzjani/Raverty, pp. 287–8, 1019–21; Juvaini/Qazvini, vol. 1, pp. 105, 137–8; Juvaini/Boyle, pp. 132, 406–7; Nuwayri, p. 255. Juzjani gives Fiku or Fitku Noyan as commanding the army. Al-Dhahabi/Negre, pp. 209–10; Nuwayri, pp. 327, 328. Al-Dhahabi, Ibn al-Athir (and Nuwayri, who uses Ibn al-Athir as a source) give Tolui as the commander. This is clearly incorrect, as he commanded forces in Khurasan at this time, independent of the army led by Chinggis Khan. The SHM gives Shiqi Qutuqtu as the commander who was defeated – see SHM-R (1984), pp. 96–7. Considering that it is thought Shiqi Qutuqtu may have written the SHM, one must wonder if he was really one of the commanders or whether he merely inserted his own name. Juvaini and Nasawi also mention the defeat of Shiqi Qutuqtu at Kandahar, but he is not killed in the battle; rather than proceeding immediately himself he apparently sent Tolui as a vanguard. See Nasawi, pp. 134–7. Thus it seems that Fiku Noyan and Shiqi Qutuqtu were the commanders of the initial force, but then Tolui, followed by Chinggis Khan, pursued Jalal al-Din to the Parwan plain. It is possible that the Fiku Noyan mentioned by Juzjani may be a combination of Tekechukh, a Mongol commander who accompanied Shiqi Qutuqtu, and Mö'etüken b. Chaghatay, who was killed at Bamiyan. Juvaini states that Chinggis Khan ordered all living beings to be killed at Bamiyan in retaliation.

28 Juzjani/Habibi, vol. 2, pp. 492–3; Juzjani/Raverty, pp. 534–6; SHM-R (1984), pp. 96–7.

29 Juzjani/Habibi, vol. 2, pp. 665–66; Juzjani/Raverty, pp. 1046–7.

30 SHM-R (1978), pp. 46–7.

31 Rashid al-Din Tabib, RD/Karimi, pp. 424–5; Rashid al-Din Tabib, *Jami'u't-Tawarikh: Compendium of Chronicles vol. 2*, p. 288; SHM-R (1978), pp. 47–9.

32 This was not Khubilai Khan, the grandson of Chinggis Khan, but rather a general.

33 SHM-R (1978), p. 49.

34 SHM-R (1978), pp. 51–3; SHM-C, pp. 122–5.

35 SHM-R (1978), p. 49. The *caragana* is a thorny shrub. The only problem is that no one really knows how these formations operated. *Caragana* has been interpreted to be in close formation, but also in a more spread formation of clumps. *Nagur*, or lake formation, has been interpreted as a spread formation, but also attacking in waves, like the caracole formation. Only the chisel formation seems fairly clear: to strike and push through the enemy line.

36 SHM-R, p. 122.

37 Zenkovsky/NC, pp. 285–6.

38 Michell, Forbes, pp. 64–5.

39 Zenkovsky, p. 194.
40 Zenkovsky-2 Nikon, p. 288.
41 Zenkovsky-2 Nikon, p. 288.
42 IL, pp. 495–7; EL, pp. 98–9; Zenkovsky, pp. 194–5.
43 Zenkovsky, p. 196; *GVC*, p. 30.
44 Dhahabi, p. 245. Allegedly 100,000 cavalry were on the rolls. This is doubtful, but it does most likely mean that the Abbasid army was sizeable.
45 Bar Hebraeus, p. 409.
46 Dhahabi, p. 265; Juzjani/Habibi, vol. 2, p. 701; Juzjani/Raverty, pp. 1229–32, 1235; RD/Thackston, vol. 2, pp. 490–1; RD/Karimi, pp. 703–5.
47 RD/Karimi, pp. 698–9; RD/Thackston, vol. 2, p. 487.
48 RD/Karimi, p. 706; RD/Thackston, vol. 2, pp. 492–3.
49 RD/Karimi, p. 707; RD/Thackston, vol. 2, p. 493.
50 Juzjani/Habibi, vol. 2, p. 707; Juzjani/Raverty, pp. 1236–7. Malik Izz al-Din ibn Fath al-Din also served as the champion of the Caliph and the commander of the right wing.
51 Bar Hebraeus, pp. 429–30; Nuwayri, pp. 381–2; RD/Karimi, p. 709; RD/Thackston, vol. 2, p. 495.
52 Juzjani/Habibi, vol. 2, p. 707; Juzjani/Raverty, p. 1238.
53 Dhahabi, pp. 266–7; Grigor, pp. 333–5; Juzjani/Habibi, vol. 2, p. 708; Juzjani/Raverty, pp. 1252–3.
54 Dhahabi, p. 267; RD/Karimi, p. 714; RD/Thackston, vol. 2, p. 499.
55 Juzjani/Habibi, vol. 2, p. 709; Juzjani/Raverty, p. 1260.
56 Wang O, pp. 61–2.
57 Wang O, pp. 66–7.
58 The Song entered the alliance because the Mongols had been at war with the Jin for 20 years. The Song emperor considered the Jin as an upstart dynasty and more of a threat than the Mongols.
59 Wang O, pp. 66–7.
60 Wang O, p. 75.
61 Wang O, pp. 80–1.
62 Wang O, pp. 80–1; SWQZL, p. 57.
63 Wang O, pp. 81–2.
64 Wang O, p. 85.
65 Wang O, pp. 90–1.
66 Wang O, p. 96.
67 Wang O, pp. 104–5.
68 Wang O, p. 113; SWQZL, p. 58.

Chapter Nine

1 For a very good analysis of what Muscovy adopted see Donald Ostrowski, *Muscovy and the Mongols: Cross Cultural Influences on the Steppe Frontier, 1304–1589* (New York: Cambridge University Press, 1998). Ostrowski gives the Mongols credit where it is due, but also dispels some myths about other, less favorable 'gifts' that the Mongols allegedly bequeathed the Russians.

2 Francis Gabriel, *Subotai the Valiant: Genghis Khan's Greatest General* (Westport: 2004), pp. 128–9.

3 Jack Weatherford, *Genghis Khan and the Making of the Modern World* (New York: Crown, 2004), p. 182; Iqtidar Alam Khan, *Gunpowder and Firearms: Warfare in Medieval India*, Aligarh Historians Society Series, edited by Irfan Habib (New Delhi: Oxford University Press, 2004), passim. Weatherford mentions the Mongols' use of gunpowder as a matter of fact, but provides no evidence to support the ubiquitous use he claims. Professor Khan is confident that the Mongols did use gunpowder on their western campaigns and cites several passages in the Persian sources which could be translated as gunpowder weapons. However, as he admits, these terms can also be translated as more conventional weapons. Khan also proposes that the Mongols are responsible for the spread of gunpowder into India, as the Sultanate of Delhi adopted its use by 1290. This is plausible, as there is evidence that gunpowder – at least in the form of fireworks, if nothing else – was in use in Central Asia in the later part of the thirteenth century.

4 B.H. Liddell Hart, *Deterrence or Defense, A Fresh Look at the West's Military Position* (New York: Frederick A. Praeger, 1960), p. 190.

5 B.H. Liddell Hart, *The Liddell Hart Memoirs*, vol. 1 (New York: G.P. Putnam's Sons, 1965), pp. 75, 272.

6 Gabriel, p. 130.

7 Liddell Hart, *Deterrence or Defense*, p. 198.

8 B.H. Liddell Hart, *Great Captains Unveiled* (Freeport, NY: Books for Libraries Press, 1967), p. 11; Liddell Hart, *Deterrent or Defense*, p. 187.

9 Liddell Hart, *Great Captains Unveiled*, p. 11.

10 Gabriel, p. 130.

11 Gabriel, p. 131.

12 Gabriel, p. 131.

13 Gabriel, p. 132.

14 John Strawson, *Hitler as Military Commander* (New York: Barnes and Noble, 1971), p. 37.

15 Strawson, p. 38.

16 Strawson, p. 38.

17 B.H. Liddell Hart, *The German Generals Talk* (New York: Quill, 1979), p. 91.

18 Strawson, p. 31.

Select bibliography

Primary sources

Abu'l-Faraj, Gregory. See Bar Hebraeus.

al-Ansari, Umar Ibn Ibrahim al-Awsi. *A Muslim Manual of War; Being Tafrij al-Kurub Fi Tadbir al-Hurub*, edited and translated by George Scanlon. Cairo: American University at Cairo Press, 1961.

al-Ansari, Umar Ibn Ibrahim al-Awsi. *Tafrij al-Kurub fi Tadbir al-Hurub (The Liberation of Sorrow in Planning of Warfare)*. Cairo: American University at Cairo Press, 1961.

Baha al-Din Ibn Shaddad. *The Rare and Excellent History of Saladin or al-Nawadir al-Sultaniyya Wa'l Mahasin al Yusufiyya*, translated by D.S. Richards. Crusades Texts in Translation, vol. 7. Aldershot: Ashgate Publishing, 2002.

Bar Hebraeus. *The Chronography of Gregory Ab U'l-Faraj 1225–1286, the Son of Aaron, the Hebrew Physician Commonly Known as Bar Hebraeus, Being the First Part of His Political History of the World*. Amsterdam: APA, 1976.

Bretschneider, Ernst, ed. and trans. *Mediaeval Researches from Eastern Asiatic Sources: Fragments Towards the Knowledge of the Geography and History of Central and Western Asia from the 13th to the 17th Century*. New York: Barnes & Noble, 1967.

Brosset, M. *Histoire de la Georgie: Depuis l'Antiquité Jusqu'au XIXe Siècle (History of Georgia from Antiquity until the 19th Century)*. St Petersburg: l'Imprimerie de l'Academie Impériale de Sciences, 1849.

Budge, Ernest, trans. *The Monks of Kublai Khan (Translation of The History of the Life and Travels of Rabban Sawma and Mar Yahbhallaha)*. London: The Religious Tract Society, 1928.

The Chronicle of Novgorod, 1016–1471, edited and translated by Robert Michell and Nevill Forbes. Camden Third Series, vol. 25. London: The Camden Society, 1914.

Clavijo, Gonzalez de. *Embassy to Tamerlane 1403–1406*, translated by Guy Le Strange. Broadway Travellers Series. London: Routledge, 1928.

Cleaves, Francis W. 'The Memorial for Presenting the Yuan Shih', *Asia Major* 1 (1988): 59–70.

Dawson, Christopher, ed. *The Mongol Mission: Narratives and Letters of the Franciscan Missionaries in Mongolia and China in the Thirteenth and Fourteenth Centuries*, translated by a nun of Stanbrook Abbey. London: Sheed and Ward, 1955.

De Bridia, C. 'The Tartar Relation' in *The Vinland Map and the Tartar Relation*, edited by R.A. Skelton et al. New Haven: Yale University Press, 1965.

Dhahabi, Muhammad ibn Ahmad, and Nègre, Arlette. *Kitab Duwal al-Islam = Les Dynasties de l'Islam (The Dynasties of Islam)*. Damas: Institut Français de Damas, 1979.

Dulaurier, M. Éd, trans. 'Les Mongols d'Apres les Historiens Armeniens: Fragments Traduits Sure les Textes Orginiaux (The Mongols according to Armenian Historians: Translated Fragments from the Original Texts)', *Journal Asiastique* 5, 11; 16 (1858; 1860).

Dulaurier, M. Éd, trans. 'Les Mongols d'Après les Historiens Arméniens: Extrait de l'Histoire (The Mongols According to Armenian Historians: Extracts of History)', *Journal Asiastique* 13 (October–November 1860): 273–315.

En-Nesawi, Mohammed. *Histoire du Sultan Djelal ed-din Mankobirti (History of Sultan Jalal al-Din Mankubirti)*, translated from the Arabic by O. Houdas. Paris: l'École des Langues Orientale Vivantes, 1895.

Ermonlinskaia Letopis' (The Chronicle of Ermonlin), edited by A.E. Tsepkov. Russkie Letopis.' Riazan': Naste Vremia, 2000.

Franke, Herbert. 'Chinese Texts on the Jurchen 1) A Translation of the Jurchen Monograph in the San-Ch'ao Pei-Meng Hui-Pien', *Zentralasiatische Studien* 9 (1975): 119–86. In Herbert Franke and Hok-lam Chan, *Studies on the Jurchens or the Chin Dynasty*. Variorum Collected Studies Series. Aldershot: Ashgate Publishing, 1997.

Gaadamba, Sh., ed. *Mongolyn Nuuts Tovchoo (The Secret History of the Mongols)*. Ulaanbaatar: Ulsiin Khevleliin Gazar, 1990.

Grigor of Akanc. 'The History of the Nation of the Archers by Grigor of Akanc', translated by R.P. Blake and R.N. Frye. *Harvard Journal of Asian Studies* 12 (1949): 269–399.

Guillelmus de Rubruc. 'Itinerarium Willelmi de Rubruc (The Journey of William of Rubruck)'. In *Sinica Franciscana: Itinera et Relationes Fratrum Minorum Saeculi XIII et XIV*, edited by P. Anastasius Van Den Wyngaert. *Sinica Franciscana* 1, 164–332. Firenze: Apud Collegium S. Bonaventurae, 1929.

al-Hamawi, Yaqut ibn Abd Allah. *Dictionnaire geographique, historique et litteraire de la Perse (Dictonary of the Geography, History, and Literature of Persia)*, translated by Charles Adrien Casimir Barbier de Meynard. Paris: Imprimerie Impériale, 1861.

Hambis, Louis. *Le Chapitre CVII Du Yuan Che*, translated by Louis Hambis. Leiden: E.J. Brill, 1954.

He Qiutao. 'Sheng Wu Qin Zheng Lu (Bogda Bagatur Bey-e-Ber Tayilagsan Temdeglel) (The Campaigns of the Holy Warrior)'. In *Bogda Bagatur Bey-e-Ber Tayilagsan Temdeglel*, edited by Asaraltu. Monggol Tulgur Bicig-un Cubural, 3–94. Qayilar: Obor Monggol-un Soyul-un Keblel-un Qoriy-a: Kolun Boyir Ayimag-un Sinquva Bicig-un Delgegur tarqagaba, 1985.

Hetoum ('Hayton'). 'La Flor Des Estoires de la Terre D'Orient'. In *RHC: Documents Armeniens*. Paris: Imprimerie Nationale, 1896–1906.

Hetoum ('Hayton'). 'The Journey of Het'um I, King of Little Armenia to the Court of the Great Khan Möngke', translated by John Andrew Boyle. *Central Asiatic Journal* 9 (1964): 175–89.

Hetoum ('Hayton'). *A Lytell Cronycle*, edited and translated by Glenn Burger. Toronto: University of Toronto Press, 1988.

Histoire Des Campagnes de Gengis Khan: Cheng-Wou Ts'in-Tcheng Loy (History of the Campaigns of Chinggis Khan), translated by Paul Pelliot and Louis Hambis. Leiden: E.J. Brill, 1951.

Hülegü. 'An Unknown Letter of Hulagu, Il-Khan of Persia, to King Louis IX of France', with a commentary by Paul Meyvaert. *Viator* XI (1980): 245–59.

The Hypatian Codex II: The Galician-Volynian Chronicle, edited and translated by George A. Perfecky. München: Wilhelm Fink Verlag, 1973.

Ibn Abi al-Hadid, Abd al-Hamid ibn Hibat Allah. *Sharh Nahi al-Balaghah (A Commentary on the Method of Eloquence)*. Beirut: Dar Maktabah al-Hayat, 1963.

Ibn al-Athir, Izz al-Din. *Al-Kamil Fi al-Tarikh (The Complete History)*. Beirut: Dar Sadr, 1965.

Ibn Batuta, edited and translated by H.A.R. Gibb, C. Defrémery, and B.R. Sanguinetti. *The Travels of Ibn Battuta, A.D. 1325–1354*. Works Issued by the Hakluyt Society. Banham, Norfolk: Archival Facsimiles Ltd, 1995.

Ibn Bibi, Nasir al-Din Husayn ibn Muhammad. *Saljuq Namah (The Book of the Saljuqs)*, translated by Muhammad Zakariya Ma'il. Silsilah-Yi Matbuat, vol. 136. Lahore: Markaz-Urdu Bord, 1975.

Ibn Bibi, Nasir al-Din Husayn ibn Muhammad. *Akhbar-i Salajiqah-i Rum (The Great Saljuqs of Rum)*. Tihran: Kitabfuushi-i Tihran, 1971.

Iohannes de Plano Carpini. 'Ystoria Mongalorum (History of the Mongols)'. In *Sinica Franciscana: Itinera et Relationes Fratrum Minorum Saeculi XIII et XIV*, edited by P. Anastasius Van Den Wyngaert. Sinica Franciscana, vol. 1, 27–130. Firenze: Apud Collegium S. Bonaventurae, 1929.

Ipat'evskaia Letopis' (Chronicle of Ipat'ev), edited by A.I. Tsenkov. Russkie Letopis', vol. 1. Ryazan': Aleksandriya, 2001.

Joinville, Jean de. *The Life of St Louis*, translated by Rene Hague. New York: Sheed and Ward, 1955.

Joinville, Jean de. *Histoire de Saint Louis (The History of Saint Louis)*. Paris: Les Libraire, 1960.

Juvaini, Ala al-Din Ata Malik ibn Muhammad. *Tarikh-i-Jahan-Gusha (The History of the World Conqueror)*, edited by Mirza Muhammad Qazvini. E.J.W. Gibb Memorial Series (3 vols). Leiden/London: Brill, 1912, 1916, 1937.

Juvaini, Ala al-Din Ata Malik ibn Muhammad. *Genghis Khan: The History of the World Conqueror*, edited and translated by J.A. Boyle. Seattle: University of Washington Press, 1997.

Juvaini, Ala al-Din Ata Malik ibn Muhammad. *The History of the World-Conqueror*, translated by J.A. Boyle. Cambridge: Harvard University Press, 1958.

Juzjani, Minhaj Siraj. *Tabaqat-i-Nasiri (Dynasties of the Helpers)* (2 vols). Lahore: Markazi Urdu Bord, 1975.

Juzjani, Minhaj Siraj. *Tabaqat-i-Nasiri (Dynasties of the Helpers)* (2 vols), edited by Abd al-Hayy Habibi. Kabul: Anjuman-i Tarikh-i Afghanistan, 1964–5.

Juzjani, Minhaj Siraj. *Tabaqat-i-Nasiri (A General History of the Muhammadan Dynasties of Asia)* (2 vols), edited and translated by Major H.G. Raverty. New Delhi: Oriental Books Reprint Corp, 1970.

Kiracos de Gantzac. 'Histoire d'Armenie (History of Armenia)'. In *Deux Historiens Arméniens: Kiracos de Gantzax, XIII S, 'Histoire d'Arménie'; Oukhtanès d'Ourha, X S, 'Histoire en Trois Parties'*, edited by M. Brousset. St Petersburg: Imperial Academy of Sciences, 1870.

Kiracos de Gantzac. 'Journey of the Armenian King Hethum to Mangoo Khan Performed in the Years 1254 and 1255, and Described by the Historian Kirakos Kandtsaketsi; Translated from the Armenian with Notes', *Asiatic Journal* 10 (1833): 137–43.

Latham, J.D., and Paterson, W.F., ed. and trans. *Saracen Archery: An English Version and Exposition of a Mameluke Work on Archery*. London: The Holland Press, 1970.

Letopis' Po Lavrentievskomu Spisku (The Laurentian Chronicle). Saint Petersburg: Arkheograficheskoi Kommissii, 1872.

'Liao Shi' (History of the Liao Dynasty). In *History of Chinese Society: Liao 907–1125*, edited and translated by Karl A. Wittfogel and Feng Chia-Sheng. Philadelphia: The American Philosophical Society, 1949.

Li Chih-Ch'ang. *The Travels of an Alchemist: The Journey of the Taoist, Ch'ang-Ch'un, from China to the Hindukush at the Summons of Chingiz Khan, Recorded by His Disciple, Li Chih-Ch'ang*, translated by Arthur Waley. London: Routledge & Sons, 1963.

Mandeville, Sir John. *The Travels of Sir John Mandeville*. London: Macmillan and Co, 1900.

al-Maqrizi, Ahmad ibn Ali. *Histoire Des Sultans Mamlouks de L'Egypte (History of the Mamluk Sultans of Egypt)*, translated by Etienne Quatremère. Paris: Oriental Translation Fund of Great Britain and Ireland, 1837, 1845.

al-Maqrizi, Ahmad ibn Ali. *Kitab al-Suluk Li-M'arifat Fi Dul al-Muluk (Introduction to the Knowledge of Royal Dynasties)*, edited by Ziyardah Muhammad Mustafi. Cairo: Lajnat al-Ta'lif wa al-Tarjamah wa al-Nashr, 1956.

Martinez, A.P. 'The Third Portion of the History of Gazan Xan in Rasidu'd-Din's Ta'rix-e Mobarake-e Gazani'. *Archivum Eurasiae Medii Aevi* VI (1988): 41–127.

Maurikos. *Maurice's Strategikon: Handbook of Byzantine Military Strategy*, translated by George T. Dennis. Philadelphia: University of Pennsylvania Press, 1984.

Nasawi, Muhammad ibn Ahmad. *Sirah al-Sultan Jalal al-Din Mankubirti (The History of Sultan Jalal al-Din Mankubirti)*. Cairo: Dar al-Fikr al-Arabi, 1953.

Nikonovskaia Letopis'. The Nikonian Chronicle (5 vols), translated by Serge A. and Betty Jean Zenkovsky. Princeton: The Kingston Press, 1984.

al-Nuwayri, Ahmad ibn Abd al-Wahhab. *Nihayat al-Arab Fi Funun al-Adab (The Conclusion of the Desires in a Variety of Humanities)*, edited by S'aid 'Ashur. Cairo: Al-hayat al Misriyyat al-'ammat lil-kitab, 1975.

Odorico de Pordenone. *Les Voyages en Asie Au XIVe Siècle Du Bienheureux Frère Odoric de Pordenone (The Voyages in the 14th Century of Friar Odoric of Pordenone)*, edited and translated by Henri Cordier and Jean de Langhe. Paris: Leroux, 1891.

Paris, Matthew. *English History*, translated by J.A. Giles. New York: AMS Press, 1968.

Peng Daya and Xu Ting. 'Hei Da Shi Lue ('Qar-a Tatar-un Tuqai Kereg-un Tobci'-Yin Tayilburilan Gerecilegsen Bicig) (Brief Account of the Black Tatar)'. In *Bogda Bagatur Bey-e-Ber Tayilagsan Temdeglel*, edited by Asaraltu. Monggol Tulgur Bicig-un Cubural, 159-256. Qayilar: Obor Monggol-un Soyul-un Keblel-un Qoriy-a: Kolun Boyir Ayimag-un Sinquva Bicig-un Delgegur tarqagaba, 1985.

Plano Carpini, John of. 'History of the Mongols'. In Dawson, Christopher, ed. *The Mongol Mission: Narratives and Letters of the Franciscan Missionaries in Mongolia and China in the Thirteenth and Fourteenth Centuries*, translated by a nun of Stanbrook Abbey. London: Sheed and Ward, 1955.

Plano Carpini, John of. *Jean de Plano Carpini: Histoire Des Mongols (History of the Mongols)*, translated by Jean Becquet and Louis Hambis. Paris: Adrien-Maisonneave, 1965.

Polo, Marco. *The Book of Ser Marco Polo*, edited and translated by Henry Yule. 3rd edition. London: J. Murray, 1929.

Polo, Marco. *La Description du Monde (Description of the World)*, edited and translated by Louis Hambis. Paris, 1955.

Polo, Marco. *The Description of the World*, translated by A.C. Moule and Paul Pelliot. London: G. Routledge, 1938.

Polo, Marco. *The Travels of Marco Polo* (2 vols), translated by Henry Yule, edited by Henri Cordier. New York: Dover Publications, 1993.

Polo, Marco. *The Travels of Marco Polo*, translated by Ronald Latham. New York: Penguin Books, 1958.

Qazwini, Hamd-allah Mustaqfi. *The Geographical Part of the Nuzhat-al-Qulub Composed by Hamd-Allah Mustaqfi of Qazwin in 740 (1340)*, edited and translated by Guy Le Strange. Leiden: Brill, 1919.

Rachewiltz, Igor de. *Index to the Secret History of the Mongols*. Bloomington: Indiana University, 1972.

Rashid al-Din Tabib. *Jami al-tawarikh (Compendium of Chronicles)* by Rashid al-Din (3 vols), edited by A.A. Alizade. Baku: NAUKA, 1957.

Rashid al-Din Tabib. *Histoire Des Mongols de la Perse (History of the Mongols of Persia)*, edited and translated by Etienne Marc Quatremère. Amsterdam: Oriental Press, 1968.

Rashid al-Din Tabib. *The Successors of Genghis Khan*, translated from the Persian by John Andrew Boyle. New York: Columbia University Press, 1971.

Rashid al-Din Tabib. *Jami al-tawarikh (Compendium of Chronicles)* by Rashid al-Din (2 vols), edited by A.A. Alizade. Moscow: NAUKA, 1980.

Rashid al-Din Tabib. *Jami' al-tawarikh (Compendium of Chronicles)*, edited by B. Karimi (2 vols). Teheran: Iqbal, 1983.

Rashid al-Din Tabib. 'The Third Portion of the History of Gazan Xan in Rasidu'd-Din's Ta'Rix-e Mobarak-e Gazani', translated by A.P. Martinez. *Archivum Eurasiae Medii Aevi* 6 (1986; 1988): 43–127.

Rashid al-Din Tabib. *Jami al-tawarikh (Compendium of Chronicles)*, edited by Muhammad Rushn Mustafi Musavi. Teheran: Nashr al-Buruz, 1995.

Rashiduddin Fazlullah. *Jami'u't-tawarikh: Compendium of Chronicles* by Rashiduddin Fazlullah, Parts 1–3. Sources of Oriental Languages and Literatures, vol. 45, translated by W.M. Thackston, edited by Sinasi Tekin and Gönül Alpay Tekin. Central Asian Sources IV. Cambridge, Harvard University: Department of Near Eastern Languages and Civilizations, 1998.

Rubruck, William of. *The Mission of Friar William of Rubruck: His Journey to the Court of the Great Khan Mongke, 1253–1255*, translated by Peter Jackson, edited by David

Morgan. Works Issued by the Hakluyt Society, 2nd Series, vol. 173. London: The Hakluyt Society, 1990.

Rubruck, William of. 'His Journey to the Court of the Greak Khan Mongke'. In *The Mongol Mission: Narratives and Letters of the Franciscan Missionaries in Mongolia and China in the Thirteenth and Fourteenth Centuries*, edited by Christopher Dawson, translated by a nun of Stanbrook Abbey. London: Sheed and Ward, 1955.

The Secret History of the Mongols, translated by Igor de Rachewiltz. In *Papers on Far Eastern History* 4 (September 1971): 115–63; 5 (March 1972): 149–75; 10 (September 1974): 55–82; 13 (March 1976): 41–75; 16 (September 1977): 27–65; 18 (September 1978): 43–80; 21 (March 1980): 17–57; 23 (March 1981): 111–46; 26 (September 1982): 39–84; 30 (September 1984): 81–160; 31 (March 1985): 21–93; 33 (March 1986): 129–37.

The Secret History of the Mongols, edited and translated by Francis W. Cleaves. Cambridge: Harvard University Press, 1982.

The History and the Life of Chinggis Khan: The Secret History of the Mongols, edited and translated by Urgunge Onon. Leiden/New York: E.J. Brill, 1990.

The Secret History of the Mongols: The Life and Times of Chinggis Khan, translated by Urgunge Onon. New edition. Richmond, Surrey: Curzon Press, 2001.

The Secret History of the Mongols, edited and translated by Igor de Rachewiltz. Leiden: Brill, 2004.

Histoire Secrete des Mongols: Restitution du Texte Mongol et Traduction Française des Chapitres I à VI (The Secret Hisotry of the Mongols. Restitution of the Mongolian Text and the French translation of Chapters 1 to 6), translated by Paul Pelliot. Oeuvres Posthumnes de Paul Pelliot vol. 1. Paris: Librairie d'Amérique et d'Orient, 1949.

Histoire Secrete Des Mongols (The Secret History of the Mongols), edited and translated by Louis Ligeti. Monumenta Linguae Mongolicae Collecta vol. 1: Budapest, 1971.

Sheng wu chin cheng lu (The Campaigns of the Holy Warrior). Ch iu-t ao Ho, Kuo-wei Wang, Kung Chao, Ta-ya P eng, T ing Hsü, Ta-heng Hsiao, Kokeondur, and Asaraltu. *Bogda Bagatur Bey-e-Ber Tayilagsan Temdeglel*. Angqadugar keb. Monggol Tulgur Bicig-un Cubural. Qayilar: Obor Monggol-un Soyul-un Keblel-un Qoriy-a Kolun Boyir Ayimag-un Sinquva Bicig-un Delgegur tarqagaba, 1985.

Simon de Saint-Quentin. *Histoire des Tartares (History of the Tatars)*. Documents Relatifs à l'Histoire des Croisades, edited by Jean Richard, vol. 8. Paris: Librarie Orientale Paul Geunther, 1965.

Smbat. *La Chronique Attribuée au Connétable Smbat (The Chronicle Attributed to the Constable Smbat)*, edited and translated by Dédéyan Gérard. Documents Relatifs à l'Histoire des Croisades. Paris: Librairie Orientaliste P. Geunther, 1980.

Ssu-ma Ch'ien. *Records of the Grand Historian*, translated by Burton Watson. New York: Columbia University Press, 1961.

Thomas of Spalato. *Istoriya Arxiyepiskopov Saloni i Splita (The History of the Archbishop of Salon and Split)*, translated by A.I. Solopov, edited by O.A. Akumovoi. Moscow: Indrik, 1997.

Umari, Ibn Fadl Allah al. *Kitab Masalik al-Absar Wa Mamalik al-Amsar: Mamalik Bayt Jinkiz Khan (Book of the Policy of Vision and Imperial Capitals: The Empire of the House of Chinggis Khan)*, edited and translated by K. Lech. Asiatische Forschungen, vol. 14. Wiesbaden: Otto Harrassowitz, 1968.

Vartan. 'Les Mongols d'après les Historiens Arméniens: Extrait de l'histoire universelle de Vartan (The Mongols according to Armenian Historians: extracted from the Universal History of Vartan)', translated and edited by M. Ed Dulaurier. *Journal Asiatique* 13 (October–November 1860): 273–315.

Villehardouin, Geoffroi de, and Joinville, Jean. *Chronicles of the Crusades*, edited and translated by Margaret R.B. Shaw. Baltimore: Penguin Books, 1983.

Voskpesenskaia Letopis' (The Chronilce of Voskpesen), edited by A.E. Tsepkov. Riazan': Pepkov Aleksandr Ivanovich, 1998.

Wang O. *The Fall of the Jurchen Chin: Wang O's Memoir on the Ts'ai-Chou Under the Mongol Siege (1233–1234)*, edited and translated by Hok-lam Chan. Münchener Ostasiatische Studien, vol. 66. Stuttgart: F. Steiner Verlag, 1993.

Yuan Shih (History of the Yuan Dynasty), Chapters 98 and 99, translated by Ch'i-ch'ing Hsiao. In *The Military Establishment of the Yuan Dynasty*, 72–124. Cambridge: Harvard University Press, 1978.

Zenkovsky, Serge A., ed. and trans. *Medieval Russia's Epics, Chronicles, and Tales*. Revised and enlarged (2nd edition). New York: Penguin Books, 1974.

Zhao Hong (Zhao Gong). *Meng-Da Bei-Lu: Polnoe Opisanie Mongolo-Tatar (Record of the Mongols and the Tatars)*, translated by Nikolai Ts. Munkuev. Moscow: Academy of Sciences (Nauka), 1975.

Zhao Hong (Zhao Gong). 'Meng-Da Bei-Lu ('Monggol-Tatar-un Tuqai Burin Temdeglel'-un Tayilburilan Gerecilegsen Bicig) (Record of the Mongols and the Tatars)'. In *Bogda Bagatur Bey-e-Ber Tayilagsan Temdeglel*, 95–158, edited by Asaraltu. Monggol Tulgur Bicig-un Cubural. Qayilar: Obor Monggol-un Soyul-un Keblel-un Qoriy-a: Kolun Boyir Ayimag-un Sinquva Bicig-un Delgegur tarqagaba, 1985.

Secondary sources

Aalto, Pentti. 'Swells of the Mongol-Storm Around the Baltic.' *Acta Orientalia Academiae Scientarium Hungaricae* 36 (1982): 5–15.

Abid, Syed Asid Ali. 'The Mongol Invasions of Persia.' *Iqbal* 7 (1959): 31–50.

Abulafia, David. *Frederick II, A Medieval Emperor*. Oxford: Oxford University Press, 1988.

Adams, Robert McCormick. *Land Behind Baghdad: A History of Settlement on the Diyala Plains*. Chicago: University of Chicago Press, 1965.

Ahmad, Aziz. 'Mongol Pressure in an Alien Land.' *Central Asiatic Journal* 6 (1961): 182–93.

Alexeev, Valery. 'Some Aspects of the Study of Productive Forces in the Empire of Chenghiz Khan.' In *The Rulers From the Steppe: State Formation on the Eurasian Periphery*, edited by Gary Seaman and Daniel Marks, 186–97. Los Angeles: University of Southern California Press, 1991.

Allen, W.E.D. *A History of the Georgian People*. New York: Barnes and Noble, 1932.

Allsen, Thomas T. 'Guard and Government in the Reign of The Grand Qan Mongke, 1251–1259.' *Harvard Journal of Asiatic Studies* 46, no. 2 (1986): 495–521.

Allsen, Thomas T. 'The Circulation of Military Technology in the Mongolian Empire.' In *Warfare in Inner Asian History, 500–1800*, edited by Nicola Di Cosmo. Handbook of Oriental Studies, Section 8: Central Asia, vol. 6, 265–94. Leiden: Brill, 2002.

Allsen, Thomas T. *Commodity and Exchange in the Mongol Empire: A Cultural History of Islamic Textiles.* Cambridge Studies in Islamic Civilization. Cambridge/New York: Cambridge University Press, 1997.

Allsen, Thomas T. *Culture and Conquest in Mongol Eurasia.* Cambridge Studies in Islamic Civilization. Cambridge/New York: Cambridge University Press, 2001.

Allsen, Thomas T. 'Ever Closer Encounter: The Appropriation of Culture and The Apportionment of Peoples in the Mongol Empire.' *Journal of Early Modern History* 1 (1997): 2–23.

Allsen, Thomas T. 'Mongol Census Taking in Rus, 1245–1275.' *Harvard Ukrainian Studies* 5, no. 1 (1981): 32–53.

Allsen, Thomas T. *Mongol Imperialism: the Policies of the Grand Qan Möngke in China, Russia, and the Islamic Lands, 1251–1259.* Berkeley: University of California Press, 1987.

Allsen, Thomas T. 'Mongolian Princes and Their Merchant Partners, 1200–1260.' *Asia Major* 2 (1989): 83–125.

Allsen, Thomas T. 'Mongols and North Caucasia.' *Archivum Eurasiae Medii Aevi* 7 (1987–91): 5–40.

Allsen, Thomas T. 'Prelude to the Western Campaigns: Mongol Military Operations in the Volga-Ural Region, 1217–1237.' *Archivum Eurasiae Medii Aevi* 3 (1983): 5–23.

Allsen, Thomas T. 'The Rise of the Mongolian Empire and Mongolian Rule in North China.' In *The Cambridge History of China*, edited by Herbert Franke and Denis Twitchett, vol. 6, *Alien Regimes and Border States, 907–1368*, 321–413. Cambridge: Cambridge University Press, 1994.

Allsen, Thomas T. 'Technician Transfers in the Mongolian Empire.' *The Central Eurasian Studies Lectures* 2 (2002).

Allsen, Thomas T. 'The Yüan Dynasty and the Uighurs of Turfan in the 13th Century.' In *China Among Equals*, edited by Morris Rossabi, 243–79. Berkeley: University of California Press, 1983.

Amitai, Reuven. 'Mongol Raids Into Palestine.' *Journal of the Royal Asiatic Society* 2 (1987): 236–55.

Amitai, Reuven. 'Whither the Ilkhanid Army? Ghazan's First Campaign Into Syria (1299–1300).' In *Warfare in Inner Asian History, 500–1800*, edited by Nicola Di Cosmo. Handbook of Oriental Studies, Section 8: Central Asia, vol. 6, 221–64. Leiden: Brill, 2002.

Amitai-Preiss, Reuven. 'Arabic Sources for the History of the Mongol Empire.' *Mongolica: An International Annual of Mongol Studies* 5 (1994): 99–107.

Amitai-Preiss, Reuven. 'Evidence for the Early Use of the Title Ilkhan Among the Mongols.' *Journal of the Royal Asiatic Society* 3rd Series 1 (1991): 353–61.

Amitai-Preiss, Reuven. 'Ghazan, Islam, and Mongol Tradition: A View from the Mamluk Sultanate.' *Bulletin of the School of Oriental and African Studies* 59 (1996): 1–10.

Amitai-Preiss, Reuven. 'In the Aftermath of Ayn Jalut: The Beginnings of the Mamluk-Ilkhanid Cold War.' *Al-Masaq* 3 (1990): 1–21.

Amitai-Preiss, Reuven. 'Northern Syria Between the Mongols and Mamluks: Political Boundary, Military Frontier, and Ethnic Affinities.' In *Frontiers in Question: Eurasian Borderlands, 700–1700*, edited by Daniel Power and Naomi Standen, 128–52. New York: St Martin's Press, 1999.

Amitai-Preiss, Reuven. 'Ayn Jalut Revisited.' *Tarih* 2 (1992): 119–50.

Amitai-Preiss, Reuven and Morgan, D.O. *The Mongol Empire and Its Legacy*. Islamic History and Civilization. Leiden/Boston: Brill, 1999.

Anderson, G.L. 'Turkish Archery.' *British Archery* 16 (1964–5): 150–1.

Asad, Talal. 'The Beduin as a Military Force: Notes on Some Aspects of Power Relations Between Nomads and Sedentaries in Historical Perspective.' In *The Desert and the Sown: Nomads in the Wider Society*, edited by Cynthia Nelson. Research Series, vol. 21. Berkeley: Institute of International Studies, 1973.

Aubin, Jean. 'L'Ethogenese Des Qaraunas.' *Turcica* 1 (1969): 65–95.

Ayalon, David. 'Discharges from Service, Banishments and Imprisonments in Mamluk Society.' *Israel Oriental Studies* 2 (1972): 25–50.

Ayalon, David. 'The Great Yasa of Chingiz Khan: A Re-Examination.' *Studia Islamica* 33 (1971): 97–140; 34 (1971): 151–80; 38 (1973): 107–56.

Ayalon, David. *Gunpowder and Firearms in the Mamluk Kingdom: A Challenge to a Medieval Society*. London: Vallentine, Mitchell and Co, 1956.

Ayalon, David. 'Mamluk.' In *Encyclopaedia of Islam*, vol. 6. Leiden: Brill, 1994.

Ayalon, David. 'Mamlukiyyat: (A) A First Attempt to Evaluate the Mamluk Military System.' *Jerusalem Studies in Arabic and Islam* 2 (1980): 321–39. Reprinted in *Outsiders in the Lands of Islam*, London: Variorum Reprints, 1988.

Ayalon, David. *Outsiders in the Lands of Islam: Mamluks, Mongols, and Eunuchs*. London: Variorum Reprints, 1988.

Ayalon, David. 'Preliminary Remarks on the Mamluk Military Instititution in Islam.' In *War, Technology, and Society in the Middle East*, edited by V.J. Parry and M.E. Yapp. London: Oxford University, 1975.

Ayalon, David. 'Studies on the Structure of the Mamluk Army.' *Bulletin of the School of Oriental and African Studies* 15 (1953): 203–28, 448–76; 16 (1954): 57–90.

Aytan, Andrew. 'Arms, Armour, and Horse.' In *Medieval Warfare*, edited by Maurice Keen, 186–208. Oxford: Oxford University Press, 1999.

Bacon, Elizabeth E. *Obok, A Study of Social Structure in Eurasia*. Viking Fund Publications in Anthropology, vol. 25. New York: Wenner-Gren Foundation for Anthropological Research, 1958.

Barfield, Thomas. 'The Devil's Horsemen: Steppe Nomadic Warfare in Historical Perspective.' In *Studying War: Anthropological Perspectives*, edited by S.P. Reyna and R.E. Downs. War and Society, vol. 2, 157–82. Amsterdam: Gordon and Breach Science Publishers, 1994.

Barfield, Thomas. *The Perilous Frontier: Nomadic Empires and China, 221 BC to AD 1757*. Studies in Social Discontinuity. Cambridge: Cambridge University Press, 1992.

Barfield, Thomas. 'Tribe and State Relations: The Inner Asian Perspective.' In *Tribes and State Formation in the Middle East*, edited by Phillip S. Khoury and Joseph Kostiner, 153–82. Los Angeles: University of California Press, 1990.

Barrett, T.H. 'The Secret History of the Mongols: Some Fresh Revelations.' *Bulletin of the School of Oriental and African Studies* 55 (1992): 115–20.

Barth, Fredrik. 'A General Perspective on Nomad-Sedentary Relations in the Middle East.' In *The Desert and the Sown: Nomads in the Wider Society*, edited by Cynthia Nelson. Research Series, vol. 21. Berkeley: Institute of International Studies, 1973.

Barthold, Vasilii Vladimirovich. *Turkestan Down to the Mongol Invasions.* 4th edition. Philadelphia: Porcupine Press, E.J.W. Gibb Memorial Trust, 1977.

Bartold, W. *An Historical Geography of Iran,* translated by Svat Soucek. Princeton: Princeton University Press, 1984.

Bergman, C.A.; McEwen. E.; and Miller, R. 'Experimental Archery: Projectile Velocities and Comparison of Bow Performances.' *Antiquity* 62 (1988): 658–70.

Biran, Michal. 'The Battle of Herat (1270): A Case of Inter Mongol Warfare.' In *Warfare in Inner Asian History, 500–1800,* edited by Nicola Di Cosmo. Handbook of Oriental Studies, Section 8: Central Asia, vol. 6, 175–220. Leiden: Brill, 2002.

Biran, Michal. 'China, Nomads, and Islam: The Qara Khitai (Western Liao) Dynasty 1124–1218.' PhD dissertation, Hebrew University, 2000.

Biran, Michal. ' "Like a Mighty Wall": The Armies of the Qara Khitai (1124–1218).' *Jerusalem Studies in Arabic and Islam* 25 (2001): 44–91.

Biran, Michal. *Qaidu and the Rise of the Independent Mongol State in Central Asia.* Surrey: Curzon, 1997.

Biran, Michal. *The Empire of the Qara Khitai in Eurasian History.* Cambridge: Cambridge University Press, 2004.

Bishop, W.E. 'On Chinese Archers' Thumbrings.' *Archery* 26, no. 11 (1954): 10–14, 33–34.

Boase, T.S.R. *The Cilician Kingdom of Armenia.* New York: St Martin's Press, 1978.

Bold, Bat-Ochir. *Mongolian Nomadic Society: A Reconstruction of the 'Medieval' History of Mongolia.* New York: St Martin's Press, 2001.

Bold, Bat-Ochir. 'The Quantity of Livestock Owned by the Mongols in the Thirteenth Century.' *Journal of the Royal Asiatic Society* 8, no. 2 (1998): 237–46.

Borchardt, Karl. 'Military Orders in East Central Europe: The First Hundred Years.' In *Autour de la Premiere Croisade,* 247–54. Paris: Publications de la Sorbonne, 1996.

Boudot-Lamotte, Antoine. *Contribution a l'Etude de l'Archerie Musulmane.* Damascus: Institut Français de Damas, 1968.

Boudot-Lamotte, A. 'Kaws.' In *Encyclopedia of Islam.* Leiden: Brill, 1978.

Bowlus, Charles R. 'Tactical and Strategic Weaknesses of Horse Archers on the Eve of the First Crusade.' In *Autour de la Premiere Croisade,* edited by Michel Balard, 149–66. Paris: Publications de la Sorbonne, 1996.

Boyle, J.A. 'The Burial Place of the Great Khan Ögödei.' *Acta Orientalia Hungarica* 33 (1970): 45–51.

Boyle, J.A. 'The Capture of Isfahan by the Mongols.' *Atti del Convegno Internazionale Sul Tema: La Persia Nel Medioevo* (1971): 331–6. Reprinted in *The Mongol World Empire,* London: Variorum Reprints, 1977.

Boyle, J.A. 'The Death of the Last Abbasid Caliph: A Contemporary Muslim Account.' *Journal of Semitic Studies* 6 (1961): 145–50. Reprinted in *The Mongol World Empire,* London: Variorum Reprints, 1977.

Boyle, J.A. 'Dynastic and Political History of the Il-Khans.' In *The Cambridge History of Iran,* edited by J.A. Boyle, vol. 5, *The Saljuq and Mongol Periods,* 303–421. Cambridge: Cambridge University Press, 1968.

Boyle, J.A. 'The Il-Khans of Persia and the Christian West.' *History Today* 23 (1973): 554–63. Reprinted in *The Mongol World Empire,* London: Variorum Reprints, 1977.

Boyle, J.A. 'Kirakos of Ganjak on the Mongols.' *Central Asiatic Journal* 8 (1963): 199–214. Reprinted in *The Mongol World Empire*, London: Variorum Reprints, 1977.

Boyle, J.A. 'The Last Barbarian Invaders: The Impact of the Mongol Conquests Upon East and West.' *Memoirs and Proceedings of the Manchester Literary and Philosophical Society* 112 (1977): 1–15. Reprinted in *The Mongol World Empire*, London: Variorum Reprints, 1977.

Boyle, J.A. 'The Mongol Commanders in Afghanistan and India According to the Tabaqat-i-Nasiri of Juzjani.' *Central Asiatic Journal* 9 (1964): 235–47. Reprinted in *The Mongol World Empire*, London: Variorum Reprints, 1977.

Boyle, J.A. 'The Mongol Invasion of Eastern Persia.' *History Today* 13 (1965): 614–23. Reprinted in *The Mongol World Empire*, London: Variorum Reprints, 1977.

Boyle, J.A. *The Mongol World Empire 1206–1370*. London: Variorum Reprints, 1977.

Boyle, J.A. 'The Mongols and Europe.' *History Today* 9 (1965): 336–43. Reprinted in *The Mongol World Empire*, London: Variorum Reprints, 1977.

Boyle, J.A. 'Some Additional Notes on the Mongolian Names in the History of the Nation of the Archers.' In *Researches in Altaic Languages Papers Read at the 14th Meeting of the Permanent International Altaistic Conference, Held in Szeged, August 22–28, 1971*, edited by Lajos Ligeti, 33–42. Budapest: Akadémiai Kiado, 1975.

Boyle, J.A. 'Turkish and Mongol Shamanism in the Middle Ages.' *Folklore* 83 (1972): 177–93.

Boyle, J.A. ed. *The Cambridge History of Iran: The Saljuq and Mongol Periods*. The Cambridge History of Iran, vol. 5. Cambridge: Cambridge University Press, 1968.

Bradford, Ernle. *The Knights of the Order*. New York: Dorset Press, 1972.

Buell, Paul D. 'The Role of the Sino-Mongolian Frontier Zone in the Rise of Cinggis-Qan.' In *Studies on Mongolia: Proceedings of the First North American Conference on Mongolian Studies*, edited by Henry Schwarz, 64–76. Bellingham: Center for East Asia Studies, Western Washington University, 1979.

Buell, Paul D. 'Cinqai (Ca. 1169–1252).' In *In the Service of the Khan: Eminent Personalities of the Early Mongol-Yuan Period (1200–1300)*, edited by Igor de Rachewiltz, Hok-lam Chan, Hsiao Ch'i-ch'ing, and Peter W. Geier, 95–111. Wiesbaden: Harrassowitz Verlag, 1993.

Buell, Paul D. 'Early Mongol Expansion in Western Siberia and Turkestan (1207–1219): A Reconstruction.' *Central Asiatic Journal* 36 (1992): 1–32.

Buell, Paul D. *Historical Dictionary of the Mongol World Empire*. Historical Dictionaries of Ancient Civilizations and Historical Eras. Lanham, MD: The Scarecrow Press, 2003.

Buell, Paul D. 'Kalmyk Tanggaci People: Thoughts on the Mechanics and Impact of Mongol Expansion.' *Mongolian Studies* 6 (1980): 41–59.

Buell, Paul D. 'Pleasing the Palate of the Qan: Changing Foodways of the Imperial Mongols.' *Mongolian Studies* 13 (1990): 57–82.

Buell, Paul D. 'Saiyid Ajall (1211–1279).' In *In the Service of the Khan: Eminent Personalities of the Early Mongol-Yuan Period (1200–1300)*, edited by Igor de Rachewiltz, Hok-lam Chan, Hsiao Ch'i-ch'ing, and Peter W. Geier, 466–79. Wiesbaden: Harrassowitz Verlag, 1993.

Buell, Paul D. 'Sino-Khitan Administration in Mongol Bukhara.' *Journal of Asian History* 13, no. 2 (1979): 121–51.

Buell, Paul D. 'Tribe, Qan, and Ulus in Early Mongol China: Some Prolegomena to Yüan History,' PhD dissertation, History, University of Washington, 1977.

Buell, Paul D.; Anderson, Eugene N.; and Husihui. *A Soup for the Qan: Chinese Dietary Medicine of the Mongol Era as Seen in Hu Szu-Hui's Yin-Shan Cheng-Yao: Introduction, Translation, Commentary and Chinese Text.* Sir Henry Wellcome Asian Series. London/ New York: Kegan Paul International, 2000.

Bulag, Uradyn Erden. 'Nationalism and Identity in Mongolia.' PhD dissertation, Social Anthropology, Cambridge University, 1993.

Bulag, Uradyn Erden. *Nationalism and Hybridity in Mongolia.* Oxford Studies in Social and Cultural Anthropology. New York: Clarendon Press, 1998.

Cahen, Claude. 'The Mongols and the Near East.' In *A History of the Crusades*, edited by R.L. Wolff and H.W. Hazard, vol. 2, *The Later Crusades, 1189–1311*, 715–34. Madison: The University of Wisconsin Press, 1969.

Cahen, Claude. 'Les Mongols dan les Balkans.' *Revue Historique* 146 (1924): 55–9.

Cahen, Claude. *Pre-Ottoman Turkey*, translated by J. Jones-Williams. New York: Taplinger Publishing, 1968.

Cahen, Claude. 'The Turks in Iran and Anatolia Before the Mongol Invasions.' In *A History of the Crusades*, edited by R.L. Wolff and H.W. Hazard, vol. 2, *The Later Crusades, 1189–1311*, 660–92. Madison: The University of Wisconsin Press, 1969.

Carruthers, Douglas. *Unknown Mongolia: A Record of Travel and Exploration in North-West Mongolia and Dzungaria.* Phildelphia: J.B. Lippincott Co, 1914.

Chahin, M. *The Kingdom of Armenia.* New York: Dorset, 1991.

Chambers, James. *The Devil's Horsemen: the Mongol Invasion of Europe.* New York: Atheneum, 1979.

Chan, Hok-lam. 'Prolegomena to the Ju-Nan i-Chih: A Memoir on the Last Chin Court Under the Mongol Siege of 1234.' *Sung Studies Newsletter* 10 (1974): 2–19.

Chan, Hok-lam. 'Siting by Bowshot: A Mongolian Custom and its Sociopolitical and Cultural Implications.' *Asia Major* 4 (1991): 53–78.

Chan, Hok-lam. 'Wang O's Contribution to the History of the Chin Dynasty (1115–1234).' *Essays in Commemoration of the Golden Jubilee of Fung Ping Shan Library (1932–1982)* (1982): 345–75. Reprinted in *China and the Mongols*, Aldershot: Ashgate Publishing, 1999.

Chan, Hok-lam. ' "The Distance of a Bowshot": Some Remarks on Measurement in the Altaic World.' *The Journal of Sung-Yuan Studies* 25 (1995): 29–46.

Chan, Hok-lam. *China and the Mongols: History and Legend Under the Yuan and Ming.* Aldershot: Ashgate Publishing, 1999.

Chase, Kenneth. *Firearms: A Global History to 1700.* New York: Cambridge University Press, 2003.

Christiansen, E. *The Northern Crusades: The Baltic and the Catholic Frontier, 1100–1525.* Minneapolis: University of Minnesota Press, 1980.

Clauson, Gerard. 'Turkish and Mongolian Horses and Use of Horses, an Etymological Study.' *Central Asiatic Journal* 10 (1965): 161–66.

Cleaves, F.W. 'A Chancellery Practice of the Mongols in the Thirteenth and Fourteenth Centuries.' *Harvard Journal of Asiatic Studies* 14 (1951): 493–526.

Cleaves, F.W. 'A Medical Practice of the Mongols in the Thirteenth Century.' *Harvard Journal of Asiatic Studies* 17 (1954): 428–44.

Commeaux, Charles. *La Vie Quotidienne Chez les Mongols de la Conquête (XIIIe Siècle)*. Paris: Hachette, 1972.

Contamine, Philippe. *War in the Middle Ages*, translated by Michael Jones. New York: Basil Blackwell, 1980.

Cordier, Henri. *Ser Marco Polo: Notes and Addenda to Sir Henry Yule's Edition, Containing the Results of Recent Research and Discovery*. London: J. Murray, 1920.

Cosmo, Nicola Di. 'State Formation and Periodization in Inner Asian History.' *World History* 10, no. 1 (1999): 1–40.

Dafeng, Qu, and Lin Jianyi. 'On Some Problems Concerning Jochi's Lifetime.' *Central Asiatic Journal* 42, no. 2 (1998): 283–90.

Dalantai. 'Menggu Singxue Yanjiu: Jian Lun Chengjisihan Yang Bing Zhi Mi.' In *The Secret History of the Mongols: The Life and Times of Chinggis Khan*, edited by Urgunge Onon, 279–87. Richmond: Curzon Press, 1996.

Dardess, J.W. 'From Mongol Empire to Yuan Dynasty: Changing Forms of Imperial Rule in Mongolia and Central Asia.' *Monumenta Serica* 30 (1972–3): 117–65.

Davis, R.H.C. *The Medieval Warhorse: Origin, Development, and Redevelopment*. London: Thames and Hudson, 1989.

Davis, Tenny L., and Ware, J.R. 'Early Chinese Military Pyrotechnics.' *Journal of Chemical Education* 24 (1947): 522–37.

Dawson, Christopher, ed. *Mission to Asia*, translated by a nun from Stanbrook Abbey. Medieval Academy Reprints for Teaching. Toronto: University of Toronto Press in association with the Medieval Academy of America, 1992.

De Rachewiltz, Igor. *Papal Envoys to the Great Khans*. London: Faber and Faber, 1971.

Delbrück, Hans. *Medieval Warfare*, translated by Walter J. Renfroe Jr. History of the Art of War, vol. 3. Lincoln: University of Nebraska Press, 1990.

DeVries, Kelly. *Medieval Military Technology*. Peterborough, Ontario: Broadview Press, 1992.

Dewey, Horace W. 'Russia's Debt to the Mongols in Suretyship and Collective Responsibility.' *Comparative Studies in Society and History* 30 (1988): 249–71.

Digby, Simon. *War-Horse and Elephant in the Delhi Sultanate: A Study of Military Supplies*. Oxford: Oxford University Press, 1971.

Dimnik, Martin. *Mikhail, Prince of Chernigov and Grand Prince of Kiev 1224–1246*. Studies and Texts, Pontifical Institute of Medieval Studies, vol. 52. Toronto: Pontifical Institute of Medieval Studies, 1981.

Doerfer, Gerhard. *Türkische und Mongolische Elemente Im Neupersischen, Unter Besonderer Berücksichtigung Älterer Neupersischer Geschichtsquellen, vor Allem der Mongolen- und Timuridenzeit*. Veröffentlichungen der Orientalischen Kommission, vol. 16. Wiesbaden: F. Steiner, 1963–75.

Dunnell, Ruth. 'The Fall of the Xia Empire: Sino-Steppe Relations in the Late 12th–Early 13th Centuries.' In *The Rulers From the Steppe: State Formation on the Eurasian Periphery*, edited by Gary Seaman and Daniel Marks, 158–85. Los Angeles: University of Southern California Press, 1991.

Dunnell, Ruth. 'The Hsi Hsia.' In *The Cambridge History of China*, edited by Herbert Franke and Denis Twitchett, vol. 6, *Alien Regimes and Border States, 907–1368*, 154–214. Cambridge: Cambridge University Press, 1994.

Dvornik, Francis. *Origins of Intelligence Services: The Ancient Near East, Persia, Greece, Rome, Byzantium, the Arab Muslim Empires, the Mongol Empire, China, Muscovy*. New Brunswick, NJ: Rutgers University Press, 1974.

Ecsedy, Hilda. 'Trade-and-War Relations Between the Turks and China.' *Acta Orientalia Hungarica* 21 (1968): 131–80.

Ecsedy, Hilda. 'Tribe and Empire, Tribe and Society in the Turk Age.' *Acta Orientalia Hungarica* 31 (1977): 3–15.

Ecsedy, Hilda. 'Tribe and Tribal Society in the 6th Century Turk Empire.' *Acta Orientalia Hungarica* 25 (1972): 245–62.

Ecsedy, Ildiko. 'Nomads in History and Historical Research.' *Acta Orientalia Hungarica* 35 (1981): 201–27.

Edbury, Peter. *The Kingdom of Cyprus and the Crusades, 1191–1374*. Cambridge: Cambridge University Press, 1991.

Edbury, Peter. 'Warfare in the Latin East.' In *Medieval Warfare*, edited by Maurice Keen, 89–112. Oxford: Oxford University Press, 1999.

Elott, M.E. 'Technique of the Oriental Release.' *Archery* (December 1962): 18–21, 43.

Endicott-West, Elizabeth. 'Hereditary Privilege in the Yuan Dynasty.' *Journal of Turkish Studies* 9 (1985): 5–20.

Endicott-West, Elizabeth. 'Imperial Governance in Yuan Times.' *Harvard Journal of Asiatic Studies* 46, no. 2 (1986): 523–49.

Endicott-West, Elizabeth. 'Merchant Associations in Yüan China: The Ortogh.' *Asia Major* 2 (1989): 127–54.

Engels, Donald W. *Alexander the Great and the Logistics of the Macedonian Army*. Berkeley: University of California Press, 1978.

Fairbank, John K. 'Introduction: Varieties of the Chinese Military Experience.' In *Chinese Ways in Warfare*, edited by Frank A. Kierman and John K. Fairbank, 1–26. Cambridge: Harvard University Press, 1974.

Faris, N.A., and Elmer, R.P. *Arab Archery*. Princeton: Princeton University Press, 1945.

Farquhar, David M. *The Government of China Under Mongolian Rule, a Reference Guide*. Münchener Ostasiatische Studien. Stuttgart: Franz Steiner, 1990.

Fennel, John. *The Crisis of Medieval Russia*. New York: Longman, 1983.

Fennel, John. 'The Tale of Baty's Invasion of North-East Rus' and its Reflexion in the Chronicles of the Thirteenth–Fifteenth Centuries.' *Russia Mediaevalis* 3 (1977): 41–78.

Fine, John V.A. *The Late Medieval Balkans: A Critical Survey from the Late Twelfth Century to the Ottoman Conquest*. Ann Arbor: University of Michigan Press, 1987.

Fletcher, Joseph. 'The Mongols: Ecological and Social Perspectives.' *Harvard Journal of Asiatic Studies* 46 (1986): 11–50.

Forbes Manz, Beatrice. 'The Office of Darugha under Tamerlane.' *Journal of Turkish Studies* 9 (1985): 69–70.

Forey, Alan. *The Military Orders from the Twelfth to the Early Fourteenth Centuries*. Toronto: University of Toronto Press, 1992.

France, John. *Western Warfare in the Age of the Crusades, 1000–1300*. Ithaca, NY: Cornell University Press, 1999.

Franke, Herbert. 'The Chin Dynasty.' In *The Cambridge History of China*, edited by Herbert Franke and Denis Twitchett, vol. 6, *Alien Regimes and Border States, 907–1368*, 215–320. Cambridge: Cambridge University Press, 1994.

Franke, Herbert. *China Under Mongol Rule*. Collected Studies. Aldershot: Variorum, 1994.

Franke, Herbert. 'Chinese Texts on the Jurchen 1) A Translation of the Jurchen Monograph in the San-Ch'ao Pei-Meng Hui-Pien.' In *Studies on the Jurchens or the Chin Dynasty*, edited by Herbert Franke and Hok-lam Chan, vol. 9, *Zentralasiatische Studien*. Variorum Collected Studies Series, 119–86. Aldershot: Ashgate Publishing, 1997.

Franke, Herbert. 'From Tribal Chieftain to Universal Emperor and God: The Legitimation of the Yüan Dynasty.' *Bayerische Akademie der Wissenshaften* 2 (1978): 3–85. Reprinted in *China Under Mongol Rule*, Aldershot: Variorum, 1994.

Franke, Herbert. 'Siege and Defense of Towns in Medieval China.' In *Chinese Ways in Warfare*, edited by Frank A. Kierman and John K. Fairbanks. Harvard East Asian Series, vol. 74, 151–201. Cambridge: Harvard University Press, 1974.

Franke, Herbert. 'Sino-Western Contacts Under the Mongol Empire.' *Journal of the Hong Kong Branch of the Royal Asiatic Society* 6 (1966): 49–72.

Franke, Herbert. 'Sung Embassies: Some General Observations.' In *China Among Equals*, edited by Morris Rossabi, 116–50. Berkeley: University of California Press, 1983.

Franke, Herbert, and Hok-lam Chan. *Studies on the Jurchens and the Chin Dynasty*. Aldershot: Ashgate Publishing, 1997.

Fügedei, Erik. *Castle and Society in Medieval Hungary (1000–1437)*, translated by J.M. Bak. Budapest: Akademiai Kiado, 1986.

Gaadamba, Sh. *Mongolyn Nuuts Tovchoo*. Ulaanbaatar: Ulsiin Khevleliin Gazar, 1990.

Gabriel, Richard A. *Subotai the Valiant: Genghis Khan's Greatest General*. Westport: Praeger, 2004.

Galstyan, A.G. 'The Conquest of Armenia by the Mongol Armies', translated by Robert Bedrosian. *The Armenian Review* 27 (1975): 356–77.

Gernet, Jacques. *Daily Life in China on the Eve of the Mongol Invasion, 1250–1276*. Stanford: Stanford University Press, 1962.

Golden, P.B. 'Cumanica I: The Qipcaqs in Georgia.' *Archivum Eurasiae Medii Aevi* 4 (1984): 45–87.

Golden, P.B. ' "I Will Give the People Unto Thee": The Cinggisid Conquests and Their Aftermath in the Turkic World.' *Journal of the Royal Asiatic Society* 10, no. 1 (2000): 21–42.

Golden, P.B. 'Cumanica II: The Ölberli (Ölperli): The Fortunes and Misfortunes of an Inner Asian Nomadic Clan.' *Archivum Eurasiae Medii Aevi* 6 (1986–8): 5–30.

Golden, P.B. 'Cumanica III: Urusoba.' In *Aspects of Altaic Civilization*, Proceedings of the Thirtieth Meeting of the Permanent International Altaistic Conference. Bloomington: Indiana University Research Institute for Inner Asian Studies, 1990.

Golden, P.B. 'Imperial Ideology and the Sources of Politcal Unity Amongst the Pre-Cinggisid Nomads of Western Eurasia.' *Archivum Eurasiae Medii Aevi* 2 (1982): 37–76.

Golden, P.B. *Nomads and Sedentary Societies in Medieval Eurasia*. Essays on Global and Comparative History Series. Washington, DC: American Historical Association, 1998.

Golden, P.B. 'Nomads and Their Sedentary Neighbors in Pre-Cinggisid Eurasia.' *Archivum Eurasiae Medii Aevi* 7 (1987–91): 41–82.

Golden, P.B. 'The Question of the Rus Qaganate.' *Archivum Eurasiae Medii Aevi* 2 (1982): 77–98.

Golden, P.B. 'Vyxod: Aspects of Medieval Eastern Slavic-Altaic Culturo-Linguistic Relations.' *Archivum Eurasiae Medii Aevi* 7 (1987-1991): 83–102.

Golden, P.B. 'War and Warfare in the Pre-Cinggisid Western Steppes of Eurasia.' In *Warfare in Inner Asian History, 500–1800*, edited by Nicola Di Cosmo. Handbook of Oriental Studies, Section 8: Central Asia, vol. 6, 105–74. Leiden: Brill, 2002.

Golden, P.B. *Ethnicity and State Formation in Pre-Cinggisid Turkic Eurasia*. The Central Eurasian Studies Lectures, vol. 1. Bloomington: Department of Central Eurasian Studies, Indiana University, 2001.

Golden, P.B. *An Introduction to the History of the Turkic Peoples: Ethnogenesis and State-Formation in Medieval and Early Modern Eurasia and the Middle East*. Turcologica. Wiesbaden: O. Harrassowitz, 1992.

Goodrich, L. Carrington. 'Early Cannon in China.' *Isis* 55 (1964): 193–5.

Goodrich, L. Carrington and Feng Chia-cheng. 'The Early Development of Firearms in China.' *Isis* 36 (1946): 114–123, 250–1.

Grousset, René. *The Empire of the Steppes: A History of Central Asia*. New Brunswick, NJ: Rutgers University Press, 1970.

Gumilev, L.N. *Searches for an Imaginary Kingdom: The Legend of the Kingdom of Prester John*. Cambridge/New York: Cambridge University Press, 1987.

Guzman, Gregory G. 'The Encyclopedist Vincent of Beauvais and His Mongol Extracts from John of Plano Carpini and Simon of Saint-Quentin.' *Speculum* 49 (1974): 287–307.

Guzman, Gregory G. 'Simon of Saint-Quentin and the Domican Mission to the Mongol Baiju: A Reappraisal.' *Speculum* 46 (1971): 232–49.

Guzman, Gregory G. 'Simon of Saint-Quentin as Historian of the Mongols and Seljuk Turks.' *Medievalia et Humanistica* 3 (1972): 155–78.

Halperin, Charles. 'The East Slavic Response to the Mongol Conquest.' *Archivum Eurasiae Medii Aevi* 10 (1998–9): 98–117.

Halperin, Charles. 'The Kipchak Connection: The Ilkhans, the Mamluks, and Ayn Jalut.' *Bulletin of the School of Oriental and African Studies* 63 (2000): 229–45.

Halperin, Charles. 'The Missing Golden Horde Chronicles and Historiography in the Mongol Empire.' *Mongolian Studies* 23 (2000): 1–16.

Halperin, Charles. 'Russia and the 'Mongol Yoke': Concepts of Conquest, Liberation, and the Chingissid Idea.' *Archivum Eurasiae Medii Aevi* 2 (1982): 99–108.

Halperin, Charles. 'Russo-Tatar Relations in the Mongol Context – Two Notes.' *Acta Orientalia Academiae Scientiarum Hungaricae* 51, no. 3 (1998): 321–39.

Halperin, Charles. '"Know They Enemy": Medieval Russian Familiarity with the Mongols of the Golden Horde.' *Jahrbücher Für Geschichte Osteuropas* 30 (1982): 161–75.

Halperin, Charles. *Russia and the Golden Horde: The Mongol Impact on Medieval Russian History*. Bloomington: Indiana University Press, 1985.

Halperin, Charles. 'Russia in the Mongol Empire.' *Harvard Journal of Asiatic Studies* 43 (1983): 239–61.

Halperin, Charles. *The Tatar Yoke*. Columbus, Ohio: Slavica Publishers, 1986.

Hamlin, H.S. 'A Study of Composite Bows.' *Archery* (April–September 1948).

Hartog, Leo De. 'The Army of Genghis Khan.' *The Army Quarterly and Defense Journal* 109 (1979): 476–85.

Hartog, Leo De. *Russia and the Mongol Yoke*. New York: I.B. Tauris Publishers, 1996.

Hartog, Leo De. *Genghis Khan, Conqueror of the World*. London: Tauris, 1989.

Heissig, Walther. *The Religions of Mongolia*, translated by Geoffrey Samuel. Berkley: University of California Press, 1980.

Henthorn, W.E. *Korea: The Mongol Invasions*. Leiden: Brill, 1963.

Henthorn, W.E. 'Some Notes on Koryo Military Units.' *Transactions of the Korean Branch of the Royal Asiatic Society* 35 (1959): 66–75.

Herman, John E. 'The Mongol Conquest of Dali: The Failed Second Front.' In *Warfare in Inner Asian History, 500–1800*, edited by Nicola Di Cosmo. Handbook of Oriental Studies, Section 8: Central Asia, vol. 6, 295–335. Leiden: Brill, 2002.

Hillenbrand, Carole. *The Crusades: Islamic Perspectives*. Edinburgh: Edinburgh University Press, 1999.

Hoang, Michael. *Gengis Khan*. London: Saqi, 1990.

Hodgson, Marshall G.S. *The Order of the Assassins*. New York: Mouton and Co, 1955.

Hoffmeyer, Ada Bruhn. 'East and West.' *Gladius* 1 (1961): 9–16.

Hoffmeyer, Ada Bruhn. 'Introduction to the History of the European Sword.' *Gladius* 1 (1961): 30–76.

Hoffmeyer, Ada Bruhn. 'Military Equipment in the Byzantine Manuscript of Scylitzes in Biblioteca Nacional in Madrid.' *Gladius* 5 (1966): 8–160.

Holt, P.M. *The Age of the Crusades: The Near East from the Eleventh Century to 1517*. London: Longman, 1986.

Housley, Norman. 'European Warfare, c.1200–1300.' In *Medieval Warfare*, edited by Maurice Keen, 113–35. Oxford: Oxford University Press, 1999.

Howarth, Stephen. *The Knights Templar*. New York: Dorset Press, 1982.

Howorth, Henry H. *History of the Mongols from the 9th to the 19th Century*. New York: B. Franklin, 1965.

Hsiao, Ch'i-ch'ing. *The Military Establishment of the Yuan Dynasty*. Harvard East Asian Monographs. Cambridge: Council on East Asian Studies, Harvard University Press, 1978.

Hsiao, Ch'i-ch'ing. 'Shih T'ien-Tse.' In *In the Service of the Khan: Eminent Personalities in the Early Mongol Yuan Period (1200–1300)*, edited by Igor de Rachewiltz, Hok-lam Chan, Hsiao Ch'i-ch'ing, and Peter W. Geier, 27–45. Wiesbaden: Harrassowitz Verlag, 1993.

Humphreys, R. Stephen. 'The Emergence of the Mamluk Army.' *Studia Islamica* 45 (1977): 67–100.

Humphreys, R. Stephen. 'The Emergence of the Mamluk Army.' *Studia Islamica* 46 (1977): 147–82.

Humphreys, R. Stephen. *From Saladin to the Mongols: The Ayyubids of Damascus, 1193–1260*. Albany: State University of New York Press, 1977.

Hung, C. 'China and the Nomads: Misconceptions in Western Historiography on Inner Asia.' *Harvard Journal of Asiatic Studies* 44, no. 2 (1981): 597–628.

Hung, William. 'The Transmission of the Book Known as The Secret History of the Mongols.' *Harvard Journal of Asiatic Studies* 14 (1951): 433–92.

Hurley, Vic. *Arrows Against Steel: The History of the Bow*. New York: Mason/Charter, 1975.

Irwin, Robert. *The Middle East in the Middle Ages*. Carbondale: Southern Illinois University Press, 1986.

Itani, Kozo. 'Jalal al-Din Khwarazmshah in Western Asia.' *Memoirs of the Research Department of the Toyo Bunko* 47 (1989): 145–64.

Jackson, Peter. 'Cormagun.' In *Encyclopedia Iranica*, 1993.

Jackson, Peter. 'The Crisis in the Holy Land in 1260.' *English Historical Review* 95 (1980): 481–513.

Jackson, Peter. *The Delhi Sultanate, A Political and Military History*. Cambridge Studies in Islamic Civilization, edited by David Morgan. Cambridge: Cambridge University Press, 1999.

Jackson, Peter. 'The Dissolution of the Mongol Empire.' *Central Asiatic Journal* 22 (1978): 186–244.

Jackson, Peter. 'From Ulus to Khanate: The Making of the Mongol State, c.1220–c.1290.' In *The Mongol Empire and Its Legacy*, edited by Reuven Amitai-Preiss and David O. Morgan, 12–38. Leiden: Brill, 2000.

Jagchid, Sechin. 'Genghis Khan's Military Strategy and Art of War.' *Chinese Culture* 5 (1963): 59–62.

Jagchid, Sechin. 'Khitan Struggles Against Jurchen Oppression – Nomadism Versus Sinicization.' *Zentralasiatische Studien* 16 (1982): 165–85. Reprinted in *Essays in Mongolian Studies*, Provo: David M. Kennedy Center for International Studies, Brigham Young University, 1988.

Jagchid, Sechin. 'The Khitans and Their Cities.' *Central Asiatic Journal* 25 (1981): 70–88. Reprinted in *Essays in Mongolian Studies*, Provo: David M. Kennedy Center for International Studies, Brigham Young University, 1988.

Jagchid, Sechin. 'Patterns of Trade and Conflict Between China and the Nomadic Peoples of Mongolia.' *Zentralasiatische Studien* 11 (1977): 177–204. Reprinted in *Essays in Mongolian Studies*, Provo: David M. Kennedy Center for International Studies, Brigham Young University, 1988.

Jagchid, Sechin. *Essays in Mongolian Studies*. Provo, Utah: David M. Kennedy Center for International Studies, Brigham Young University, 1988.

Jagchid, Sechin. 'Some Notes on the Horse-Policy of the Yuan Dynasty.' *Central Asiatic Journal* 10 (1965): 246–68. Reprinted in *Essays in Mongolian Studies*, Provo: David M. Kennedy Center for International Studies, Brigham Young University, 1988.

Jagchid, Sechin and Bawden, C.R. 'Notes on Hunting of Some Nomadic Peoples of Central Asia.' In *Die Jagd bei Den Altaischen Volkern*, 90–102. Wiesbaden: Harrassowitz Verlag, 1968.

Jagchid, Sechin and Hyer, Paul. *Mongolia's Culture and Society*. Boulder: Westview Press, 1979.

Jagchid, Sechin and Symons, Van Jay. *Peace, War, and Trade Along the Great Wall: Nomadic-Chinese Interaction Through Two Millennia*. Bloomington: Indiana University Press, 1989.

Kaegi, Walter Emil Jr. 'The Contribution of Archery to the Turkish Conquest of Anatolia.' *Speculum* 39 (1964): 96–108.

Kafesoglu, Ibrahim. *A History of the Seljuks: Ibrahim Kafesoglu's Interpretation and the Resulting Controversy*, translated by Gary Lieser. Carbondale: Southern Illinois University, 1988.

Kahn, Paul. 'Instruction and Entertainment in the Naiman Battle Text: An Analysis of §189 Through §196 of The Secret History of the Mongols.' In *Culture Contact, History and Ethnicity in Inner Asia*, edited by Michael Gervers and Wayne Schlepp, 106–14. Toronto: Joint Centre for Asia Pacific Studies, 1996.

Kahn, Paul, and Cleaves, Francis Woodman. *The Secret History of the Mongols: The Origin of Chinghis Khan: An Adaptation of the Yuan Ch Ao Pi Shih, Based Primarily on the English Translation by Francis Woodman Cleaves*. San Francisco: North Point Press, 1984.

Kaszuba, Sophia C. 'Wounds in Medieval Mongol Warfare: Their Nature and Treatment in The Secret History, with Some Notes on Mongolian Military Medicine and Hygiene.' *Mongolian Studies* 19 (1996): 59–68.

Keen, Maurice, ed. *Medieval Warfare*. Oxford: Oxford University Press, 1999.

Kennedy, Hugh. *Mongols, Huns and Vikings: Nomads at War*. Cassell's History of Warfare, edited by John Keegan. London: Cassell, 2002.

Khan, Abdoul-Ghazi Behadour. *Histoire des Mongols et des Tatares*, translated by Petr. I. Desmaisons. Amsterdam: Philo Press, 1970.

Khan, Iqtidar Alam. 'Coming of Gunpowder to the Islamic World and North India: Spotlight on the Role of the Mongols.' *Journal of Asian History* 30, no. 1 (1996): 27–45.

Khan, Iqtidar Alam. 'The Turko-Mongol Theory of Kingship.' *Medieval India* 2 (1972): 8–18.

Khan, Iqtidar Alam. *Gunpowder and Firearms: Warfare in Medieval India*. New Delhi: Oxford University Press, 2004.

Khazanov, Anatoly M. 'Muhammad and Jenghiz Khan Compared: The Religious Factor in World Empire Building.' *Comparative Studies in Society and History* 35, no. 3 (1993): 461–80.

Khazanov, Anatoly M. 'Muhammad and Jenghiz Khan Compared: The Religious Factor in World Empire Building.' *Proceedings of the British Academy* 82, 149–70. Oxford: Oxford University Press, 1993.

Khazanov, Anatoly M. *Nomads and the Outside World*, translated by Julia Crookenden. Cambridge/New York: Cambridge University Press, 1984.

Khazanov, Anatoly M. 'The Spread of World Religions in Medieval Nomadic Societies of the Eurasian Steppes.' *Toronto Studies in Central and Inner Asia* 1 (1993): 11–33.

Khowaiter, Abdul-Aziz. *Baibars the First: His Endeavours and Achievements*. London: Green Mountain Press, 1978.

Khudyakov, Yu. C. *Vooruzheniye Tsentral'no-Aziatskikh Kochyevnikov v Epokhu Rannyego i Razvitogo Spegnyevekov'ya*. Novosibirsk: Academy of Sciences, 1991.

Klaproth, M. 'Apercu des Entreprises des Mongols en Georgie et en Armenie dans le XIIIe Siècle.' *Journal Asiatique* 12 (1833): 194–214.

Koprulu, Mehmed Fuad. *Islam in Anatolia After the Turkish Invasion (Prolegomena)*, translated by Gary Leiser. Salt Lake City: University of Utah Press, 1993.

Kotwicz, Wladyslaw. 'Contributions à l'Hisotire de l'Asie Centrale.' *Rocznik Orientalistyczny* (1939–49): 159–95.

Kotwicz, Wladyslaw. 'Les Mongols, Promoteurs de l'Idée de Paix Universelle au Début du XIIIe Siècle.' *Rocznik Orientalistyczny* 16 (1950): 428–34.

Kotwicz, Wladyslaw. 'Quelques Données Nouvelles sur les Relations Entre les Mongols et les Ouigour.' *Rocznik Orientalistyczny* 2 (1919–24): 240–47.

Krader, Lawrence. 'The Cultural and Historical Position of the Mongols.' *Asia Major* 3 (1952): 169–83.

Krader, Lawrence. 'Feudalism and the Tatar Policy of the Middle Ages.' *Comparative Studies in Society and History* 1 (1958): 76–99.

Krader, Lawrence. 'The Origin of the State Among the Nomads of Asia.' In *Pastoral Production and Society*, L'Équip Écologie et Anthropologie de Société Pastorale, 221–34. Cambridge: Cambridge University Press, 1979.

Krader, Lawrence. 'Qan-Qagan and the Beginnings of Mongol Kingship.' *Central Asiatic Journal* 1 (1955): 17–35.

Krader, Lawrence. *Social Organization of the Mongol-Turkic Pastoral Nomads*. The Hague: Mouton, 1963.

Krader, Lawrence. 'The Tatar State: Turks and Mongols.' In *The Formation of the State*, 82–103. Englewood Cliffs: Prentice-Hall, 1968.

Krollman, Christian. *The Teutonic Order in Prussia*, translated by Ernst Horstmann. Leipzig: Offizin Haag-Drugulin, 1938.

Krueger, John R. 'Chronology and Bibliography of the Secret History.' *Mongolia Society Bulletin* 5 (1966): 25–31.

K'uan-chung, Huang. 'Mountain Fortress Defence: The Experience of the Southern Sung and Korea in Resisting the Mongol Invasions.' In *Warfare in Chinese History*, edited by Hans Van de Ven. Sinica Leidensia Series, vol. 47, 222–51. Leiden: Brill, 2000.

Kwanten, Luc. 'The Career of Muqali: A Reassessment.' *The Bulletin of Sung and Yüan Studies* 14 (1978): 31–8.

Kwanten, Luc. 'Chingis Khan's Conquest of Tibet: Myth or Reality?' *Journal of Asian History* 8 (1974): 1–20.

Kwanten, Luc. 'The Role of the Tangut in Chinese-Inner Asian Relations.' *Acta Orientalia Hungarica* 39 (1978): 191–9.

Lambton, Ann K.S. 'Mongol Fiscal Administration in Persia.' *Studia Islamica* 65 (1957): 97–124.

Lambton, Ann K.S. *Continuity and Change in Medieval Persia: Aspects of Administrative, Economic and Social History, 11th–14th Century*, edited by Ehsan Yershater. Columbia Lecutres on Iranian Studies, vol. 2. Albany: The Persia Heritage Foundation, 1988.

Lambton, Ann K.S. *Landlord and Peasant in Persia*. London: Oxford University Press, 1953.

Lambton, Ann K.S. *State and Government in Medieval Islam*. Oxford: Oxford University Press, 1981.

Lane, George. *Early Mongol Rule in Thirteenth Century Iran: A Persian Renaissance*. Studies in the History of Iran and Turkey, edited by Carole Hillenbrand. London: Routledge Curzon, 2003.

Lang, David Marshall. *The Armenians*. London: George Allen & Unwin, 1981.

Lang, David Marshall. *The Georgians*. London: George Allen & Unwin, 1966.

Langlois, J.D., Jr., ed. *China Under Mongol Rule*. Princeton: Princeton University Press, 1981.

Latham, J.D. 'Notes on Mamluk Horse-Archers.' *Bulletin of the School of Oriental and African Studies* 32 (1969): 257–69.

Latham, J.D.; Paterson, W.F.; and Taybugha. *Saracen Archery: An English Version and Exposition of a Mameluke Work on Archery (Ca. A.D. 1368)*. London: Holland Press, 1970.

Lattimore, Owen. 'Chingis Khan and the Mongol Conquests.' *Scientific American* 209 (1963): 55–68.

Lattimore, Owen. 'The Geography of Chingis Khan.' *Geography Journal* 129 (1963): 1–7.

Lattimore, Owen. 'Inner Asian Defensive Empires and Conquest Empires.' Reprinted in *Studies in Frontier History*, edited by Owen Lattimore, London: Oxford University Press, 1962.

Lazarescu-Zobian, Maria. 'Cumania as the Name of Thirteenth Century Moldavia and Eastern Wallachia: Some Aspects of Kipchak-Rumanian Relations.' *Journal of Turkish Studies* 8 (1984): 265–72.

Le Strange, Guy. *The Lands of the Eastern Caliphate*. London: Frank Cass, 1966.

Le Strange, Guy. *Mesopotamia and Persia under the Mongols in the 14th Century A.D. from the Nuzhat al Kulub of Hamd-Allah Mustawofi*. London: Royal Asiatic Society, 1903.

Ledyard, G. 'The Establishment of Mongolian Military Governors in Korea in 1231.' *Phi Theta Papers* 6 (1961): 1–17.

Ledyard, G. 'The Mongol Campaigns in Korea and the Dating of The Secret History of the Mongols.' *Central Asiatic Journal* 9 (1964): 1–22.

Legrand, Jacques. 'Conceptions de l'Espace Division Territorial et Divisions Politiques Chez les Mongols de l'Époque Post-Impériale (XIVe-XVIIe Siècles).' In *Pastoral Production and Society*, L'Equip Écologie et Anthropologie de Société Pastorale, 155–70. Cambridge: Cambridge University Press, 1979.

Lessing, Ferdinand, et al. *Mongolian English Dictionary*, edited by Ferdinand Lessing. Bloomington: The Mongolia Society, 1995.

Lewicki, Marian. 'Turcica et Mongolica.' *Rocznik Orientalistyczny* 15 (1939–49): 239–67.

Lewis, Archibald. *Nomads and Crusaders: A.D. 1000–1368*. Bloomington: Indiana University Press, 1988.

Lewis, Bernard. *The Assassins: A Radical Sect in Islam*. New York: Oxford University Press, 1987.

Lewis, Bernard. 'The Mongols, the Turks, and the Muslim Polity.' In *Islam in History*, 179–98, 324–35. London: Alcove Press, 1973.

Liddell Hart, B.H. 'Jenghiz Khan and Sabutai.' In *Great Captains Unveiled*. Freeport: Books for Libraries, 1967.

Liddell Hart, B.H. *The Liddell Hart Memoirs 1895–1938*. New York: G.P. Putnam's Sons, 1965.

Liddell Hart, B.H. *The German Generals Talk*. New York: Quill, 1979.

Liddell Hart, B.H. *Deterrent or Defense: A Fresh Look at the West's Military Position*. New York: Frederick A. Praeger, 1960.

Ligeti, Louis. *Histoire Secrete Des Mongols*. Monumenta Linguae Mongolicae Collecta, vol. 1. Budapest, 1971.

Ligeti, Louis. 'Le Lexique Mongol de Kirakos de Gandzak.' *Acta Orientalia Hungarica* 18 (1965): 241–98.

Lindner, R.P. 'Nomadism, Horses and Huns.' *Past and Present* 92 (1981): 3–19.

Lindner, R.P. *Nomads and Ottomans in Medieval Anatolia*. Bloomington: Indiana University Press, 1983.

Lindner, R.P. 'What Was a Nomadic Tribe?' *Comparative Studies in Society and History* 24, no. 4 (1982): 689–711.

Lippard, Bruce G. 'The Mongols and Byzantium, 1243–1341.' PhD dissertation, Uralic and Altaic Studies, Indiana University, 1983.

Little, D.P. 'The Founding of Sultaniyya: A Mamluk Version.' *Iran: Journal of the British Institute of Persian Studies* 16 (1978): 170–5.

Liu, James T.C. 'The Jurchen-Sung Confrontation: Some Overlooked Points.' In *China Under Jurchen Rule*, edited by Hoyt Cleveland Tillman and Stephen H. West. Albany: SUNY Press, 1995.

Lockhart, L. 'The Relations Between Edward I and Edward II of England and the Mongol Il-Khans of Persia.' *Iran: Journal of the British Institute of Persian Studies* 6 (1968): 25–31.

Lot, Ferdinand. *L'Art Militaire et les Armees Au Moyen Age en Europe et dans Le Proche Orient*. Paris: Payot, 1956.

Love, Ronald S. ' "All the King's Horsemen": The Equestrian Army of Henri IV, 1585–1598.' *Sixteenth Century Journal* 22, no. 3 (1991): 510–33.

Lutaa, B. 'Old Songs of Arrows.' *Mongolia Today Online Magazine*, no. 7 (9 August 2002). <http://www.mongoliatoday.com/issue/7/archery.html>.

Luttwak, Edward N. 'Logistics and the Aristocratic Idea of War.' In *Feeding Mars: Logistics in Western Warfare from the Middle Ages to the Present*, edited by John A. Lynn, 3–8. Boulder: Westview Press, 1993.

Lynn, John A. 'Tactical Evolution in the French Army, 1560–1660.' *French Historical Studies* 14, no. 2 (1985): 176–91.

Lynn, John A. ed. *Feeding Mars: Logistics in Western Warfare from the Middle Ages to the Present*. Boulder: Westview Press, 1993.

Maalouf, Amin. *The Crusades Through Arab Eyes*. New York: Schocken Books, 1985.

Marek, Jiri; Knizkova, Hana; and Forman, W. *The Jenghiz Khan Miniatures from the Court of Akbar the Great*, 40–2. London: Spring Books, 1963.

Marshall, Christopher. *Warfare in the Latin East, 1192–1291*. Cambridge: Cambridge University Press, 1992.

Marshall, Robert. *Storm from the East from Ghenghis Khan to Khubilai Khan*. Berkeley: University of California Press, 1993.

Martin, Henry Desmond. *The Rise of Chingis Khan and His Conquest of North China*. Baltimore: Johns Hopkins, 1950.

Martinez, A.P. 'Some Notes on the Il-Xanid Army.' *Archivum Eurasiae Medii Aevi* 6 (1986): 129–242.

Martinez, A.P. 'The Third Portion of the History of Gazan Xan in Rasidu'd-Din's Ta'rix-e Mobarake-e Gazani.' *Archivum Eurasiae Medii Aevi* 6 (1988): 41–127.

Matsuda, Kochi. 'On the Ho–Nan Mongol Army.' *Memoirs of the Research Department of the Toyo Bunko* 50 (1992): 29–56.

May, Timothy. 'The Mechanics of Conquest and Governance: The Rise and Expansion of the Mongol Empire, 1185–1265.' PhD dissertation, Department of History, University of Wisconsin–Madison, 2004.

Mayer, H.E. *The Crusades*, translated by John Gillingham. London: Oxford University, 1972.

Mayers, W.F. 'On the Introduction and Use of Gunpowder and Firearms Among the Chinese.' *Journal of the North China Branch of the Royal Asiatic Society* 6 (1869–70): 73–104.

McNeill, William H. *The Pursuit of Power: Technology, Armed Force, and Society Since A.D. 1000*. Chicago: University of Chicago Press, 1982.

Melville, Charles. ' "Sometimes by the Sword, Sometimes by the Dagger": The Role of the Ismailis in Mamluk-Mongol Relations in the 8th/14th Century.' In *Mediaeval Ismaili History and Thought*, edited by Farhad Daftary. New York: Cambridge University Press, 1996.

Meserve, Ruth I. 'An Historical Perspective of Mongol Horse Training, Care and Management: Selected Texts.' PhD dissertation, Uralic and Altaic Studies, Indiana University, 1987.

Meserve, Ruth I. 'On Medieval and Early Modern Science and Technology in Central Eurasia.' In *Culture Contact, History and Ethnicity in Inner Asia*, edited by Michael Gerver and Wayne Schlepp. Toronto Studies in Central and Inner Asia, vol. 2, 49–70. Toronto: Joint Centre for Asia Pacific Studies, 1996.

Meserve, Ruth I. 'Some Remarks on the Turkmen Horse.' In *Aspects of Altaic Civilization*, Proceedings of the Thirtieth Meeting of the Permanent International Altaistic Conference, Indiana University Bloomington, Indiana June 19–25, 1987. Bloomington: Indiana University Research Insitute for Inner Asian Studies, 1990.

Meyvaert, Paul. 'An Unknown Letter of Hulagu, Il-Khan of Persia, to King Louis IX of France.' *Viator* 11 (1980): 245–59.

Miller, David B. 'The Many Frontiers of Pre-Mongol Rus'.' *Russian History* 19 (1992): 231–60.

Miller, William. *Trebizond, the Last Greek Empire of the Byzantine Era, 1204–1461*. Chicago: Argonaut Inc, 1969.

Minorsky, Vladimir. 'Caucasia II: 1. The Georgian Maliks of Ahar.' *Bulletin of the School of Oriental and African Studies* 13 (1951): 869–79.

Minorsky, Vladimir. 'Caucasia III: The Alan Capital Magas and the Mongol Campaigns.' *Bulletin of the School of Oriental and African Studies* 16 (1952): 215–38.

Minorsky, Vladimir. 'Caucasia IV.' *Bulletin of the School of Oriental and African Studies* 15 (1953): 504–30.

Minorsky, Vladimir. 'Mongol Place-Names in Mukri Kurdistan.' *Bulletin of the School of Oriental and African Studies* 19 (1957): 58–81.

Minorsky, Vladimir. 'Nasir al-Din Tusi on Finance.' In *Iranica*, 292–305. Teheran, 1964.

Minorsky, Vladimir. 'Pur-I Bahas "Mongol" Ode.' *Bulletin of the School of Oriental and African Studies* 18 (1956): 261–78.

Minorsky, Vladimir, and Bartold, V.V. *Hudud-al Alam: 'The Regions of the World'*. London: Luzac & Co, E.J.W. Gibb Memorial, 1937.

Moffet, Samuel Hugh. 'Beginnings to 1500.' In *A History of Christianity in Asia*. New York: Harper Collins, 1992.

Molnár, Ádám. *Weather-Magic in Inner Asia*. Bloomington, Indiana: Research Institute for Inner Asian Studies, Indiana University, 1994.

Montgomery, James A. *The History of Yaballaha III, Nestorian Patriarch, and of His Vicar Bar Sauma, Mongol Ambassador to the Frankish Courts at the End of the Thirteenth Century*. Columbia University Records of Civilization, vol. 8. New York: Columbia University Press, 1966.

Morel, H. 'Les Campagnes Mongoles Au XIIIe Siecle.' *Revue Militaire Française* 4 (1922): 348–68.

Morgan, David O. 'Cassiodorus and Rashid al-Din on Barbarian Rule in Italy and Persia.' *Bulletin of the School of Oriental and African Studies* 44, no. 1 (1981): 120–5.

Morgan, David O. 'The Mongol Armies in Persia.' *Der Islam* 56 (1976): 80–96.

Morgan, David O. 'Mongol or Persian: The Government of Ilkanid Iran.' *Harvard Middle Eastern and Islamic Review* 3 (1996): 62–76.

Morgan, David O. 'The Mongols in Syria, 1260–1300.' In *Crusade and Settlement*, edited by P.W. Edbury, 191–6. Cardiff: University College Cardiff Press, 1985.

Morgan, David O. *The Mongols*. Oxford: Basil Blackwell, 1986.

Morgan, David O. 'Persian Historians and the Mongols.' In *Medieval Historical Writings in the Christian and Islamic Worlds*, 109–24. London: School of Oriental and African Studies, 1982.

Morgan, David O. 'Who Ran the Mongol Empire?' *Journal of the Royal Asiatic Society* (1982): 124–36.

Morgan, David O. 'The "Great Yasa of Chingiz Khan" and Mongol Law in the Ilkhanate.' *Bulletin of the School of Oriental and African Studies* 49, no. 1 (1986): 163–76.

Moses, Larry. 'Legends by the Numbers: The Symbolism of Numbers in the Secret History of the Mongols.' *Asian Folklore Studies* 56 (1996): 73–98.

Moses, Larry. 'The Quarrelling Sons in the Secret History of the Mongols.' *Journal of American Folklore* 100 (1987): 63–9.

Moses, Larry. 'A Theoretical Approach to the Process of Inner Asian Confederation.' *Etudes Mongoles et Sibériennes* 5 (1974): 113–22.

Moses, Larry. 'Triplicated Triplets: The Number Nine in the Secret History of the Mongols.' *Asian Folklore Studies* 45 (1986): 287–94.

Moule, A.C. 'Bibliographical Notes on Odoric.' *T'oung Pao* 20 (1922): 387–93.

Moule, A.C. 'A Life of Odoric of Pordenone.' *T'oung Pao* 20 (1921): 275–90.

Moule, A.C. 'Marco Polo.' *Journal of the Royal Asiatic Society* (1932): 603–25.

Moule, A.C. 'The Siege of Saianfu and the Murder of Achmach.' *Journal of the North China Branch of the Royal Asiatic Society* 58 (1927): 1–35.

Moule, A.C. 'A Small Contribution to the Study of the Bibliography of Odoric.' *T'oung Pao* 20 (1921): 301–22.

Muir, William. *The Mameluke or Slaves Dynasty of Egypt A.D. 1260–1517*. Amsterdam: Oriental Press, 1968.

Muldoon, James. *Popes, Lawyers, and Infidels: The Church and the Non-Christian.* Philadelphia: University of Pennsylvania Press, 1979.

Murphey, Rhoads. *Ottoman Warfare 1500–1700.* New Brunswick: Rutgers University Press, 1999.

Nacagdorz, S. 'L'Organization Sociale et son Dévelopement Chez les Peuples Nomades d'Asie Centrale.' *Etudes Mongoles et Sibériennes* 5 (1974): 135–44.

Nam, Seng Geung. 'A Study of Military Technics of the Thirteenth Century Mongols.' *Mongolica: An International Annual of Mongol Studies* 5 (1994): 196–205.

Nasonov, A.H. *Mongoli' i Rus': Istoria Tatarsko' Politiki Na Rusi.* Moscow: Izdatel'stvo Akademii HAUK SSSR, 1940.

Nersessian, Sirarpie Der. *The Armenians.* London: Thames and Hudson, 1969.

Nersessian, Sirarpie Der. 'The Kingdom of Cilician Armenia.' In *A History of the Crusades,* edited by R.L. Wolff and H.W. Hazard, vol. 2, *The Later Crusades, 1189–1311,* 630–60. Philadelphia: University of Pennsylvania Press, 1962.

Nicolle, David. *Arms and Armour of the Crusading Era, 1050–1350.* White Plains: Kraus International Publications, 1988.

Nicolle, David. *Early Medieval Islamic Arms and Armour. Gladius.* Jarandilla: Instituto de Estudios sobre Armas Antiguas, Consejo Superior de Investigaciones Cientificas, Patronato Menendez y Pelayo, 1976.

Nicolle, David. *Lake Peipus 1242: Battle of the Ice.* London: Osprey, 1996.

Nicolle, David. 'Medieval Warfare: The Unfriendly Interface.' *The Journal of Military History* 63 (1999): 579–600.

Nicolle, David. *The Mongol Warlords: Genghis Khan, Kublai Khan, Hülegü, Tamerlane.* Poole: Firebird, 1990.

Nicolle, David. *Medieval Warfare Source Book,* vol. 1, *Warfare in Western Christendom.* London: Arms and Armour, 1995.

Nishimura, D. 'Crossbows, Arrow-Guides, and the Solenarion.' *Byzantion* 58 (1988): 422–35.

Noonan, Thomas. 'Rus', Pechenegs, and Polovtsy: Economic Interaction Along the Steppe Frontier in the Pre-Mongol Era.' *Russian History* 19 (1992): 301–27.

Noonan, Thomas. 'Medieval Russia, the Mongols, and the West: Novgorod's Relations with the Baltic, 1100–1300.' *Medieval Studies* 37 (1975): 316–39.

Noonan, Thomas S. *The Islamic World, Russia and the Vikings, 750–900, the Numismatic Evidence.* Aldershot: Variorum, 1998.

Norwich, John Julius. *A Short History of Byzantium.* New York: Alfred A. Knopf, 1997.

Ohsson, Constantin d'. *Histoire des Mongols, Depuis Tchinguiz-Khan Jusqu'à Timour Bey ou Tamerlan.* Amsterdam: F. Muller, 1852.

Olschki, L. *Gilaume Boucher: A French Artist at the Court of the Khans.* Baltimore: University of Johns Hopkins Press, 1946.

Olschki, L. *Marco Polo's Asia: An Introduction to His 'Description of the World' Called 'Il Milione'.* Los Angeles: University of California Press, 1960.

Olschki, L. *Marco Polo's Precursors.* New York: Octagon Books, 1972.

Olschki, L. 'Olun's Chemise: An Episode from the "Secret History of the Mongols".' *Journal of the American Oriental Society* 67 (1947): 54–6.

Oman, Charles. *A History of the Art of War in the Middle Ages* (2 vols). New York: Burt Franklin, 1924.

Ostrowski, Donald. 'City Names of the Western Steppe at the Time of the Mongol Invasion.' *Bulletin of the School of Oriental and African Studies* 61 (1998): 465–75.

Ostrowski, Donald. 'The Mongol Origins of Muscovite Political Institutions.' *Slavic Review* 49 (1990): 525–43.

Ostrowski, Donald. 'The Tamma at the Dual-Administrative Structure of the Mongol Empire.' *Bulletin of the School of Oriental and African Studies* 61 (1998): 262–77.

Ostrowski, Donald. *Muscovy and the Mongols: Cross-Cultural Influences on the Steppe Frontier, 1304–1589.* Cambridge: Cambridge University Press, 1998.

Paladi, Kovacs. 'Hungarian Horse-Keeping in the 9th and 10th Centuries.' *Acta Ethnographica Hungarica* 41 (1996): 55–66.

Patton, Douglas. 'Badr al-Din Lu'lu' and the Establishment of a Mamluk Government in Mosul.' *Studia Islamica* 74 (1991): 791–803.

Payne-Gallway, Ralph. *The Projectile-Throwing Engines of the Ancients and Turkish and Other Oriental Bows.* Totowa: Rowman and Littlefield, 1973.

Payne-Gallway, Ralph. *The Book of the Crossbow.* New York: Dover Publications, 1995.

Pelenski, J. 'The Contest Between Lithuania-Rus' and the Golden Horde.' *Archivum Eurasiae Medii Aevi* 2 (1982): 303–21.

Pelliot, Paul. 'Les Mongols et la Papauté.' *Revue de l'Orient Chrétien* 4 (1924): 225–335.

Pelliot, Paul. *Notes on Marco Polo.* Paris: A. Maisonneuve, 1959–1973.

Pelliot, Paul. *Notes on Marco Polo.* Paris: Imprimerie Nationale, 1959.

Petrushevsky, I.P. 'Socio-Economic Conditions of Iran Under the Il-Khans.' In *Cambridge History of Iran*, edited by J.A. Boyle. Cambridge: Cambridge University Press, 1968.

Pikov, G.G. *Zapadn'ie Kidani.* Novosibirsk: Izgatel'stvo Novosibirskogo Universiteta, 1989.

Prawdin, Michael. *The Mongol Empire, Its Rise and Legacy.* New York: Free Press, 1967.

Qu, Da-Feng. 'A Study of Jebe's Expedition to Tung Ching.' *Acta Orientalia Hungarica* 51 (1998): 171–7.

Rachewiltz, Igor de. 'Some Reflections on Cinggis Qan's Jasaq.' *East Asian History* 6 (1993): 91–104.

Rachewiltz, Igor de. *In the Service of the Khan: Eminent Personalities of the Early Mongol-Yüan Period (1200–1300).* Asiatische Forschungen. Wiesbaden: Harrassowitz, 1993.

Rachewiltz, Igor de. *Index to the Secret History of the Mongols.* Uralic and Altaic Series. Bloomington: Indiana University, 1972.

Ratchnevsky, Paul. *Genghis Khan: His Life and Legacy*, translated by Thomas Nivison Haining. Oxford: Blackwell, 1991.

Rice, David Talbot; Gray, Basil; and Rashid al-Din Tabib. *The Illustrations to the World History of Rashid al-Din.* Edinburgh: Edinburgh University Press, 1976.

Robinson, H. Russell. *Oriental Armour.* New York: Walker and Co, 1967.

Rockstein, Edward. 'The Mongol Invasions of Korea.' *The Mongolia Society Bulletin* 11, no. 2 (1972): 55–75.

Rogers, Greg S. 'An Examination of Historians' Explanations For the Mongol Withdrawal from East Central Europe.' *East European Quarterly* 30 (1996): 3–26.

Rossabi, Morris, ed. *China Among Equals: The Middle Kingdom and Its Neighbors, 10th and 14th Centuries*. Berkeley: University of California Press, 1983.

Rossabi, Morris, ed. *Khubilai Khan: His Life and Times*. Berkeley: University of California Press, 1988.

Roux, Jean-Paul. 'Le Chaman Gengiskhanide.' *Anthropos* 54 (1959): 401–32.

Roux, Jean-Paul. *Histoire de l'Empire Mongol*. Paris: Fayard, 1993.

Rudolph, R.C. 'Medical Matters in an Early Fourteenth Century Chinese Diary.' *Journal of the History of Medicine and Allied Sciences* 2 (1947): 209–306.

Ruotsala, Antti. *Europeans and Mongols in the Middle of the Thirteenth Century: Encountering the Other*. The Finnish Academy of Science and Letters Humaniora Series, vol. 314. Helsinki: Academia Scientiarum Fennica, 2001.

Salia, Kalistrat. *History of the Georgian Nation*, translated by Katherine Vivian. Paris: L'Academie Francias, 1980.

Sarközi, Alice. 'A Mongolian Hunting Ritual.' *Acta Orientalia Hungarica* 25 (1972): 191–208.

Saunders, J.J. *The History of the Mongol Conquests*. Philadelphia: University of Pennsylvania Press, 2001.

Saunders, J.J. 'The Nomad as Empire Builder: A Comparison of the Arab and Mongol Conquests.' *Diogenes* 52 (1965): 79–103.

Savvides, Alexes G.K. *Byzantium in the Near East: Its Relations with the Seljuk Sultanate of Rum in Asia Minor, the Armenians of Cilicia and the Mongols A.D. c.1192–1237*. Byzantina Keimena Kai Meletai. Thessaloniki: Kentron Byzantinon Ereunon, 1981.

Schamiloglu, Uli. 'Preliminary Remarks on the Role of Disease in the History of the Golden Horde.' *Central Asian Survey* 12, no. 4 (1993): 447–57.

Schamiloglu, Uli. 'The Qaraci Beys of the Later Golden Horde: Notes on the Organization of the Mongol World Empire.' *Archivum Eurasiae Medii Aevi* 4 (1984): 283–97.

Schurmann, H.F. *Economic Structure of the Yuan Dynasty*. Cambridge: Harvard University Press, 1956.

Schurmann, H.F. 'Mongolian Tributary Practices of the Thirteenth Century.' *Harvard Journal of Asiatic Studies* 19 (1956): 304–89.

Schütz, Edmond. 'The Decisive Motives of Tatar Failure in Ilkhanid-Mamluk Fights in the Holy Land.' *Acta Orientalia Hungarica* 45, no. 1 (1991): 3–22.

Schütz, Edmond. 'Tangsux in Armenia.' *Acta Orientalia Hungarica* 17 (1964): 105–12.

Schwartz, Henry. 'Otrar.' *Central Asian Survey* 17 (1998): 5–10.

Schwartz, Henry. 'Some Notes on the Mongols of Yunnan.' *Central Asiatic Journal* 28 (1994): 100–18.

Sedelko, Paul L. 'Western Embassies to the Mongols and the Prospects for Their Conversion, 1245–1253.' In *Culture Contact, History and Ethnicity in Inner Asia*, edited by Michael Gerver and Wayne Schlepp. Toronto Studies in Central and Inner Asia, vol. 2, 71–9. Toronto: Joint Centre for Asia Pacific Studies, 1996.

Seidler, G.L. 'The Political Doctrine of the Mongols.' *Annales Universitatis Mariae Curie-Sklodoska* 6 (1959): 249–74.

Serruys, Henry. 'Mongol Altan "Gold" = "Imperial".' *Monumenta Serica* 21 (1962): 357–78.

Setton, Kenneth M. 'The Papal Interregnum, Gregory X, and the Second Council of Lyon (1268–1383).' In *The Papacy and the Levant (1204–1571)*, edited by Kenneth M. Setton. Philadelphia: The American Philosophical Society, 1976.

Sheppard, E.W. 'Military Methods of the Mongols.' *Army Quarterly* 18 (1929): 305–15.

Silfen, Paul Harrison. *The Influences of the Mongols on Russia: A Dimensional History*. Hicksville, NY: Exposition Press, 1974.

Simon, Edith. *The Piebald Standard: A Biography of the Knights Templars*. Boston: Little, Brown, and Co, 1959.

Simon, Robert. 'Symbiosis of Nomads and Sedentaries on the Character of Middle Eastern Civilization.' *Acta Orientalia Hungarica* 35 (1981): 229–42.

Sinor, Denis. 'History of the Mongols in the 13th Century. (Notes on Inner Asian Bibliography, Part 4).' *JASH* 23 (1989): 26–70.

Sinor, Denis. 'Horse and Pasture in Inner Asian History.' *Oriens Extremus* 19 (1972): 171–84.

Sinor, Denis. *Inner Asia and Its Contacts with Medieval Europe*. London: Variorum Reprints, 1977.

Sinor, Denis. 'The Inner Asian Warriors.' *Journal of the American Oriental Society* 101, no. 2 (1981): 133–44.

Sinor, Denis. 'The Mongols and Western Europe.' In *A History of the Crusades*, edited by Kenneth M. Setton, vol. 3, *The Fourteenth and Fifteenth Centuries*, 513–44. Madison: University of Wisconsin Press, 1975.

Sinor, Denis. 'On Mongol Strategy.' In *Proceedings of the Fourth East Asian Altaistic Conference*, edited by Ch'en Chieh-hsien. Taipai, 1971.

Sinor, Denis. 'Un Voyageur du Treizieme Siècle: Le Dominicain Julien de Hongrie.' *Bulletin of the School of Oriental and African Studies* 14, no. 3 (1952): 589–602.

Sinor, Denis and Francis, David. *Aspects of Altaic Civilization: Proceedings of the Fifth Meeting of the Permanent International Altaistic Conference, Held at Indiana University, June 4–9, 1962*. Westport: Greenwood Press, 1981.

Skelton, R.A., et al, ed. *The Vinland Map and the Tatar Relation*. New Haven: Yale University Press, 1965.

Smail, R.C. *Crusading Warfare (1097–1193)*. Cambridge Studies in Medieval Life and Thought. Cambridge: Cambridge University Press, 1956.

Smail, R.C. and Marshall, Christopher. *Crusading Warfare, 1097–1193*. 2nd edition. Cambridge: Cambridge University Press, 1994.

Smith, John Masson. *The History of the Sarbadar Dynasty, 1336–1381 A.D. and its Sources*. The Hague: Mouton, 1970.

Smith, John Masson, Jr. 'Demographic Considerations in Mongol Siege Warfare.' *Archivum Ottomanicum* 13 (1993–4): 329–35.

Smith, John Masson, Jr. 'Mongol and Nomadic Taxation.' *Harvard Journal of Asiatic Studies* 30 (1970): 46–85.

Smith, John Masson, Jr. 'Mongol Campaign Rations: Milk, Marmots, and Blood?' *Journal of Turkish Studies* 8 (1984): 223–8.

Smith, John Masson, Jr. 'Mongol Manpower and Persian Population.' *Journal of the Economic and Social History of the Orient* 18, no. 3 (1975): 271–99.

Smith, John Masson, Jr. 'Mongol Nomadism and Middle Eastern Geography: Qishlaqs and Tümens.' In *The Mongol Empire and Its Legacy*, edited by Reuven Amitai-Preiss and David O. Morgan, 39–56. Leiden: Brill, 2001.

Smith, John Masson, Jr. 'Mongol Society and Military in the Middle East: Antecedents and Adaptations.' In *War and Society in the Eastern Mediterranean, 7th–15th Centuries*, edited by Yaacov Lev. The Medieval Mediterranean Peoples, Economies, and Cultures, 400–1453, vol. 9. Leiden: Brill, 1996.

Smith, John Masson, Jr. 'The Mongols and World Conquest.' *Mongolica: An International Annual of Mongol Studies* 5 (1994): 206–14.

Smith, John Masson, Jr. 'Obstacles to the Mongol Conquest of Europe.' *Mongolica: An International Annual of Mongol Studies* 10 (2000): 461–70.

Smith, John Masson, Jr. 'Ayn Jalut: Mamluk Success or Mongol Failure?' *Harvard Journal of Asiatic Studies* 44 (1984): 307–45.

Somogyi, Joseph de. 'A Qasida on the Destruction of Baghdad by the Mongols.' *Bulletin of the School of Oriental and African Studies* 7 (1933–5): 41–8.

Stang, H. 'The Baljuna Revisited.' *Journal of Turkish Studies* 9 (1985): 229–36.

Stawson, John. *Hitler as Military Commander*. New York: Barnes & Noble, 1971.

Stein, Aurel. 'Marco Polo's Account of a Mongol Inroad Into Kashmir.' *Geography Journal* 54 (1919): 92–103.

Suny, Ronald Grigor. *The Making of the Georgian Nation*. Bloomington: Indiana University Press, 1994.

Sweeney, James Ross. 'Thomas of Spalato and the Mongols: A Thirteenth-Century Dalmatian View of Mongol Customs.' *Florelegium* 4 (1982): 156–83.

Swietoslwski, Witold. *Arms and Armour of the Nomads of the Great Steppe in the Times of the Mongolian Expansion (12th–14th Centuries)*. Studies on the History of the Ancient and Medieval Art of Warfare. Lodz: Oficyna Naukowa MS, 1999.

Szczesniak, B. 'Hagiographical Documentation of the Mongol Invasions of Poland in the Thirteenth Century, Part 1, the Preaching Friars.' *Memoirs Research Department of the Toyo Bunko* 17 (1958): 167–95.

Tang, Chi. 'On the Administration System of the Mongol Empire in China Recorded in Jame' el-Tevarih.' Paper presented at the The International Conference on China Border Area Studies. National Chengchi University, Taipai, Taiwan, 1984.

Tao, Jing-Shen. *The Jurchen in Twelfth-Century China: A Study in Sinicization*. Seattle: University of Washington Press, 1976.

Tao, Jing-Shen. *Two Sons of Heaven: Studies in Sung-Liao Relations*. Tucson: The University of Arizona Press, 1988.

Tapper, Richard L. 'The Organization of Nomadic Communities in Pastoral Societies of the Middle East.' In *Pastoral Production and Society*, L'Équip Écologie et Anthropologie de Société Pastorale, 43–66. Cambridge: Cambridge University Press, 1979.

Thorau, Peter. 'The Battle of 'Ayn Jalut: A Re-Examination.' In *Crusade and Settlement*, edited by P.W. Edbury, 236–41. Cardiff: University College Cardiff Press, 1985.

Thorau, Peter. *The Lion of Egypt: Sultan Baybars I and the Near East in the Thirteenth Century*. London: Longman, 1992.

Tikhvinskii, Sergei Leonidovich. *Tataro-Mongoly v Azii i Evrope Sbornik Statei.* 2nd edition. Moskva: Nauka, 1977.

Tillman, Hoyt Cleveland. 'An Overview of Chin History and Institutions.' In *China Under Jurchen Rule*, edited by Hoyt Cleveland Tillman and Stephen H. West. Albany: SUNY Press, 1995.

Tillman, Hoyt Cleveland and Stephen H. West, eds. *China Under Jurchen Rule: Essays on Chin Intellectual and Cultural History.* SUNY Series in Chinese Philosophy and Culture. Albany: SUNY Press, 1995.

Togan, Isenbike. *Flexibility and Limitation in Steppe Formations: The Kerait Khanate and Chinggis Khan.* The Ottoman Empire and Its Heritage Series, edited by Suraiya Faroqhi and Halil Inalcik, vol. 15. Leiden: Brill, 1998.

Tsevel, Ya. *Monggol Khelnii Tovch Tailbar Tol*, edited by Kh. Luvsanbaldan. Ulaanbaatar: Ulsiin Khevleliin Khereg Erkhlekh Khoron, 1966.

Tsoodol, Ichinkhorloogiin. *Mongol Ulsyn Miangan Zhiliin Gaikhanshig.* Ulaanbaatar: Soëmbo Khevleliin Gazar, 1992.

Turan, Osman. 'The Ideal of World Domination Among the Medieval Turks.' *Studia Islamica* 4 (1955): 77–90.

Ullman, Manfred. *Islamic Medicine.* Islamic Surveys, vol. 11. Edinburgh: Edinburgh University Press, 1978.

Uray-Kölhalmi, Catherine. 'La Périodisation de l'Histoire des Armements des Nomades des Steppes.' *Etudes Mongolews et Sibériennes* 5 (1974): 145–55.

Van de Ven, Hans, ed. *Warfare in Chinese History.* Sinica Leidensia Series, edited by W.L. Idema, vol. 47. Leiden: Brill, 2000.

Vasary, Istvan. 'The Golden Horde Term Daruga and its Survival in Russia.' *Acta Orientalia Hungarica* 30 (1976): 187–97.

Vasary, Istvan. 'Mongolian Impact on the Terminology of the Documents of the Golden Horde.' *Acta Orientalia Hungarica* 48 (1995): 479–85.

Vasary, Istvan. 'The Origin of the Institution of Basqaqs.' *Acta Orientalia Hungarica* 32 (1978): 201–6.

Verbruggen, J.F. *The Art of Warfare in Western Europe During the Middle Ages from the Eighth Century to 1340.* 2nd edition. Woodbridge: The Boydell Press, 1997.

Vernadsky, George. *The Mongols and Russia.* New Haven: Yale University Press, 1953.

Vernadsky, George. 'The Scope and Contents of Chingis Khan's Yasa.' *Harvard Journal of Asiatic Studies* 3 (1938): 337–60.

Vladimirtsov, B.I. *Le Régime Social Des Mongols: Le Féodalisme Nomade*, translated by René Grousset. Paris: Librarie d'Amerique et d'Orient, 1948.

Vladimirtsov, B.I. *Gengis-Khan.* Paris: Librairie d'Amerique et d'Orient, 1948.

Vladimirtsov, B.I. *Le Régime Social Des Mongols: Le Féodalisme Nomade.* Paris: A. Maisonneuve, 1948.

Voegelin, Eric. 'The Mongol Orders of Submission to European Powers.' *Byzantion* 15 (1970): 378–413.

Von Gabain, Annemarie. 'Horse and Rider in the Middle Ages.' *Central Asiatic Journal* 10 (1965): 228-43.

Vyronis, Speros Jr. 'Byzantine and Turkish Societies and Their Sources of Manpower.' In *War, Technology, and Society in the Middle East*, edited by V.J. Parry and M.E. Yapp, 125–52. London: Oxford University Press, 1975.

Walker, Cyril Charles. *Jenghiz Khan*. London: Luzac, 1939.

Wang, Ling. 'On the Invention and Use of Gunpowder and Fire-Arms in China.' *Isis* 37 (1947): 160–78.

Werner, E. 'The Burial Place of Genghis Khan.' *Journal of the North China Branch of the Royal Asiatic Society* 56 (1925): 80–6.

White, Lynn Jr. 'The Crusades and the Technological Thrust of the West.' In *War, Technology, and Society in the Middle East*, edited by V.J. Parry and M.E. Yapp, 97–112. London: Oxford University Press, 1975.

Whitman, Captain J.E.A. *How Wars Are Fought*. London: Oxford University Press, 1941.

Williams, Alan R. 'The Manufacture of Mail in Medieval Europe: A Technical Note.' *Gladius* 15 (1980): 105–35.

Wittfogel, Karl A., and Feng Chia-Sheng. *History of Chinese Society: Liao (907–1125)*. Philadelphia: The American Philosophical Society, 1949.

Woods, John E. 'A Note on the Mongol Capture of Isfahan.' *Journal of Near East Studies* 36 (1977): 49–51.

Wu, Chaolu. 'Tree Worship in Early Mongolia.' In *Culture Contact, History and Ethnicity in Inner Asia*, edited by Michael Gerver and Wayne Schlepp. Toronto Studies in Central and Inner Asia, vol. 2, 80–95. Toronto: Joint Center for Asia Pacific Studies, 1996.

Yamada, Nobuo. 'Formation of the Hsiung-Nu Nomadic State.' *Acta Orientalia Hungarica* 36 (1982): 572–82.

Yao, Tao-Chung. 'Ch'iu Ch'u-Chi and Chinggis Khan.' *Harvard Journal of Asiatic Studies* 46, no. 1 (1986): 201–19.

Zaky, A. Rahman. 'Introduction to the Study of Islamic Arms and Armour.' *Gladius* 1 (1961): 17–29.

Zaky, A. Rahman. 'Islamic Armour: An Introduction.' *Gladius* 2 (1963): 69–74.

Index

Acknowledgements

There are a number of people who have been involved in this book in one way or another, and I wish to express my gratitude for their assistance. First and foremost is David Morgan of the University of Wisconsin-Madison. Not only did he read and re-read previous versions of this work when it appeared as part of my dissertation, but he recommended me to Pen & Sword Publishing. And of course, his assistance in clarifying certain passages in the Persian texts was enlightening.

Michael Chamberlain, who served as the chair of my dissertation committee, encouraged me to examine the Mongol military beyond traditional means. My examination of how one transforms a tribal levy into a regular operational military force is greatly influenced by the challenge he set for me. I also owe him my thanks for his assistance when my Arabic failed me. I also owe much to the advice of Uli Schamiloglu, David McDonald, Charles Halperin, Thomas Allsen, Michal Biran, Reuven Amitai, Christopher Atwood, Morris Rossabi and Kemal Karpat. Their comments, answers to questions, and general advice were of great value. Special thanks are extended to Paul Buell, not only for his comments on earlier drafts, but also his patience as I had to place other writing projects on hold in order to finish this one.

At my own institution, North Georgia College and State University, I owe the chair of my department, Dr Georgia Mann, and the dean of the School of Arts and Letters, Dr Christopher Jespersen, my gratitude for providing not only encouragement, but for reducing my course load in order that I could complete this project. Of course the interlibrary loan staff at North Georgia College and State University as well as those at the University of Wisconsin-Madison have my eternal thanks. Without them, this work would have been impossible. My esteemed colleague, Dr Richard Byers, has my thanks not only because he increased my understanding of the training of the Wehrmacht, but because he also put up with my endless ramblings about the Mongol military and its legacy. I am indebted, too, to the students from my Mongol Conquest classes during the spring semesters of 2005 and 2006, not only for developing an interest in the Mongols, but also for asking a plethora of questions, many unanticipated, regarding the Mongol military – some of which forced me to rethink my conclusions. One of my students, Lee Modlin also provided a line drawing.

This work could never have been completed without the diligence and seemingly endless patience of my editor at Pen & Sword Publishing, Rupert Harding. His suggestions have been appreciated since the beginning and his assistance in navigating me through the publishing process has been simply invaluable. Of course, while the above were instrumental in writing this work, I alone am responsible for any errors.

I do not have the words to express my gratitude to my beautiful wife Michaeline and my children for their sustained support. Michaeline helped create time for me to write when it seemed impossible, while my children, Aidan, Victoria, and Kira, made sure I stopped occasionally to enjoy life away from the keyboard.